# The Historical Muhammad

# The Historical Muhammad

Irving M. Zeitlin

polity

First published in 2007 by Polity Press
Reprinted in 2007

Polity Press
65 Bridge Street
Cambridge CB2 1UR, UK

Polity Press
350 Main Street
Malden, MA 02148, USA

ISBN-10: 0-7456-3998-4
ISBN-13: 978-07456-3998-7
ISBN-10: 0-7456-3999-2 (pb)
ISBN-13: 978-07456-3999-4 (pb)

A catalogue record for this book is available from the British Library.

Typeset in 11 on 12.5 pt Ehrhardt
by Servis Filmsetting Ltd, Manchester
Printed and bound in the United States by Odyssey Press Inc., Gonic, New Hampshire

For further information on Polity, visit our website: www.polity.co.uk

# Contents

# Preface

It is entirely coincidental that this effort of mine to understand the Muhammad of history is seeing the light of day at a time when certain political individuals and groups are in the news, presuming to speak for and represent Islam. I need, therefore, to inform the reader that I began this project before the subject-matter might have been considered "topical," and that I had intended it from the beginning as a scholarly affair. It was and continues to be my aim to catch a few relatively reliable glimpses of the birth of Islam and the role played by its extraordinary founder, Muhammad.

Islam, as its Prophet came to conceive it, was a strict and absolute monotheism. And since I am a student of religion and of the monotheistic religions in particular, I felt an inner need to study the origins of Islam carefully from a historical–sociological standpoint. In the course of my academic career, my primary intellectual interests have been in the history of social and political thought and the sociology of religion. I consider it my good fortune, then, that in my previously published studies of the two earlier monotheistic religions, I was able to employ some of the insights and conceptual tools of certain classical social theorists. The first such study I called *Ancient Judaism*, an analysis of key issues in the interpretation of the Hebrew Bible (the Old Testament) as history. The second such study was titled *Jesus and the Judaism of His Time*, the aim of which was to gain an understanding of the man Jesus by situating him in the context of first-century Judaism.

During the last few years, as I began to immerse myself in the scholarly literature on Muhammad and early Islam, it occurred to me that more than thirty years ago, in my studies of the development of social thought, I had discovered Ibn Khaldun, who may be regarded as one of the greatest social thinkers of all time, and whose sociology anticipated the major theoretical contributions of several of the outstanding thinkers who wrote centuries later. One of Ibn Khaldun's chief concerns was with what he termed the interplay between the desert and the sown, between the denizens of the desert, wherever they happen to be on this planet, and the neighboring sedentary cultures. The more I reflected on the literature on Muhammad and nascent Islam, the more I came to recognize the relevance and analytical power of Ibn Khaldun's theory of that interplay as applied both to the pre-Islamic condition of the Arabian Peninsula, and to the Medinan phase of Muhammad's prophetic career. Hence, it is Ibn Khaldun's *Muqaddima* that constitutes, in a large measure, the theoretical framework guiding my quest for the historical Muhammad.

IMZ

## ACKNOWLEDGEMENT

For their helpful editorial suggestions and for the graciousness with which they offered them, I am grateful to John Thompson, Emma Hutchinson and Susan Beer. I want also to thank Tony Giddens for having read an early draft of the manuscript, for finding it interesting and for encouraging me to pursue the project. My being pre-industrial where computers are concerned, has meant that I have had to impose frequently on Ruth Z. Ellman in handling my email correspondence, and for that I thank her much. Finally, I need to acknowledge the essential role my typist, Gloria Rowe, has played in transcribing, impeccably, my hardly legible handscript. She has typed all my manuscripts for the past thirty years.

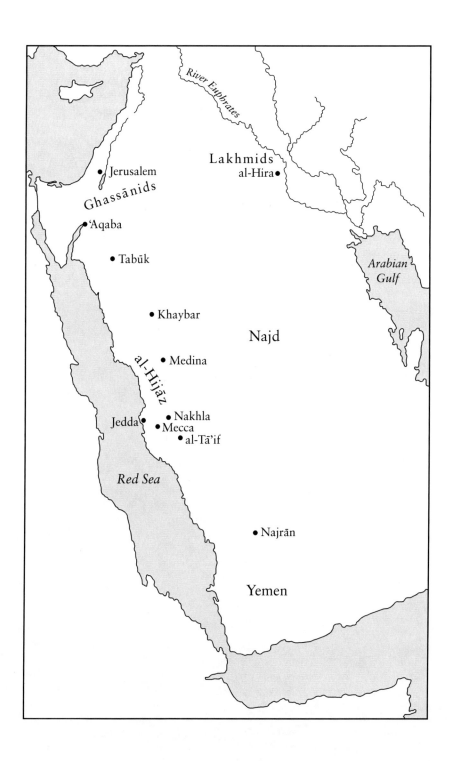

*To the great Ibn Khaldun*

# Introduction and Overview of the Life of Muhammad

If consequences – political and cultural – are the criteria by which to assess the role of an individual in history, then it is quite evident that Muhammad, the founder of Islam, was an extraordinary historical individual. Indeed, there is a sense in which he made history, for he initiated the process that led to a world empire and a world religion. Muhammad had set the process in motion that made it possible for his first two successors, Abu Bakr (632–4) and Umar (634–44), to conquer Mesopotamia, Syria, Palestine, and Egypt in only twelve years after the Prophet's death. And already in the reign of al-Walid (705–15), only 73 years after the Prophet's death, the Islamic Empire reached its greatest extent, embracing all the lands from the Pyrenees through Spain and North Africa to the Indus Valley in the east.

It is probably true that we know little or nothing about the childhood and early youth of any of the great founders of the world religions. The likely reason is that no one took any special interest in them until they grew into adults and became known for their theory and practice. For example, we hear in the Hebrew Bible the story about Moses as an infant in the rushes of the marsh, but we learn nothing more about him until he has reached adulthood. In the New Testament we read about the birth of the man Jesus and his encounter, at age twelve, with wise men in the Temple. But we hear nothing about his youth, meeting him again at age thirty, when he already has begun his mission. The Gospels thus frustrate us with this eighteen-year-long gap, leaving us to speculate concerning Jesus' education, work and general activities during those years. This lack of information appears to be true of Muhammad's childhood and youth as well.

The distinguished contemporary scholar, F. E. Peters, has observed, that with regard to Muhammad's Meccan period, practically nothing is known for sure except his marriage and his preaching. The Quran itself provides no coherent biographical narrative, and as Peters aptly observes, "For Muhammad, unlike Jesus, there is no Josephus to provide a contemporary

political context, no literary apocrypha for a spiritual context and no
Qumran scrolls to illuminate a Palestinian 'sectarian milieu.' "[1]

The earliest biographer of Muhammad was Ibn Ishaq who died in 767
CE, which means that he lived and wrote about 145 years after the Hijra,
that is, after Muhammad's emigration from Mecca and his move to Medina
in 622 CE. The original text of Ibn Ishaq's biography was lost, and no
extant copy of the original exists. All we have is the recension by Ibn
Hisham who died more than 200 years after the Hijra. These earliest
"biographies" were written from a religious–ideological standpoint, and
are based on the oral traditions (*hadiths*) that had developed from the time
of Muhammad's death. The biographers' narratives concerning the
Prophet's childhood and youth are a fusion of legendary and factual elements, obliging the scholar to distinguish between them.

The truth, then, is that the quest for the historical Muhammad is beset
with difficulties and problems, the chief of which is the nature of the
sources. One of the most recent and enlightening discussions of the sources
is found in Fred M. Donner's *Narratives of Islamic Origins*.[2] It is the first
half-century of Islamic history, from about 610 to about 660 CE, that is
most problematic despite its importance. According to Islamic tradition, it
was during those years that the formative events in the life of the Islamic
community occurred: the preaching of Islam's Prophet, Muhammad; the
creation under his leadership of the first community of believers in Arabia;
the rapid military expansion of that community throughout Western Asia
following Muhammad's death; the emergence of the first Islamic Empire;
and the codification of Islam's holy book, the Quran. Muslims of all eras
have looked upon this period of Islamic origins as a "golden age," from
which to seek guidance in how to live their lives.

From the standpoint, however, of modern, intellectually rigorous historical research – carried out, ideally, in an objective attitude – the sources are
highly problematic. Indeed, uncertainty about the reliability of the Islamic
sources has tended to undermine historians' confidence in almost every
aspect of the traditional view of Islamic origins. Some sources, touching
upon the rise of Islam, were produced outside the Islamic tradition, and
scholars justifiably have tried to use them. But those sources too, are, for the
most part, neither contemporary with the events they purport to describe,
nor consistent in what they say. So Donner begins his critical analysis by
turning our attention first to the copious literary sources in Arabic that
purport to inform us about the earliest phase of Islamic history. These
include, among other items, collections of *hadiths*, or sayings, attributed to
the Prophet and his companions, in addition to the text of the Quran itself.
The *hadiths* are also not contemporary sources, some having been written

centuries after the events they discuss. Moreover, one finds in these collections chronological discrepancies, implausibilities, and contradictions. Many accounts are anachronistic; others show evidence not only of embellishment, but outright invention to serve some sort of political or religious purpose.

The first approach taken by Western scholars toward early Islamic history was to accept the traditional picture of Islamic origins presented by the Muslim sources. This was, of course, a decisive advance in historical method over the anti-Islamic polemic that dominated Western writing about Islam from the Middle Ages until the eighteenth century, and which had ignored Muslim sources. When Western scholars began to try to be more objective, they worked with three main assumptions about the Muslim sources: (1) that the text of the Quran contained documentary value for the life and teaching of the Prophet Muhammad; (2) that the *akhbar*, or copious reports making up the narratives about Islamic origins found in Muslim chronicles were reliable for reconstructing "what actually happened"; and (3) that the many *hadiths* attributed to the Prophet were a *religious* literature distinct from the *akhbar* and, therefore, not directly relevant to the task of historical reconstruction of the early Islamic period.

Donner reminds us that this approach has resulted in the fact that the majority of Western surveys of Islamic history have presented the story of Islamic origins along lines remarkably similar to those laid down in the traditional Islamic sources. He cites as examples a long list of such studies, including some on which I rely in my own re-examination of issues in the present work. Donner illustrates the reliance on traditional Islamic sources by showing that it applies not only to early works like those of William Muir and Philip K. Hitti, but also to recent works by G. E. von Grunebaum, M. A. Shaban, M. G. S. Hodgson, Hugh Kennedy, Albert Hourani, and many others. This comfortable replication of the Islamic tradition's own view, Donner remarks, would be perfectly acceptable if it could withstand critical scrutiny. But it became more and more evident in the late nineteenth and early twentieth centuries, that the Islamic texts contained contradictions among different sources, logical and chronological absurdities, implausibilities, and, on top of it all, patent sectarian political bias.

This gave rise to a second approach that Donner calls the *Source-Critical Approach*. It was a central premise of this "school" that the existing narrative sources contained much accurate, early historical material, but that it was intermixed with unreliable material, presumably also of early date. The aim, therefore, was somehow to distinguish between the trustworthy, less trustworthy and untrustworthy accounts. A second premise was, that non-Muslim sources (particularly Christian sources in Syriac and Greek) provided an independent source of evidence against which one could compare specific accounts in the Muslim narratives, to determine whether they were reliable. The third and fourth assumptions of this school were that the *hadith* material was of marginal importance because of its non-historical and religious concerns. Famous scholars like Julius Wellhausen sought to distinguish reliable from unreliable sources, thus establishing tentative criteria for fairly comprehensive syntheses of early Islamic history; he addressed, in particular, the *ridda* wars (the revolt of certain Arabian tribes after the death of Muhammad), the early Islamic conquests, and the history of the Umayyads, subject-matter for which the evidence seemed to be more sound. He refrained, however, from tackling directly the life of the Prophet Muhammad, perhaps, Donner surmises, "because of uncertainty over how to use the *hadith* material" (11). This source-critical approach, Donner avers, contributed some sound insights that continue to be of value, such as the role of later interpolation for dogmatic or political reasons, the misplacement of individual accounts, and the question of the interdependence of different written sources. This method marked a definite advance over the approach of simply relying on and repeating the traditional Muslim narratives.

However, although this source-critical method was an advance, it was most useful only as applied to cases where one could safely assume that the texts in question were transmitted in written form. As it became evident, however, that in the earliest period of Islamic writing first and second centuries AH, i.e., After the *Hijra*, material was often if not usually transmitted orally or in only partially written form, a new methodological approach emerged, which Donner dubs the *traditional-critical approach*, inaugurated by the publication in 1890 of Ignaz Goldziher's epochal study of *hadith*. Donner describes this study as

> the first by a Western scholar to view the *hadith* in the context of conflicting political, religious, and social interests in the Islamic community during its first several centuries, and thus to see it [the *hadith*] as of central importance to an understanding of the whole of early Islamic civilization. Goldziher demonstrated convincingly that many of the *hadiths*, far from being authentic sayings of the Prophet, could only be understood as reflections of those later interests, despite the fact that each *hadith* was equipped with an *isnad*, or chain of informants, who were supposedly the ones through whom the saying had been handed down from the Prophet to later generations of *hadith* collectors. (13–14)

What made Goldziher's findings especially significant is that he had analyzed the supposedly sound *hadiths*, many of which turned out to be forgeries. His work therefore called into question the whole corpus of *hadiths* and the presumed authenticity of *isnads* as records of a *hadith's* origins and transmission.

Goldziher, however, despite his deep skepticism regarding the transmission of the *hadiths*, remained quite positive where the reliability of the Islamic historiographical tradition was concerned. He and some of the later critical scholars continued to maintain that there was a valid "historical kernel" in the traditional material, even if uncovering it in the mass of accretions was an extraordinarily difficult task. But there were also scholars who contended that the application of the source-critical and tradition-critical methods to reports about Islamic origins seemed to reduce the "historical kernel" to the vanishing point. "It was pointed out," Donner writes,

> That *isnads* were found not only in the *hadiths*, but also in many historical accounts, and that it had been on the basis of such *isnads* that source-critics like de Goeje and Wellhausen had relied to identify their different historiographic "schools." If some *hadiths* could be shown by various means to be not the words of the Prophet, but inventions of the second, or third, or fourth centuries A. H., despite an apparently flawless chain of transmitters, how could we be sure that other *hadiths* were not also forgeries which had simply escaped detection? And if forgeries were rife among even the most apparently trustworthy *hadiths*, how could we be sure that other kinds of accounts, including apparently early historical ones relying on similar chains of authorities for their warrant of authenticity, were not also merely later fabrications made for political, religious, or other ends? (19–20)

This gave rise to what Donner calls the *skeptical approach*. Like the tradition-critics, the skeptics view the traditions about Islamic origins as the products of long and partly oral development, but unlike the tradition-critics, "they deny that there is any recoverable kernel of historical fact that might tell us 'what actually happened'" (20). Donner cites as a precursor of the radically skeptical position the works of the Jesuit scholar Henri Lammens who around the beginning of the twentieth century published a series of detailed studies of the background and rise of early Islam. It was his conviction that the *Sira* material, the traditional biography of the Prophet, was not an independent set of recollections of the Prophet's life, but rather an outgrowth of earlier works of Quran commentary (*tafsir*) and *hadith*, or sayings, attributed to the Prophet, most of the latter of which were, in Lammens' view, false. Donner applies the term "skeptical" to this school because "they exhibit a radical skepticism toward the whole received picture of Islamic origins" (20, fn. 47). Among contemporary scholars, it is Patricia Crone whom Donner regards as the most articulate of the recent wave of skeptical writers. In her study, *Slaves on Horses*, she contends that "whether one approaches Islamic historiography from the angle of the religious or the tribal tradition, its overall character remains the same: the bulk of it is debris of an obliterated past" (Crone, p. 10).

Donner cites in addition to Crone, several other skeptics whose names one runs across in the specialist literature: John Wansbrough, Michael Cook, Suliman Bashear, Gerald Hawting, Moshe Sharon, Judith Koren and Yehuda D. Nevo, and Norman Calder. Underlying the work of these radical skeptics are three propositions: (1) the Quran was codified as a closed canon of sacred text much later than assumed by the Muslim tradition – during the second or even the third century A. H., not in the first century as Muslims and most Western scholars have assumed. The Quran itself, therefore, cannot be used as evidence for the origins of Islam, but only for its later development. (2) The narratives of Islamic origins are idealized or polemicized visions of the past that originated in a later period; they contain no "kernel" of historical information, for such information "either was never conveyed, or was completely suppressed, or if it did survive is inextricably entangled with later interpolations" (23). (3) The narratives about the life of the Prophet contain no evidence about Islamic origins independent of the Quran text itself or of later legal traditions. Of these three revisionist propositions, the notion that the Quranic text crystallized generations or perhaps even centuries after Islam's beginnings is the most radical. What the radical, skeptical position implies, in effect, is either that one should look elsewhere for evidence or give up trying altogether.

### Donner's Reply to the Skeptics

Donner counters the extreme methodological pessimism of these skeptics by reminding them and us that it is quite unlikely, a priori, that the whole tradition has been totally reshaped. For such a notion implies that certain unnamed "authorities," "whoever they were, could have tracked down every book and tradition contained in every manuscript in the whole Islamic community, from India to Spain, so that no view dissenting from the standard orthodox position was allowed to survive" (27). For Donner, the traditional material, taken as a whole, and notwithstanding extensive redaction of particular portions of it, contains within it enough material to enable us to catch at least a few reliable glimpses of the early Islamic period. For, as Donner convincingly observes, there are many accounts in the Islamic tradition that seem to contain vestigial evidence of very early historical matters relevant to our quest for the historical Muhammad. We can, for example, glimpse in the sources some of the very early tensions in the community of believers: the rivalry between the *Muhajirun*, Muhammad's emigrants from Mecca, and the *Ansar*, his helpers in Medina; concerns over the proliferation of wealth among the believers during the conquest period, and more.

One of Donner's most persuasive arguments against the radical skeptics is based on his comparative analysis of the Quran and the *hadiths*. He calls attention to their radically different content in order to defend the Quran text as a literary product of the earliest community of believers in Arabia. One of the most striking aspects of the corpus of the *hadith* is the degree to which it reflects the salient *political* issues of the first and second centuries A. H. Donner remarks on a humorous anachronism: that in the *hadith* literature the Prophet even has a considerable amount to say about the Caliphate, even though the office of the Caliph (Khalifa) did not arise until after his death. In sharp contrast, however, to the deep concerns in the *hadith* literature over questions of political leadership, the Quran text has almost nothing to say about political or religious leadership except as it relates to Muhammad himself. The discrepancy between the Quran and *hadith*, where political leadership is concerned, suggests strongly that the two bodies of material came not from a so-called common "sectarian milieu," but from different historical contexts. Moreover, Donner avers, a "much more natural way to explain the Quran's virtual silence on the question of political leadership is to assume that the Quran text, as we now have it, *antedates* the political concerns enshrined so prominently in the *hadith* literature" (45). Donner notes, in addition, the frequent references in the *hadith* to such figures as Muhammad's cousin Ali, his uncles Abu Talib and al-Abbas, the Meccan clan chief, Abu Sufyan, and more; while the Quran, in contrast, makes absolutely no mention of these figures, even in the most innocuous way. And the most telling of Donner's critical responses to the radical skeptics is his recognition of the most obvious and fundamental discrepancy between the Quran and *hadith*: "the fact that the Quran itself is totally devoid of obviously anachronistic references to people, groups, or events dating to periods long after the life of Muhammad" (47–8).

Still another indisputable contrast between the Quran and *hadith*, is their fundamentally different treatments of Muhammad. The overwhelming majority of Quranic passages involving prophets and prophethood are devoted to the many prophets who preceded Muhammad, not to Muhammad himself. In the Quran Muhammad's mortality is affirmed; and although he is the recipient and vehicle of God's revelations, he is in all other respects an ordinary mortal. Indeed, as Donner observes, "the Quran presents Muhammad as suffering indignities from those who, in view of

Muhammad's ordinariness and the absence of miracles, could not believe he was truly a prophet: they say: 'what is with this apostle? He eats food and walks in the market. Why has no angel been sent down to be a warner (*nadhir*) with him?'" (Sura 25; Donner, 51). In the *hadith*, in contrast, Muhammad is no ordinary mortal. There he is frequently portrayed as a miracle-worker who, in Donner's words,

> is able to feed multitudes, heal the sick with his spittle, procure water by pressing the ground with his heel, see behind himself, predict the future, or divine hidden knowledge such as the names of people whom he has not yet met or the origins of a piece of stolen meat served to him. This vision of Muhammad . . . does not coincide with the Quranic image of Muhammad as a normal man, and once again casts doubt on Wansbrough's [and other radical skeptics'] proposition that the Quran originated in the same cultural environment that produced the countless miracle-stories related in the *hadith* literature and origins narratives. (51–2)

In Donner's superb analysis of the issues concerning the narratives of Islamic origins, he makes a strong case for not giving up the quest for the historical Muhammad. A historical–sociological method can, perhaps, help us in this quest – a method derived from the great Ibn Khaldun, whose substantive and methodological insights will be presented in chapter 1 to illustrate their fruitfulness. But first we need a brief overview of the life of Muhammad, basing it on traditional sources while trying to take into account their problematic character.

### Enter Muhammad: An Overview

Fortunately, the biographical narratives regarding the Prophet's Medinan period are largely reliable; for as F. E. Peters explains, the biographies by Ibn Ishaq and the others, were little more than accounts of the " . . . raids conducted by or under Muhammad; and they took the watershed battle of Badr as their starting point and anchor, and dated major events in Muhammad's life from it. But for the years from Badr (624 CE) back to the migration to Medina (622 CE) there is great uncertainty and, for the entire span of the Prophet's life at Mecca, hardly any chronological data at all (264)." In what follows, then, we shall rely not only on Ibn Hisham, Tabari, and other Muslim historians, but also on outstanding Western scholars.

According to tradition, a child was born to the Quraysh at Mecca in or about 570 or 571 CE, and called by his tribe al-Amin, "the faithful," apparently an honorific title. In the Quran (3: 138; 33: 40; 48: 29; 47: 2) his name is Muhammad (highly praised), a quite common name, and he is referred to once as Ahmad. The baby's father, Abdullah, died before the child's birth, and the mother, Aminah, when he was about six years of age. It therefore became the responsibility of the grandfather, Abd-al-Muttalib, to raise the boy and, after the grandfather's death, the duty fell upon Muhammad's uncle, Abu-Talib.

The tradition tells us that when Muhammad was twelve years old, he accompanied his uncle on a caravan journey to Syria where he met a Christian monk to whom legend has given the name Bahira. We use words like "tradition" and "legend" because there is no way to confirm the reliability of stories about the Prophet's early life. There are no non-Arabic, non-Muslim sources for the early period of nascent Islam. The first Byzantine chronicle to record some events of Muhammad's career was Theophanis who wrote in the ninth century.

What does seem to be a fact, however, is Muhammad's marriage at the age of twenty-five to a wealthy widow named Khadijah, fifteen years his senior. She was a member of the Quraysh tribe and a well-to-do merchant's widow – now conducting the business herself and independently – who employed Muhammad and gave him considerable responsibility. Thus lifted out of the relative poverty of his childhood, Muhammad now had the leisure to follow his inclinations, and was often noticed secluding himself and meditating in a small cave on a hillside called Hira, outside of Mecca. Sura 93 seems to confirm that before marrying Khadijah he had been poor, and that until the age of forty or thereabouts, he followed the religion of his tribe and countrymen: "Did He [the Lord] not find thee an orphan and gave thee a home? And found thee erring and guided thee, and found thee needy and enriched thee."

It was during one of those periods of seclusion that he is said to have heard a voice commanding him to "recite" in the name of the Lord. The word *qaraa*, which is the root of the word Quran, parallel to the rabbinic *mikra*, means to recite or address, and its etymology and use in related dialects means *to call, cry aloud, proclaim*. The speaker in this as in most of the Suras, is Gabriel of whom Muhammad had, as he believed, a vision on the hill, Hira. After a brief interval, the second vision came, and Muhammad, feeling the chill of great emotional stress, rushed home to Khadijah, asking her to enwrap him in his mantle. The call and the message he was told to recite was this: God is one, all-powerful and the creator of the universe. There is a judgment day at which great rewards in paradise await those who obey God's commandments; and terrible punishments in hell await those who ignore or disobey them.

Now regarding himself as the messenger (*rasul*) of Allah, Muhammad began to go among his own people, preaching, teaching, and bringing his new message. But they failed to take him seriously, and even laughed at his pretension, which turned him into a *nadhir*, a "warner" (Quran 67: 26; 51: 50, 51) aiming to win over converts by means of vivid descriptions of the joys of paradise and the terrors of hell. That is the impression we get from the early revelations, the Meccan Suras. However, he gained few converts, and it was his wife Khadija, influenced by her *hanif* or Christian cousin Waraqa–ibn–Nawfal, who became the first of the few who responded to his call. Muhammad's cousin Ali and his kinsman Abu-Bakr followed; but Abu-Sufyan, representing the privileged and influential Umayyad branch of Quraysh, continued to oppose the Prophet. For them, Muhammad's views not only flouted the sacred principles of their polytheism, but also threatened the economic interests of the Quraysh as custodians of the center for Arabian pilgrimages. It seems to be highly probable that Muhammad's few other converts came primarily from the slave and lower strata, and were even what Ibn Hisham calls a "despised minority."[2] The reaction of the Quraysh leaders to Muhammad's success with these recruits was to switch from sarcasm and ridicule, which had become less-than-effective weapons, to active persecution. This, in turn, prompted the new converts to flee to Abyssinia and to seek refuge there.

In the year 615, eleven Meccan families followed by 83 other men, found asylum in the domain of the Christian Negus, who adamantly refused to deliver them into the hands of their oppressors (Ibn Hisham, pp. 146–51). The beliefs of these fugitives were so close in some ways to those of the Christians, that the Negus might have viewed them as Christians. Meanwhile, revelations continued to descend upon Muhammad.

Soon Umar ibn-al-Khattab (also transliterated as Omar), who would later play a key role in establishing the Islamic state, became a follower of the Prophet's new view of Allah. It was in this period too, about three years before the Hijra, that the Prophet's beloved Khadija died, followed soon afterward by Abu-Talib, who though he never professed Islam, never ceased to defend his nephew, his protégé. Abu-Talib's defense and protection of Muhammad explains why he had no need to flee with the other persecuted Muslims to Abyssinia. In reality it was the Prophet's clan and not merely his uncle who protected him in accordance with the powerful Arabian custom. The fact that Muhammad's followers had to flee from persecution suggests strongly that they were, as Ibn Hisham stated, a "despised minority" recruited from slaves and the lowest strata of Meccan society. In this pre-Hijra period there also occurs the dramatic *isra*, the night journey in which the Prophet is said to have been carried from the sacred temple of Mecca "to the temple that is more remote," that is, Jerusalem (Sura 17: 1). Although Muslim tradition interprets the phrase, "temple that is more remote" as referring to Jerusalem, the city's name does not actually appear in the passage. Nevertheless, Jerusalem, already sacred to the Jews and Christians, became in the Muslim world, the third holiest city after Mecca and Medina.

In the year 620 some people from Yathrib-Medina, mainly of the Khazraj tribe, or perhaps from both the Aws and the Khazraj tribes, met Muhammad at the Ukaz fair and showed interest in what he had to say. Living in close proximity to the Medinan Jews, they had learned that the Jews were looking forward to the coming of a Messiah. The men of the Arab tribes, having heard by this time of the Prophet of Mecca, believed that he might in fact be the prophet eagerly awaited by the Jews. The Yathribites hoped that by inviting Muhammad to make Medina his home, they would accomplish two things to their advantage: they would win him over to their cause instead of that of the Jews; and they would gain a prophet-mediator who might succeed in reconciling the mutually hostile Aws and Khazraj tribes. Muhammad, on his part, having had even less success in Taif than in his native town, allowed or encouraged about 200 followers to escape from the Quraysh and make their way to Medina. He himself followed soon afterward, arriving there on September 24, 622 – the famous *Hijra*, the migration that apparently had been carefully considered for two years. It was the second Caliph, Umar, who, seventeen years later, designated the lunar year in which the Hijra had taken place, as the official beginning of the Muslim era.

The Hijra definitely marked a turning point in the life of Muhammad. He left the city of his birth as a despised prophet and entered his newly adopted city as an honored chief. The prophet-preacher in him now recedes, and the man of practical politics comes to the fore. What becomes most salient in Medina is his role as political leader, military strategist and warrior. We come now to the circumstances that led to the battle of Badr, and its long-range consequences. It was under the leadership of the new chief, during the months of the "holy truce," that the Medinan Muslims, now termed *Ansar* (supporters), developed a scheme by which to offer sustenance to the *Muhajirun* (emigrants). They intercepted a summer caravan on its return from Syria to Mecca. The caravan leader, Abu-Sufyan, had got wind of the scheme and sent to Mecca for reinforcements. The clash between the reinforcements and the Medinans, mostly Emigrants, took place at Badr, 85 miles southwest of Medina in Ramadan, 624 CE. The victory of the Medinans under the inspired leadership of the Prophet, acquired long-range, religious significance; for it was a complete victory of

300 Muslims over 1,000 Meccans of the Quraysh. The solidarity of the Medinan Muslims was immeasurably strengthened by the meaning assigned to the victory as divine sanction of the new faith. As Philip Hitti observed, "the spirit of discipline and contempt of death manifested at this first armed encounter of Islam proved characteristic of it in all its later and greater conquests."[3]

In the following year (625), however, the Muslims suffered defeat at the battle of Uhud (Ibn Hisham, pp. 370f). The Meccans, under the leadership of Abu-Sufyan, avenged their earlier defeat and even wounded the Prophet. But this proved to be only a temporary setback, for after Uhud, Islam recovered and turned from the defensive to the offensive in which military victories and the propagation of its faith went hand-in-hand and seemed always assured. In Mecca, nascent Islam was a religion; in Medina after Badr, it became more than a religion – it became what the world has ever since recognized it to be, a religion and a militant polity.

## The Battle of the Trench

In 627, some three years after Badr, an alliance which the Quran calls "confederates," consisting of Meccans, Bedouins, and Abyssinian mercenaries, gathered for the invasion of Medina (Sura 33: 9–25). In the face of so formidable a force, it seemed to the Medinans that there was no way they could successfully defend themselves against it. But a Persian follower, it is said, advised Muhammad to dig a wide trench around Medina, a military innovation that struck the Bedouins as the most unfair tactic they had ever seen. Disgusted, they lifted the month-long siege and withdrew with the loss of some twenty men on both sides.

We come now to Muhammad's relations with the Yathrib–Medinan Jewish tribes, to which later chapters will be devoted. After the besiegers in the Battle of the Trench withdrew, Muhammad launched a campaign against the Jewish tribes on the pretext of their having "sided with the confederates." To grasp adequately the underlying socioeconomic causes of the growing antagonism between Muhammad and the Jews, we have to invoke Ibn Khaldun's theory of the interplay between the desert and the sown, between Bedouins and sedentary cultures, a theory discussed in detail in the next chapter. In the context of Yathrib–Medina and its environs, the Jews represented the sown and were correspondingly better off than the Emigrants and the Medinan supporters of Muhammad. It was, therefore, not merely religious–ideological differences, but also and, primarily, material economic and political differences that resulted in the killing of between 600 and 900 men of the Jewish tribe, Banu-Qurayza, and the selling of the women and children into slavery. These men were systematically beheaded after they had surrendered, which appears to have been an unprecedented atrocity in the Hijaz. Muhammad then turned over the now-ownerless date plantations of the Jews to the Emigrants. A year before the massacre, Muhammad had sent into exile the Banu-al-Nadir, a second Jewish tribe of Medina, and confiscated their land as well. The Jews of Khaybar, a strongly fortified oasis north of Medina, came next. Most of the settlements surrendered in the year 628, and, in order to save their lives, agreed to pay as tribute 50 percent of their yield. Muhammad agreed to this arrangement, most likely because by this time he had come to understand that he had more to gain from such an arrangement than from killing or expelling the Khaybar Jews: he realized that his Bedouin followers possessed neither the knowledge, the skills, nor the will to engage in agricultural labor.

It was in the Medinan period that Muhammad decisively severed his relationship with both Judaism and Christianity. More than earlier his self-understanding defined him as a prophet sent to the Arabs, which meant that all the institutions of the new religion ought to be Arabianized so as to appeal to the latent Arabian national sentiment. This was the apparent motive behind the substitution of Friday for the Jewish and Christian Sabbaths; for the *adhan* (the call from the minaret) in place of trumpets and gongs; for Ramadan as a definite month of fasting; for Mecca as the *qibla* (the direction faced in prayer) instead of Jerusalem; for the pilgrimage to the Kaaba; and for sanctioning the kissing of the Black Stone, a pre-Islamic fetish. In sum, Muhammad's Arabianization of Islam was accomplished by retaining virtually all of the key elements of the old faith and by infusing these elements with new meaning – a meaning that would not only continue to resonate with the ethnic sentiments of the Bedouin, but create an *inter-tribal* "group feeling" in Ibn Khaldun's sense.

Muhammad's "group feeling" or solidarity with his own tribe never waned. On the contrary, it remained strong and intense in spite of their treatment of him and his followers. He had left Mecca and his tribe as a prophet without honor. But now that he was an armed prophet, he was determined to regain his honor with the Quraysh. His attachment to his tribe is so great that he eventually places them in positions of leadership and privilege in his militant Islamic polity. In the year 628 Muhammad deliberately led a *small* group of some 200 followers – so as not to appear intent upon aggression – to a settlement, al-Hudaybiya, nine miles from Mecca, where he exacted a pact from the Meccans in which they and the Muslims were to be treated on equal terms. This treaty brought to an end the war with his own people, the Quraysh. Members of his tribe, including several who had been the Prophet's bitter opponents, were recruited to his cause. Most notable were Khalid ibn-al-Walid and Amr ibn-al-As, who became the two "mighty swords" of militant Islam. In January 630, the murder of a Muslim by a Meccan in what appears to have been a personal quarrel, served as *casus belli* for the final attack and conquest of Mecca. Entering its sanctuary, Muhammad smashed the hundreds of idols and exclaimed that "truth has come and falsehood has vanished" (Hitti, 118; Quran 17: 83).

Another sign of the affection Muhammad felt for his tribe, is the magnanimity with which he treated the people. Scholars propose that it was at this time that Muhammad declared the environs of the Kaaba as *haram* (sacred), and dictated the passage in Sura 9: 28: "O Believers! Only those who join gods with God are unclean! Let them not, therefore, after this . . . year, come near the sacred Temple." This verse was evidently intended to forbid only polytheists from approaching the Kaaba during the annual pilgrimage, but the verse was later interpreted as prohibiting all non-Muslims from approaching the sacred shrine.

In 631, Muhammad's forces were numerous and strong enough for him to station a garrison as far north as Tabuk on the frontier of the Ghassanids, and without a single military engagement to conclude peace treaties with the Christian chief of Aqaba and the Jewish tribes of the oases to the south. The Jews and the Christians were now taken under the protection of the Islamic community in return for a payment of tribute later called *jizyah*. This became a precedent largely followed by the Caliphs. It was also in the years 630–1 that delegations came even from great distances to offer allegiance to the Prophet who had now become a prince. Tribes joined largely out of material considerations – the allure of booty – and the extent of their religious conviction was demonstrated by a brief verbal profession of faith and a payment of *zakah* (poor tax). Arabia, which had never before bowed to the will of one man, appeared now willing to be ruled by Muhammad and incorporated into his political and religious movement.

Ten years after the Hijra, Muhammad, at the head of the annual pilgrimage, entered Mecca, his new religious capital, peacefully. Three months after his return to Medina, he became ill and, complaining of a headache, died (June 8, 632). Scholars agree that even in the height of his glory, Muhammad had led a modest and unpretentious life. He was often seen mending his own clothes, and he stayed at all times within the reach of his people.

The new community of Emigrants and Supporters that Muhammad had established in Medina was the first attempt in the history of Arabia at a social organization based on religion rather than on kinship. In his last sermon, Muhammad enjoined his followers to take these words to heart, that every Muslim is a brother to every other Muslim. As Hitti observes,

> thus by one stroke the most vital bond of Arab relationship, that of tribal kinship, was replaced by a new bond, that of faith; a sort of Pax Islamica was instituted for Arabia . . . Its mosque was its public forum and military drill ground as well as its place of common worship. The leader in prayer, the *Imam*, was also to be commander-in-chief of the army of the faithful, who were enjoined to protect one another against the entire world. All Arabians who remained heathen were outside the pale, almost outlaws. Islam cancelled the past. Wine and gambling – next to women the two indulgences dearest to the Arabian heart – were abolished in one verse [Quran 5: 92] . . . (Hitti, 120–1).[4]

In this brief overview, much of importance has been left unsaid. So we need to start again and address key questions, problems and issues. And to do so most effectively, we need to introduce the great Ibn Khaldun.

# 1

# Ibn Khaldun's Social and Economic Theory

## Bedouins and Sedentary Peoples

For Ibn Khaldun, Bedouins and sedentary peoples are what he calls "natural groups," by which he means socio-economically determined groups.[1] The differences of condition among people are largely the result of the different ways in which they make their living. Social organization enables them to cooperate, starting with the provision of the basic necessities of life. From the earliest periods of history, some people were able to adopt agriculture – the cultivation of vegetables and grains – as their way of making a living, while others adopted animal husbandry, the raising of sheep, goats, bees, and silkworms for breeding and for their products. Those who live by animal husbandry cannot avoid the call of the desert. Their way of life seldom takes them beyond the bare subsistence level. If and when they do produce surpluses, they use them to build large houses and towns for their protection. This brings with it comfort and ease and the development of luxurious customs. They thus become sedentary, the inhabitants of cities, some adopting crafts as their way of making a living, others choosing commerce. They therefore earn more and live more comfortably than Bedouins.

In contrast to sedentary peoples, the Arabs[2] use tents of hair and wool, or houses of wood, clay or stone, and provide themselves with the other bare necessities of life: food, shade, and shelter, and nothing beyond that. All this was true of the Arabs of pre-Islamic Arabia. Those who cultivate grain and practice agriculture are bound to remain stationary, settling in small communities and villages. In early history they were predominantly non-Arabs. Those who raise sheep, goats, and cattle are frequently on the move, seeking pasture and water for their animals. They go not deep into the desert because good pastures are rare there. But those who make their living by raising camels, as did the Arabs of the Hijaz (the region about Mecca and

Medina), wander deep into the desert where the camels are capable of feeding on desert shrubs and drinking the salty desert water. In winter, the camels are driven even deeper into the desert, fleeing the cold and seeking the warm desert air. It is also in the warm desert sands that the female camels can find hospitable places in which to give birth to their young.

Because the Arabs of the Arabian Peninsula live almost exclusively on camels, they are more deeply rooted in desert life than are other groups who live for the most part on sheep and cattle, but on camels as well. Temporally, Bedouins are prior to sedentary people. The toughness of desert life precedes the relative softness of sedentary life. Bedouins are more courageous than settled peoples because the latter become used to ease, laziness, and luxury, entrusting their safety and the defense of their property to a ruler and his armed men. They rely on the fortified walls surrounding them, and they become so carefree that they carry no weapons. The Bedouins, in contrast, being remote from the sedentary ruler's militias, walls, and gates, provide their own defense, and are always armed. Their chief characteristics are fortitude and courage.

## Asabiyah

Ibn Khaldun now introduces one of his key concepts, *asabiyah*, which may be translated as "group feeling" or "solidarity." As Franz Rosenthal, the distinguished translator of the *Muqaddimah* observes: "Islam generally condemned *asabiyah* if it took the form of 'a blind support for one's group without regard for the justice of its cause.' As such, any show of *asabiyah* is deprecated as an atavistic survival of the pagan, pre-Islamic mentality" (vol. I, lxxi). Ibn Khaldun was, of course, aware of this negative connotation; but he distinguishes between this objectionable form and the natural *asabiyah* that is a part of being human. The latter is the affection one feels for others when they are treated unjustly or killed. Nothing can take it away. It is equivalent in some ways to what Rousseau later referred to as the natural pity or compassion one feels for one's fellows, or even for other sentient creatures. This form of *asabiyah* is not forbidden by Muslim religious law. On the contrary, it is something desirable and useful in connection with the holy war (*Jihad*) and with propaganda for Islam (lxxix). A preponderance of *asabiyah* renders one group stronger than others.

Ibn Khaldun stresses that only tribes held together by group feeling and loyalty can live in the desert. They have to be united because they are in a state of conflict, actual or potential, with other tribes due to the scarcity of pasture and water. Group feeling results from "blood" ties, or something corresponding to it – the notion or fact of common descent. The advantage of such a notion or fact consists in the group feeling or solidarity that derives from it, and which leads to mutual affection, devotion, and aid – and unity against hostile external forces.

Owing, then, to the strength of their *asabiyah*, savage peoples are better able to achieve superiority than others. Savage groups, like the Arab–Bedouin, are braver than others. They are therefore better able to achieve superiority in battle and to rob things that are in the hands of other peoples. It is the socio-economic condition of their daily lives that accounts for their superiority in that respect. Just as it is the socio-economic condition of people who settle in the fertile valleys and begin to live in luxury that accounts for their diminished bravery. Ibn Khaldun now gives us an additional insight: "Superiority," he avers, "comes to peoples through enterprise and courage. The more firmly rooted in desert habits and the wilder a group is, the closer does it come to achieving superiority over others, if both parties are approximately equal in number, strength, and group feeling" (vol. I, 283). We shall see, in due course, how fruitful this insight is for an understanding of early Islam.

Ibn Khaldun now proceeds to provide historical evidence to support his theoretical proposition. Tribes that remained in the desert longer than others successfully took away and appropriated what the other tribes and groups possessed. Sustained desert habits tended to preserve the strength of the successful groups' feeling. And it is such groups that eventually become the most powerful among the Arabs. Ibn Khaldun now anticipates Thomas Hobbes by recognizing another implication of group feeling in the desert context of tribal particularism. According to their nature, Ibn Khaldun writes,

> human beings need someone to act as a restraining influence and mediator in every social organization, in order to keep the members from fighting each other. That person must, by necessity, have superiority over others in the matter of group feeling. If not, his power to exercise a restraining influence could not materialize. Such superiority is royal authority (*mulk*). It is more than leadership. Leadership means being a chieftain, and the leader is obeyed, but has no power to force others to accept his rulings. Royal authority [a leviathan or common power in Hobbes' terms] means superiority and the power to rule by force [if necessary].(I, 284)

Ibn Khaldun goes further in anticipating Hobbes' view of the international arena as existing in what he calls a "state of nature and war of each against all." Even if an individual tribe has several clans and households, and allegiances to them, "still there must exist a group feeling that is stronger than all the other [particular] group feelings combined, that is superior to them all and makes them subservient, and in which all the diverse group feelings coalesce . . . to become one greater group feeling. Otherwise, splits would occur and lead to dissension and strife" (vol. I, 285). Furthermore, once such an overarching group feeling has established itself under a central authority, it will strive to gain superiority over other groups. If the two groups are relatively equal, each will maintain its sway over its own domain and people "as is the case with tribes and nations all over the earth" (Ibid.). Moreover, if one such solidified group overpowers the other and makes it subservient to itself, the two group feelings add power to the victorious group feeling, thus setting its goal of superiority and domination higher than before. This process continues until the power of the victor becomes a ruling dynasty. But then a new tendential law becomes operative, and in time the ruling dynasty grows senile; and if no defender arises from among its friends who share in its group feeling, a new and oppositional group feeling takes over, deprives the preceding dynasty of its power and displaces it.

In Ibn Khaldun's theory of this historical process, it is the very victory of the group that tends to undermine the conditions that had led to its victory; for the victorious group has now gained control over a considerable amount of wealth, and comes to share the prosperity and luxuries of which the vanquished group has been dispossessed. Now, members of the victorious group are primarily concerned with leading an easy, restful life, with the result that the toughness of desert life is lost and the virtue of courage declines steadily in succeeding generations; and the formerly victorious group's new vulnerability is such that it invites its own destruction. Meekness and docility – due to the relaxed and luxurious way of life – that become more and more characteristic of the settled cultures and their dynasties, tend to undermine the vigor and strength of their group feeling. Meekness and docility are, then, for Ibn Khaldun, an effect rather than a cause, for when a people has become meek and docile, that shows that their group feeling is lost. They do not become meek until they have become too weak to defend themselves.

Still reflecting on the Arabs of both pre-Islamic and Islamic history, Ibn Khaldun proposes that when a people is savage, as are the Arabs of the desert, its power is more effective, for they are, among human beings, as beasts of prey among domestic animals. Savage peoples, moreover, have no permanent homelands that they might use as fertile pasture, and therefore no fixed base. All regions and places are the same to them. Hence, they do not restrict themselves to the possession and protection of their own and neighboring regions. Instead, they swarm across distant zones and achieve superiority over faraway nations, at least temporarily.

Arabs or Bedouin, Ibn Khaldun observes, can gain control most easily over flat territory, because they "plunder and cause damage. They plunder whatever they are able to lay their hands on without having to fight or to expose themselves to danger. They then retreat to their pastures in the desert" (I, 302). What is quite striking and remarkable in the following characterization of the Arab-Bedouins, is Ibn Khaldun's scholarly object-ivity. He states that "places that succumb to the Arabs are quickly ruined" (I, 302). "The reason for this," he writes,

> is that the Arabs[3] are a savage nation, fully accustomed to savagery and the things that cause it. Savagery has become their character and nature. They enjoy it, because it means freedom from authority and no subservience to rulers. Such a . . . disposition is the negation and antithesis of civilization. All the customary activities of the Arabs lead to travel and movement. This is the antithesis and negation of stationariness, which produces civilization. For instance, the Arabs need stones to set them up as supports for their cooking pots. So, they take them from buildings which they tear down to get the stones, and use them for that purpose. Wood, too, is needed by them for props for their tents and for use as tent poles for their dwellings. So, they tear down roofs to get the wood for that purpose. (vol. I, 303)

Furthermore, it is their socially determined second nature "to plunder whatever other people possess. Their sustenance lies wherever the shadow of their lances falls. They recognize no limit in taking the possessions of other people . . ." (Ibid.). And "since they use force to make craftsmen and professional workers do their work, they do not see any value in it and do not pay them for it . . ." (Ibid.).

In his characterization of the Arab–Bedouins, there are several more "furthermores."

> Furthermore, the Arabs are not concerned with laws . . . They care only for the property that they might take away from people through looting and imposts. When they have obtained that, they have no interest in anything further, such as taking care of people, looking after their interests, or forcing them not to commit misdeeds . . . (vol. I, 304).
>
> Furthermore, every Arab is eager to be the leader. Scarcely a one of them would cede his power to another, even to his father, his brother, or the eldest member of the family. (Ibid.)
>
> It is noteworthy how civilization always collapsed in places the Arabs took over and conquered, and how such settlements were depopulated and the very earth there turned into something that was no longer earth. The Yemen

where the Arabs live is in ruins, except for a few cities. Persian civilization in the Arab Iraq is likewise completely ruined. The same applies to contemporary Syria. (vol. I, 305)

It is, of course, Ibn Khaldun as an Arab here speaking, for he claims Arab descent through the male line. On that subject, Franz Rosenthal writes:

> While Ibn Khaldun's Arab descent has occasionally been questioned, it has also been considered a major influence in forming his outlook on life and history. Neither point of view has anything to recommend it. Ibn Khaldun's claim to Arab descent through the male line cannot reasonably be doubted . . . Decisive in itself is the fact that he believed himself to be of Arab descent, a circumstance that, in a sense, conferred title of nobility. However, even if Ibn Khaldun was proud of his ancient Arab lineage, there is no indication that it colored his historical views or influenced his reactions to his environment . . . In fact, it would seem that not his Arab descent, but his Spanish origin was the crucial factor in his intellectual development and outlook . . . (vol. I, xxxiv)

It is certainly Ibn Khaldun's consistent striving for objectivity and his hard-headed realism that is so impressive even when discussing the Arab–Bedouin character, or perhaps one should say especially when discussing that subject. Perhaps his realistic, unsentimental view of desert Arabs was colored by the fact that he belonged to a clan of *South* Arabian origin, for there was a world of difference between the south-Arabian, sedentary cultures and the north-Arabian desert Arabs of the Hijaz. The clan Khaldun, from whom the family name was derived, is believed to have immigrated to Spain in the eighth century, in the early years of the Muslim conquest. Hence, Ibn Khaldun's experience in the high Muslim culture of Spain at the time may have influenced *not* his objective views of the desert Arab–Bedouin, but, perhaps, the way he expressed his views, which sound, occasionally, as if they are derogatory (Rosenthal, vol. I, lxxxiii).

As we continue with a few more of Ibn Khaldun's observations, it becomes evident that he is interpreting the results of Muhammad's mission in the Arabian Peninsula. "Arabs," he writes, "can obtain royal authority [and inter-tribal unity] only by making use of some religious coloring, such as prophecy, or sainthood, or some great religious event in general" (vol. I, 305). "The reason for this," Ibn Khaldun explains, "is that because of their savagery, the Arabs are the least willing of nations to subordinate themselves to each other, as they are rude, proud, ambitious, and eager to be the leader . . . But when there is religion among them through prophecy or sainthood, then they have some restraining influence in themselves. The qualities of haughtiness and jealousy leave them. It is then easier for them to subordinate themselves and unite as a social organization. This is achieved by the common religion they now have" (vol. I, Ibid.).

Again employing a proto-Hobbesian proposition, Ibn Khaldun explains why the Arabs are of all peoples most remote from "royal leadership." Due to the attributes acquired in the deep desert, they remain remote from the inter-tribal unity made possible by the establishment of a "common power" or leviathan in Hobbes' sense, which Ibn Khaldun calls "royal leadership." Again referring implicitly to Muhammad's contribution, Ibn Khaldun writes that the Arabs attain "royal leadership" " . . . only once their nature has undergone a complete transformation under the influence of some religious coloring that . . . causes them to have a restraining influence on themselves . . ." (vol. I, 307). This is illustrated by the Arab dynasty in Islam where religion cemented leadership with the religious law and its ordinances, which are concerned with what is good for civilization. As the Caliphs followed one another, the royal authority and government of the Arabs became great and strong. But writing in the fourteenth century after careful reflection on the history of the Arabs, Ibn Khaldun recognized that the particularistic, centrifugal forces of the desert-Arabian tribes had never ceased to operate in spite of Islam, which proved to be only a temporarily unifying ideology. For the Arabs neglected their religion, and eventually lost the central political leadership or common power that is the *sine qua non* of inter-tribal solidarity. They thus returned to their desert, and to domination by the adjacent, neighboring populations.

For Ibn Khaldun, "royal authority" or what Hobbes calls a "common power," is attained only through a strong group feeling. The reason is clear: both aggressive and defensive strength are obtained only through a group feeling which creates real mutual affection and willingness to fight and die for one another. Such willingness applies not merely to one's own clan or tribe, but to the larger organization of several or many tribes. How did this come about in the history of the Arabs?

Ibn Khaldun's answer is, that what he calls "religious propaganda" gives a social organization a substantial increment of power in addition to that of the group feeling it had possessed owing to the number of its supporters. The acceptance of Islam, therefore, not only diminished the inter-tribal conflicts of the desert Arabs, it created a higher form of solidarity among them. This he illustrates with the experience of the Arabs at the beginning of Islam during the Muslim conquests. Though the Persians and the Byzantines under Heraclius vastly outnumbered the Arabs, neither of the two imperial armies was able to withstand the Arabs who routed them and seized their possessions. Ibn Khaldun further clarifies his point by maintaining that "religious propaganda cannot materialize without group feeling" (vol. I, 322).

To appreciate the profundity of this insight we have to understand it to mean that the higher form of solidarity cannot result from just any kind of religious propaganda. The new religious ideas have, rather, to resonate with the basic values, sentiments, and interests of the groups in question, in this case the tribes of northern Arabia. Following this logic, we can say that Muhammad's preaching at Mecca for thirteen years, had failed, apparently, to resonate with the sentiments and interests of the majority of Meccans, for he succeeded in producing there only a small sect of followers, who had ultimately to flee from persecution. When did Muhammad's message begin to capture the imagination of the Arab tribes of the Hijaz? The answer, as we shall soon demonstrate in detail, is that it was only in Medina that his message began to acquire an increasingly wide appeal, which was due to the new strategy he adopted, the sword instead of the sermon, or more correctly, the sword *and* the sermon. Hence, as Ibn Khaldun observed, when God united the power of the Arabs in Islam, it enabled them to take possession of the realms of the Persians and the Byzantines who were the greatest powers of the time – "as well as the realms of the Turks in the East, of the European Christians and Berbers in the West (Maghrib), and of the Goths in Spain. They [the Arab Muslims] went from the Hijaz to as-Sus in the far West, and from Yemen to the Turks in the farthest north. They gained possession of all seven zones" (I, 330).

Charles Issawi[4] has provided a splendid summary of Ibn Khaldun's theoretical framework with which we can appropriately conclude this introductory discussion and prepare for the detailed analyses of the forthcoming chapters.

The social life of the pre-Islamic desert Arabs was, on the whole, "solitary, poor, nasty, brutish and short," owing to the tribal wars of each against all. Hence, where *asabiyah* is concerned, it existed only within each tribe, but not as a force unifying the tribes with one another. Moreover, the poverty of the desert means that little or nothing ties them to the land of their birth. A new religion can establish itself only by *strife*, and will succeed only if it enlists the help of a powerful social solidarity; but once established, a religion can not only greatly reinforce social solidarity within each tribe, but even create an overarching social solidarity to the extent of eliminating the war of each against all, at least for a time.

The new, religiously determined inter-tribal solidarity mobilizes and concentrates a multitude of wills and emotions around a common purpose. The combination of religious and inter-tribal solidarity is formidable, and to it Ibn Khaldun attributes the rapid and sweeping conquests of the

Muslim Arabs of the seventh century. But if inter-tribal solidarity can found empires, it can also check them. Ibn Khaldun contrasts the easy task of ruling sedentary peoples like Egypt with the difficulties encountered in Morocco, owing to the existence of many independent tribes; or the struggle of the Israelites to subjugate the tribes of ancient Canaan. His general sociological proposition, then, is that the extent of an empire will vary directly with the strength of the original solidarity that created it, and inversely with the strength of the solidarities it encounters. Although this proposition may now appear to be obvious or merely common-sensical, it emerged from Ibn Khaldun's careful study of history.

A state can arise only on the basis of some original solidarity. Once established, however, the need for solidarity decreases, as the unquestioned power of the ruler secures the required acquiescence and obedience of the subjects. But the State, like any other social institution, is subject to the laws of change, and, indeed, decline. The State, created originally by inter-tribal solidarity, is characterized in its early stages by a cohesiveness and comradeship that enables the people to participate in government. But owing to the disintegrating effects of sedentary and luxurious living, the ruler seeks to make his power absolute. The pattern Ibn Khaldun perceived was that the ruler now created a new class of clients personally attached to him, and substituted mercenary soldiers for his erstwhile primitive comrades in arms and counsel. What follows is an increase in pomp and ceremony, the concentration of power in the hands of the ruler, and a fundamental estrangement between ruler and subjects. The pomp and luxury lead to financial crises; taxes are raised, and the pay of the officials and soldiers becomes overdue, thus creating fertile soil for violent uprisings, civil war or external aggression and a change of rulers.

In underscoring the originality of this theory, Issawi notes that although Ibn Khaldun cites outstanding Muslim historians such as Tabari, Masudi, Waqidi, and others, they rarely rise above the level of chroniclers. It is therefore almost certain that Ibn Khaldun could not have derived from them his sociological search for general patterns and tendencies.

As we reflect, then, on Ibn Khaldun's extraordinary contribution to our understanding of history in general, and of Arab and Muslim history in particular, it is easy to see why we shall rely on him periodically in this quest for the historical Muhammad. Ibn Khaldun has been favorably compared with Thucydides and Machiavelli for his realism and objectivity. And Arnold Toynbee, in his *Study of History*, stated that the *Muqaddima* " . . . is undoubtedly the greatest work of its kind that has ever been created by any mind in any time or place."

# 2

# Pre-Islamic Arabia

The Arabian Peninsula comprises an area of almost continental proportions, being as large as Europe west of the Vistula, including the British Isles. This great expanse, however, is about nine-tenths desert. It is only here and there that one might find fertile spots, the most extensive of which is the strip along the Red Sea. Before Muhammad, as we have seen, the Peninsula was inhabited principally by nomadic, Bedouin tribes without a common government. They lived a pastoral life, herding sheep, goats, and cattle, and moving from one grassy plot to another. The most absorbing interests of their lives were cattle and caravan raiding and intertribal conflicts over pasture lands. During four months of the year, however, on the occasion of religious pilgrimages, festivals, and fairs, a truce was called during which raiding, by common agreement, was prohibited. At all times, however, the custom of according hospitality even to the most inveterate enemy – an unwritten and unbreakable law – was observed. These Bedouin tribes had no literature or plastic arts, but the poets or bards who recited in sonorous language the heroic exploits of their tribes, were greatly honored.

Not all tribes lived a nomadic life. In the fertile strip along the Red Sea were a number of settlements, the most important of which were Mecca and Medina. They were inhabited by the more sedentary Arabs who – according to an earlier view – were mainly engaged in commerce. There appeared to have been a much traveled caravan route extending from the southwestern tip of Arabia northward through Mecca and Medina into Syria and Mesopotamia. The conventional view is that along that route passed caravans carrying goods from India and perhaps even China, a view which needs to be challenged in a later context. The inhabitants of Mecca also profited from the fact that their settlement or town possessed a famous shrine called the Kaaba. In addition to numerous idols, the shrine contained a black stone that was the special object of veneration of the surrounding tribes. According to legend, it had fallen from heaven, which suggests that it might have been a meteorite. Polytheism, therefore, may be the appropriate term with which to describe the religion of the Arabs of the Hijaz.

Arabia is one of the driest and hottest of regions. In the Hijaz, the birth-place of Islam, droughts can last as long as three or four years. Rain, when it occurs, takes the form of violent storms of short duration, following which the hardy pastoral flora of the desert makes its appearance. In the northern Hijaz it is the few isolated oases, the largest covering an area of 10 square miles, that are the only support of settled life. Most of these fertile tracts were cultivated at the time of Muhammad by Jews. Apart from the springs that exist in the few oases, there is no other major source of water. The Peninsula possesses not a single river of significance that flows constantly and reaches the sea. The absence of a system of rivers means that the inhabitants rely on a network of wadis to carry away the flood waters. The wadis tend to determine the routes of the caravans and the pilgrimages. The dry air and the salty soil inhibit the possibility of any luxurious growth, although the Hijaz oases are rich in dates. Indeed, the date-palm tree, most probably introduced by the oasis-dwelling Jews, who were experienced in agriculture, bears the most common and esteemed fruit (*tamr*). It is this fruit which, together with milk, constitutes the chief item in the Bedouins' daily diet; and except for the occasional meal of camel flesh, is his only solid food.

The Bedouins' principal domestic animals are the camel, the ass, the watch dog, the greyhound, the cat, the sheep and the goat. Although the horse has become renowned in Muslim literature, it was a late importation into ancient Arabia. The horse is an animal of luxury whose feeding and care is difficult for the denizen of the desert. Its possession requires wealth and its main value lies in providing the speed necessary for a successful Bedouin raid. Moreover, the horse in the Arabian environment, requires water even more frequently than humans. So it is the camel, from the nomad's standpoint, that is the most useful. Without this animal, humans would find the deeper regions of the desert uninhabitable. Philip Hitti explains just how essential is the camel to the Bedouin's way of life: "It is the Bedouin's constant companion, his *alter ego*, his foster parent. He drinks its milk instead of water (which he spares for the cattle); he feasts on its flesh; he covers himself with its skin; he makes his tent of its hair. Its dung he uses as fuel, and its urine as a hair tonic and medicine."[1] The paramount importance of the camel in the economic life of the Arab–Bedouin is dramatically illustrated by the fact that there may be as many as one-hundred names for the camel in the Arabic language. This animal can serve his master without water, if necessary, for about twenty-five days in winter and five in the summer. The camel was a factor accounting for the success of the early Muslim conquests, for in providing more mobility, it became a definite advantage over the settled peoples.

The Arab–Bedouin represents the best human adaptation to Near Eastern desert conditions. As Ibn Khaldun was among the first to observe, the interaction between the desert and the settled peoples was dictated by self-interest and self-preservation. The nomad feels no compunction about taking from his more favorably situated neighbor whatever he himself lacks. He does so, for the most part, by means of violence – raids. Hunting and raiding are his staple occupation and to his mind the only occupations worthy of a man. As he regards himself as a noble warrior, he looks with contempt on agriculture and all forms of trade and craft. We have already mentioned the principle of hospitality, which together with fortitude and manliness are considered supreme virtues. We need, however, to add another principle that was honored in pre-Islamic Arabia. Although the sharp competition for water and pasturage had split the desert populace into warring tribes, there were, nevertheless, rules of the game: no blood should be shed except in cases of extreme necessity. The relevance of this important fact will become clear in a later discussion of raids and war in early Islam.

Clan organization is the basis of Bedouin society. Each family lives in a tent; an encampment of tents forms a *hayy*; members of one *hayy* make up a clan (*qawm*). A number of kindred clans constitute a tribe (*qabilah*). "Banu" (children of) is the title with which clan and/or tribal members prefix their joint name. *Asabiyah* in the pre-Islamic era, implied unconditional, chauvinistic loyalty to fellow clansmen. Hitti, stating what we have already learned from Ibn Khaldun, writes:

> This ineradicable particularism in the clan, which is the individualism of the member of the clan magnified, assumes that the clan or tribe, as the case may be, is a unit by itself, self-sufficient and absolute, and regards every other clan or tribe as its legitimate victim and object of plunder . . . The unsocial features of individualism and *asabiyah* were never outgrown by the Arab character as it developed and unfolded itself after the rise of Islam, and were among the determining factors that led to the disintegration and ultimate downfall of the various Islamic states. (Hitti, 27–8)

## The Hijaz on the Eve of the Rise of Islam

Muslim scholars refer to the pre-Islamic era as the *Jahiliyah* period, the "time of ignorance" or "barbarism," the period in which Arabia had no inspired prophet, no revealed book. As the Arabs of the Hijaz had no system of writing, our sources are limited to legends, traditions, proverbs, and above all to poems, all of which were committed to writing two-to four-hundred years after the events which they were supposed to commemorate. Eloquence, the ability to express oneself forcefully and well in both prose and poetry, was as essential an attribute of the perfect man as excellence in archery and horsemanship. In this heroic age of the Hijaz, prior to the emergence of a system of writing, poetry was the only means of literary expression. The poet served diverse functions. In battle, his tongue raised his tribe's morale by singing its praise and by denigrating its opponents. There is a sense in which the Bedouin character itself is expressed in poetry. Alan Jones, in his *Early Arabic Poetry*[2] illustrates how central was the role of the poet in the life of the Bedouin. Jones opens by citing the views of early Muslim commentators: "In the days of Ignorance verse was to the Arabs the register of all they knew, and the utmost compass of their wisdom; with it they began their affairs, and with it they ended them" (Year 845). More illuminating are the words of another early Muslim commentator:

When there appeared a poet in a family of the Arabs, the other tribes round about would gather together to that family and wish them joy for their good luck. Feasts would be got ready, the women of the tribe would join together in bands, playing upon lutes, as they were wont to do at bridals, and the men and boys would congratulate one another; for a poet was a defense to the honor of them all, a weapon to ward off insult from their good name, and a means of perpetuating their glorious deeds and of establishing their fame for ever. And they used not to wish one another joy but for three things – the birth of a boy, the coming to light of a poet, and the foaling of a noble mare. (Year 1070)

Jones comments that both passages accurately reflect the basic importance of poetry in early Arabic tribal society. The poetry of a tribe helped to distinguish it from other tribes. "It was a projection into words," Jones writes,

of the life of the tribe, its solidarity and its aspirations, its fears and its sorrows . . . Poetry helped to emphasize a tribe's uniqueness and its virtues and to vaunt them against similar claims made by neighboring rivals. Moreover, poetry had a quality not possessed by a tribe's worldly possessions. Land, camels, goods and chattels, even members of the tribe could be seized or destroyed by enemies; but as long as the collective memory survived, so would the tribe's poetry, together with two other bulwarks of separate identity, both close to the hearts of the *bedu*: *ansab* "genealogies" and *akhbar* "legends of the tribe's history." However, neither *ansab* nor *akhbar* had the force, the quasi-magical power of poetry. (1)

Philip Hitti explains the quasi-magical role of the Arabian poet: "The Arabian poet (*shair*), as the name indicates, was originally one endowed with knowledge hidden from the common man, which knowledge he received from a demon, his special *shaytan* (Satan). As a poet he was in league with the unseen powers and could by his curses bring evil upon the enemy. Satire (*hija*) was therefore a very early form of Arabic poetry" (94). Hitti remarks in a footnote that Balaam of the Hebrew Bible (Num. 23:7) was a type of primitive Arabian satirist. Jones, agreeing with Hitti, writes that "poetry had a number of facets that took it into the realm of magic. First, each poet was believed to be inspired by his own spirit, who was one of the *jinn* (equivalent to the Greek *daimon*). Secondly, a poet's poetic utterances were believed to have a magical force." Jones then cites approvingly Hitti's strong statement about the Arabic language:

> No people in the world, perhaps, manifest such enthusiastic admiration for literary expression and are so moved by the word, spoken or written, as the Arabs. Hardly any language seems capable of exercising over the minds of their users such irresistible influences as Arabic. Modern audiences in Baghdad, Damascus, and Cairo can be stirred to the highest degree by the recital of poems, only vaguely comprehended, and by the delivery of orations in the classical tongue, though it be only partially understood. The rhythm, the rhyme, the music, produce on them the effect of what they call "lawful magic." (Hitti, 90)

Early Arabic poetry, then, is essentially tribal poetry, the substance of which reflects what we have learned so far about the Bedouin's way of life – their nomadic character, their dependence on camels and to a lesser extent on their sheep and goats; their environs in the desert and semi-desert areas, and the surrounding mountains; their tribal raids and feuds and the consequent outlook on life as hard and dangerous. From the poetry we also learn that a complex code of social conduct regulated both intra-tribal and inter-tribal relationships, and that there was an ethical code based on the notion of *muruwwa* (manliness).

## Pre-Islamic Religion

Alan Jones, in his Introduction to the Quran (Koran),[3] observes that the Bedouin had an outlook on life that was dominated by the concept of FATE, what the ancient Greeks called *moira*. "Their poetry makes it clear," Jones writes, that there basic belief was that Fate ruled their destiny and that sooner or later Fate would bring death. They knew about gods and idols, but there are lines of poetry that show that the gods, even Allah, were less important to the *bedu* than Fate . . .

Though the *bedu* seem to have had little expectation that Fate might be pro-pitiated in this manner [by means of rituals and pilgrimages], they appear to have sought to avoid its final, fatal appearance in somewhat less formal ways, and divination and soothsayers (*kahins*) were all popular. (Jones, *Koran*, xii)

Jones stresses that throughout the early Muslim period, right up to the first Caliphates, the majority of poets were *bedu* and

poetry was associated much more with nomadic life than it was with settled places. That is not to say that such centers as Mecca and Medina were without poets, but they do not appear to have flourished in the way that their nomadic counterparts did. It is not fortuitous that all the poets represented in this book were *bedu* – that appears to have been the case even with the unknown women – and only one, Labid, ever moved to a settlement, and that under the influence of Islam. (Jones, *Early Arabic* . . . p. 6)

The religious beliefs and practices of the pre-Islamic Bedouin may be characterized as a form of polytheism, which included the expectation of reciprocity in a human's relationship with a deity. This expectation is rec-ognized in classical sociological studies of religion. Henri Hubert and Marcel Mauss, in their study of sacrifice,[4] took for their central theme a Vedic principle that sacrifice is a gift that compels the deity to make a return: I give so that you may give. It is likely that this earlier work by Hubert and Mauss inspired Mauss' later classic study *The Gift*, in which he documents his thesis of a morally sustained gift cycle upholding the cycle of social life. The gift cycle in social life, with its obligatory reciprocity, became the model for the human being's relation to the divine. Following Mauss' work, subsequent research suggested that hopes and expectations of reciprocity from a deity is a rather general phenomenon. It is notewor-thy in this regard, that a distinguished specialist in Islamic studies, Marshall G. S. Hodgson, has discerned this phenomenon in pre-Islamic Mecca. He writes:

The prevailing religious climate in Mecca was still not far removed from Bedouin paganism round about. Relations with fetishes or with deities were chiefly on the basis of bargaining – for the offering I give you lord, you will give me that favor in return. That was little removed from magic. Lots were cast at the Kaaba to foretell fortunes, and vows and sacrifices were made to assure success.[5]

That the hope and expectation of reciprocity is a general phenomenon and evident in the monotheistic religions as well, can be illustrated where one might least expect it – in the Book of Job. If anyone had an exquisite love of the Divine, it was certainly Job. But even the most exquisite such love carries with it a concern for oneself and one's loved ones, and a trust that the Deity will reciprocate for the offerings made to him. We are told in the Book of Job that when he learned that his sons had invited their sisters to a feast, he "sanctified them and rose up early in the morning, and offered burnt offerings according to the number of them all; for Job said: 'It may be that my sons have sinned, and blasphemed God in their hearts.' Thus did Job continually" (1: 5). This strongly suggests that in making his offering, Job expected a reciprocal consideration from the Deity.

In the pre-Islamic, Arabian context, a deity's or oracle's failure to provide a wished-for response might even have evoked anger. Hitti relates the tale concerning Imru-al-Qays who set out to avenge the murder of his father, and stopped at a shrine to consult the oracle by means of drawing arrows, a ritual later explicitly forbidden by Islam (Quran 5: 4, 92). Upon drawing the response "abandon" thrice, he hurled the broken arrows at the idol, shouting "Accursed one! Had it been thy father who was murdered, Thou wouldst not have forbidden my avenging him" (Hitti, 96).

It appears that for any knowledge at all about pre-Islamic religion in the Hijaz, we have to rely on the references in the poetry and primarily on the few allusions to polytheism in the Islamic literature. The Bedouins' religion was basically animistic in the sense introduced by the pioneer anthropologist, E. B. Tylor. Even after the notion of deities in the form of spirits and idols had emerged, the Bedu continued to regard natural objects such as trees, wells, caves and stones, as sacred objects, either as fetishes or as media through which the individual could get in touch with the deity. Spring water, not surprisingly, early acquired such a sacred character, as did the spring in the desert, with all of its life-supporting qualities. The famous well of Zamzam, of which we shall hear more, became holy, according to Arabian authors such as Ibn Hisham, long before the emergence of Islam, and went back to the time that it supplied water to Hagar and Ishmael. In due course we shall address the question whether the presumed association of Abraham, Hagar and Ishmael with Zamzam and the Kaaba at Mecca is historical.

The moon in whose light the Bedouin grazed his flocks was the center of his astral beliefs. It seems to be true that moon-worship or veneration is characteristic of pastoral societies, while sun-centered worship emerged at a later agricultural period. The beliefs of desert Bedouins included, as already mentioned, animistic spirits, or beings called *jinn* or demons. While the deities are believed to be, on the whole, benevolent, the *jinn* are viewed as hostile. With Islam the number of *jinn* increased as the polytheistic deities were then degraded into such beings. Among the settled peoples of the Hijaz, which constituted a small fraction of the total population, the astral stage of polytheism was evident early. The three daughters of Allah, Al-Uzza, al-Lat and Manat, had their sanctuaries in the region that later became the birthplace of Islam.

Just as the historicity of Abraham's connection with the Kaaba requires clarification, so does the question of whether Muhammad, in his early conception of monotheism, had believed it was compatible with the three daughters of Allah as intercessors with him. Certain early Muslim writers such as Tabari, have related that having become thoroughly estranged from the members of his own tribe, the Quraysh, he sought to win them over by making the concession of recognizing these powerful goddesses of Mecca as associates of Allah. As Hitti writes:

> In a weak moment, the monotheistic Muhammad was tempted (Quran, 22: 51–2; 17: 74–6) to recognize these powerful deities . . . and make a compromise in their favor, but afterwards he retracted and the revelation is said to have received the form now found in Sura 53: 19–20. Later theologians explained the case according to the principle of *nasikh* and *mansukh*, abrogating and abrogated verses, by means of which God revokes and alters the announcements of His will; this results in the cancellation of a verse and the substitution of another for it (Quran, 2: 100). (Hitti, 99)

This issue will receive a fuller analysis in a later chapter.

The Meccan Kaaba, the chief deity of which was Hubal (from the Aramaic word for vapor or spirit), was represented in human form. A soothsayer (*kahin* also Aramaic), on duty with the ritual arrows used for divination, drew lots by means of them. The pre-Islamic Kaaba, according to tradition, was an unpretentious cube-like (hence the name) structure of primitive simplicity, originally roofless, serving as the domicile for a black meteorite venerated as a fetish. With the emergence of Islam the structure was rebuilt, presumably with the aid of an Abyssinian, from the wreckage of a Byzantine ship destroyed on the shore of the Red Sea. The territory around the Kaaba and even beyond it, was regarded as sacred (*haram*). The traditional pilgrimages were made there and special sacrifices offered. Muslim tradition maintains that the Kaaba was originally built by Adam according to a celestial prototype, and, after the Deluge, rebuilt by Abraham and Ishmael (Quran, 2: 118–21). The Kaaba, according to tradition, remained in Ishmael's descendants charge until the polytheistic tribe, Banu-Jurhum, and later the Banu-Khuzaah, took possession of it and introduced idol worship.

Allah (meaning "the god") appears to have been the principal deity of Mecca, and to the best of our knowledge, there was no iconic representation of him. Hitti informs us that "the name is an ancient one. It occurs in two South Arabia inscriptions, one a Minaean found at al-Ula and the other a Sabaean, but abounds in the form HLH in the Lihyanite inscriptions of the fifth century BC . . . The name occurs as Hallah in the Safa inscriptions five centuries before Islam and also in a pre-Islamic Christian Arabic inscription found in Umm-al-Jimal, Syria, and ascribed to the sixth century. The name of Muhammad's father was "Abd-Allah (Abdullah, the slave or worshipper of Allah)" (Hitti, 101).

The pre-Islamic Meccans regarded Allah as the creator and supreme provider and *the* deity to be invoked in times of peril or need. Those are the qualities attributed to Allah by several Quranic passages: 31: 24, 31; 6: 137, 109; 10: 23. The Kaaba and its environs made the Hijaz the most important religious area in north Arabia.

The Bedouins, especially during the four months of "holy truce," frequented the settled towns of the Hijaz and there picked up some of the urban beliefs and were thus introduced to the ritualistic practices of the Kaaba and the offering of sacrifices – camels and sheep at Mecca, and at idols and altars in the vicinity. The pilgrimage to a notable shrine of the settled Arabs was a most important religious practice of the desert-dwelling Arabs. Of the four months of the holy truce, the first three were devoted to religious observance, while the fourth was set aside for trade. The central location of the Hijaz on what appears to have been a main caravan route running north and south, offered hospitable conditions for both religious and commercial activity – I say "appears to have been," because we shall have to call attention to serious challenges to this notion in our later discussion of Muhammad at Mecca.

The Hijaz, meaning "barrier," is so called because it is in fact barren country standing like a barrier between the uplands of Najd and the low coastal region called Tihamah (low land). We know of only three urban settlements in the region – Mecca, Medina (earlier called Yathrib) and Taif. The third of these, situated at an altitude of 6000 feet, and rich in shady trees and a variety of succulent fruits, was a summer resort for the Meccan elite. The products of this settlement included honey, watermelons, bananas, figs, grapes, almonds, peaches, and pomegranates. Its roses were known for the attar from which some Meccans produced perfume. The vines of Taif, we learn from Hitti, citing al-Aghani, were introduced by a Jewish woman who offered the first slips as a present to the local chief. Hitti remarks that "of all places in the Peninsula al-Taif came nearest to the Koranic description of paradise in Sura 47: 16–17" (103).

The name "Mecca," meaning "sanctuary," suggests that it owes its foundation to some religious group, and that the settlement had been some sort of religious center long before Muhammad was born. It lies in the southern Hijaz, about 48 miles east of the Red Sea in a barren, rocky valley described in the Quran (14: 40) as "unfit for cultivation." Hence, the Meccans or more correctly its chief tribe, the Quraysh, sought their prosperity from another source. For it was under their leadership, as the custodians of the Kaaba, that it became a national shrine and, indeed, a commercially profitable one.

Yathrib, some 295–300 miles north of Mecca, was, as Hitti remarks, much more favored by nature than its southern sister. It was a veritable oasis and, as mentioned earlier, well adapted for the cultivation of date palms. Now, because the Jewish tribes of Yathrib and Khaybar are a necessary subject in any adequate discussion of Muhammad at Medina, we will first present Hitti's description of the role of the Jews in Yathrib, and then, in a later chapter, analyze in some detail the Prophet's relationship with them. Hitti writes:

> In the hands of its Jewish inhabitants, the banu-Nadir and banu-Qurayza, the town became a leading agricultural center. Judging by their proper names and the Aramaean vocabulary used in their agricultural life these Jews must have been mostly Judaized clans of Arabian and Aramaean stock, though the nucleus may have been Israelites who fled from Palestine at the time of its conquest by the Romans in the first century after Christ [70 CE] It was possibly these Aramaic-speaking [and Arabic-speaking] Jews who changed the name Yathrib into Aramaic Medinta, the explanation of the name al-Madinah (Medina) as "the town" (of the Prophet) being a comparatively late one. The two leading non-Jewish tribes were the Aws and the Khazraj, who came originally from al-Yaman. (104)

Hitti calls attention in this context to another possible phenomenon in the Hijaz: that in addition to Judaism, Christianity, and polytheism, there may have existed a form of monotheism or quasi-monotheism that was distinct from Judaism and Christianity. The Muslim sources use the term *hanif* to describe an adherent of a monotheism of that sort. Hitti alerts us to an inscription (542–3 CE) of Abraha, a version of the name Abraham, the Abyssinian viceroy, dealing with the alleged break of the Marib Dam.

It begins with the words: "In the power and grace and mercy of the merciful [Rahman-an] and His Messiah and of the Holy Spirit." The word *Rahman-an* is especially significant because its northern equivalent, *al-Rahman*, later became a prominent attribute of Allah and one of His names in the Quran and in Islamic theology. The word *Rahman* is also Hebrew and Aramaic, meaning compassionate and merciful; and there is the related *Rahmanah*, meaning God the merciful. Later we shall have to explore in detail the proposition that there had existed in pre-Islamic Arabia some form of non-Judaic, non-Christian monotheism.

In the century prior to the birth of Islam, Zoroastrian Persia contended with Christian Abyssinia for control of Yemen. Persian military arts were passing into Arab hands from the south and also from the north through Persian Arabia, with its capital al-Hira near the Euphrates. Muslim tradition relates that it was Salman the Persian who instructed the Prophet on how to dig a trench for the defense of Medina. Al-Hira was the main conduit through which not only Persian cultural influences but, later, Aramaean Nestorian influences penetrated Arabia of the pre-Islamic era. It was the Nestorians who transmitted northern cultural ideas of an Aramaic, Persian and Hellenistic origin into polytheistic Arabia; just as it was, apparently, the Nestorians who later conveyed Hellenistic concepts to nascent Islam. The kind of influence the Nestorians of al-Hira had on the Arabs near the Persian border, was exerted by the Monophysites of Ghassanland upon the people of the Hijaz. For several centuries prior to the rise of Islam, these Syrianized, Christian Arabs had been bringing the Arabian Bedouins of the Peninsula in touch not only with Syria, but also with Byzantium. Hence we find that such personal names as Dawud (David), Sulayman (Solomon), Isa (Jesus), were fairly common among the pre-Islamic Arabians. We shall need, then, in a separate chapter, to assess the influence of Christianity on nascent Islam.

Hitti stresses, however, that one must not overestimate the Christian influence in forming the *hanif* monotheism or quasi-monotheism of Arabia. That the Jews were ubiquitous in the Hijaz most scholars would agree; and Jewish colonies flourished in Medina and in the various other oases of the northern Hijaz, such as Khaybar. *Jibril* (Gabriel), *Surah*, the word for "chapter" in the Quran, *jabbar* (Heb. *Gibbor*, "most powerful"), illustrate Hebrew words in the Arabic vocabulary. Hitti agrees that there were individuals in the Peninsula, and individuals in the settlements or towns, who had acquired vague monotheistic concepts and went by the name of *Hanifs*: "Umayyah ibn-abi-al-Salt (624 CE), through his mother a second cousin of the Prophet, and Waraqah ibn-Nawfal, a cousin of Khadija, were such Hanifs, though several sources make Waraqah a Christian" (Hitti, 108).

# 3

# The Role of Abraham, Hagar, and Ishmael

According to Islamic tradition and the Quran, Abraham[1] was neither a Jew nor a Christian; he was a Hanif, who first preached the Divine Unity and thus became the original Muslim, that is, the first to surrender to God. It was Abraham and his son Ishmael who, purportedly, had built the original mosque and made Mecca a permanent habitat. If we had to state the Islamic view concerning Abraham, Hagar, and Ishmael, it would read something like the following summary.[2]

Abraham was born in Mesopotamia to a father whose occupation was carpentry and the making and selling of idols for worship. As Abraham grew up and witnessed his father at work, he was astonished by the people's worship of pieces of wood. He developed serious doubts that these icons, wrought from wood, were truly deities. He asked his father how *he* could worship the products of his hands, and being dissatisfied with the reply, he shared his doubts with his friends. This aroused his father's fears that if the word got out that his son was questioning the beliefs and practices of the people, it would not only threaten his own trade and means of livelihood, but also place Abraham's life in jeopardy. Abraham refused, however, to silence himself, and went about seeking to convince his people of the foolishness and futility of idol worship. Once, when he noticed that the worshippers were absent from the shrine, he seized the opportunity and destroyed all the idols but one, the one revered as the principal deity. When he was accused publicly of this offense and asked whether it was he who had destroyed the community's gods, he replied: "No, it was the chief god who destroyed the others. Ask them, for they would speak, wouldn't they?"

Abraham thus recognized that the idols were no-gods, but not knowing, as yet, who ought to be the true object of devotion, he began his search. When night came and he saw a star rise, he thought for the moment that it might be the true God. But then the star set, so he asked himself, how can that have been the true God if it disappeared? Then the moon appeared and shone brilliantly, and he thought, perhaps that is the God. But when the moon also disappeared, he was again disappointed. Later, Abraham observed the sun in all of its glory, and thought to himself, surely it is the greatest of all and must be the master of the world. But then it, too, set and disappeared, which brought Abraham the insight that the sun worship common among his people was no less fallacious than worshipping the products of one's hands. In that way, Abraham, it is said, arrived at the conclusion that it is only He who had created the heavens and the earth who is God. Thereafter, Abraham became a *hanif* and dedicated himself to the worship of the one true God.

Although Abraham had thus liberated *himself* from polytheism, he had failed to liberate his people from their foolish and futile notions. Indeed, the people tried to punish him for his iconoclasm by throwing him into the fire, but God rescued him and allowed him to escape to Canaan together with his wife, Sarah. From Canaan (Palestine) they moved on to Egypt where the Hyksos or Amalekite kings ruled and were wont to take into their households and harems beautiful women even if they were married.

Abraham, learning of this and fearing for his life, said to Sarah, you are a fair woman to look upon, and it may come to pass that when the Egyptians will see you, they will say, "she is his wife," and they will kill me and make you their captive. So say that you are my sister, so that I may be protected. The King, however, did take Sarah, and when he later discovered that she was Abraham's wife, the King blamed him for his lie, returned Sarah to him with gifts, one of which was a slave girl named Hagar. As Sarah remained barren for many years, she urged Abraham to go into Hagar, which he did, and she bore him his son Ishmael. Later, when Ishmael was a youth, Sarah bore Abraham a son called Ishaq (Isaac).

## Who was the Sacrificial Son?

Ishmael, according to Islamic tradition, was the sacrificial son. The only disagreement among Islamic historians is whether it took place before or after the birth of Isaac; and whether it took place in Palestine or in the Hijaz. Jewish historians insist, of course, that the sacrificial son was Isaac, not Ishmael. So Haykal rejects the biblical view, citing the work of Shaykh Abd al Wahhab al Najjar, *Qisas al Anbiya*, who concluded that the sacrificial son was Ishmael. His evidence he drew from the Quran itself where the text states that the sacrificial son was Abraham's "unique son," who could only be Ishmael, and only as long as Isaac had not yet been born. Explaining the difference of opinion among Muslim historians, Haykal writes:

> For with the birth of Ishaq, Ibrahim would have no "unique" son but two, Ismail and Ishaq. But to accede to this evidence implies that the sacrifice should have taken place in Palestine. This would be equally true in case the sacrificial son was Ishaq, for the latter remained with his mother Sarah in Palestine and never left for the Hijaz. On the other hand, the report [i.e., a *Hadith* or traditional report] which makes the sacrifice take place on the mountain of Mina near Makkah [Mecca] identifies the sacrificial son as Ismail. The Quran did not mention the name of the sacrificial son, and hence Muslim historians disagree in this regard. (Haykal, 24–5)

In the Quranic version of Abraham's readiness to sacrifice his son (37: 100f.), Abraham saw in a dream God commanding him to sacrifice his son to Him. Therefore in the morning he took his son and went out to fulfill the command. When they reached the destination Abraham said, "my son, I saw in a dream God commanding me to offer you up as a sacrifice. What will you say to that?" Ishmael replied: "Fulfill whatever God has commanded; for by God's will you will find me patient." When Abraham then threw his son to the ground and prepared for the procedure, God called out to him: "O Abraham, you have already fulfilled the commandment by intending to obey Me. We shall reward you as we reward the virtuous. You have manifestly succeeded in your travail. We ransomed him with a worthy sacrificial animal" (Haykal, 25).

## The Islamic Theory that Abraham, Ishmael, and Hagar Traveled to the Valley of Mecca

Isaac grew up with his brother Ishmael. Abraham loved both sons equally, but Sarah was displeased with this equation of her son with the son of the slave girl, Hagar. In time, Sarah refused to live in the same household with Hagar, so Abraham, taking her and Ishmael, traveled south until they arrived at the valley of Mecca. Although Mecca was a resting place for caravans that came in season, this place was empty at all or most other times. Abraham deposited Ishmael and Hagar there and left them some sustenance. Hagar set up a tent in which she and her son settled, and where Abraham could visit when he returned. When water and food were exhausted, Hagar set out to find the necessities of life, but found none. As the *hadiths* or story-tellers of the tradition relate what happened next,

Hagar ran towards the valley searching for water, and finding none, ran in another direction. Running thus back and forth between Safa and Marwah, she returned in despair to her son and was delighted to discover that he, having scratched the earth with his foot, had miraculously uncovered a spring, from which mother and son drank to their satiety. It was this discovery of the spring called Zamzam, that made it possible for mother and son to continue to live in Mecca, and, indeed, to provide water to cara-vaneers and other Arab travelers.

In some versions of the story, the Zamzam attracted tribes to the area, among which the Jurhum was the first to settle in Mecca. Other versions say that Jurhum was already settled in Mecca even before Hagar and Ishmael arrived. The most favored tradition, however, is that no tribes settled there until Zamzam had sprung forth and made life possible in this otherwise barren valley. When Ishmael became a man, he married a woman of the Jurhum tribe and lived with this tribe until he built the holy shrine, around which the town of Mecca arose.

In his discussion of these traditional stories, Haykal states that although Muslim historians disagree on details, there is a consensus among them that Abraham and Ishmael had in fact emigrated to Mecca. The only ques-tions on which the historians disagree, as mentioned earlier, is whether, when Hagar and Ishmael arrived, the Zamzam was already a live spring, and whether the Jurhum tribe had already occupied the place and had wel-comed Hagar and her son to live in their midst. Muslim historians also propose that when Ishmael married a Jurhum woman and had several sons with her, it was this mixture of Hebrew, Egyptian, and Arab blood that gave Ishmael's descendants the resoluteness, courage and other virtues of the native Arabs, Hebrews, and Egyptians combined.

Haykal now employs as a foil the famous pioneer Western scholar, Sir William Muir, who not only doubts the whole story of Abraham's and Ishmael's trip to the Hijaz, but denies it altogether. Summarizing Muir's view, Haykal writes that Muir claims that it is one of the Israelitisms which the Jews had invented long before Islam emerged in order to create a con-nection with the Arabs by making them descendants of Abraham as father of all. As the Jews regarded themselves as descendants of Isaac, they would become the cousins of the Arabs and therefore entitled to Arab hospitality if the Arabs were declared the sons of Isaac's brother, Ishmael. Such a theme, properly advocated, was probably thought to establish the legit-imacy of the Jewish presence in the Hijaz. In making this claim, says Haykal, Muir assumed that the religious situation in Arabia was far removed from the religion of Abraham. The former was pagan whereas Abraham was a monotheist. In response to Muir, Haykal writes: "For our part, we do not think that this is sufficient reason to deny a historical truth. Our evidence for the paganism of the Arabs is centuries later than the arrival of Abraham and Ishmael to the scene. It cannot therefore constitute any proof that at the time of Abraham's arrival to the Hijaz and his building of the Kaaba with his son Ishmael that the Arabs were pagan" (28–9).

In his attempted rebuttal of Muir, then, Haykal questions that the religion of the Arabs was pagan at the time. Haykal argues that had Abraham called the Arabs to monotheism, as earlier he had called his own people of Mesopotamia without success, the Arabs thus remaining idol worshippers, they would not have allowed Abraham and Ishmael to settle in Mecca. Haykal believes that this argument tends to corroborate the traditional Muslim reports (*hadiths*). For Haykal it is logical to assume that "Abraham, the man who left Iraq to escape from his people and traveled to Palestine and Egypt, was a man who knew how to travel and was familiar with desert crossing. The road between Palestine and Mecca was one trodden by the caravans for ages. There is, therefore, no reason to doubt a [purportedly] historical event which [traditional Islamic] consensus has confirmed, at least in its general themes" (29).


## Abraham, Ishmael, and the Kaaba

That Abraham and Ishmael had laid the foundations of the Kaaba, and that it was the first house built for public worship, is a fundamental element of the Islamic faith. Consequently, Haykal feels the need to address this question: "How did it happen that Abraham built the house as a place of refuge and security for the people so that the believers in God alone might use it for prayer, and then it became a pantheon full of statues for idol worship?" (30)

Haykal supports the traditional view that Abraham's and Ishmael's monotheism had preceded any form of paganism. He asks, therefore, how and when Abrahamic monotheism was superseded by polytheism. He acknowledges, however, that it is in vain that one turns the pages of Muslim history books for an answer. In effect, Haykal finds it impossible to answer the question. All we find in the Muslim *hadiths* "are presumptions which their authors think are reports of facts" (30).

Haykal nevertheless presents some of those presumptions. The Sabeans, for example, are said to have been star worshippers, and they enjoyed great popularity and prestige in Arabia. But the Sabeans did not always worship the stars for their own sake. At an earlier time, they had worshipped God alone and venerated the stars as signs of His creation and power. However, as the majority of the people were not cultivated enough to understand the transcendent nature of the Godhead, they confused the stars with God and took them as gods. Also, some of the volcanic or meteoric stones appeared to men to have fallen from heaven, and therefore to be astral in nature. Consequently, they were taken as manifestations of the astral divinities and sanctified as such. Later on they were venerated for their own sake, and then worshipped as divinities. "In fact, the Arabs venerated these stones so much," Haykal writes, "that not only did they worship the Black Stone in the Kaaba, but they would take one of the stones of the Kaaba as a holy object [fetish] in their travels, praying to it and asking it to bless every move they made. Thus all the veneration and worship due to the stars, or to the creator of the stars, were now conferred upon these stones. It was in a development similar to this, that paganism was established in Arabia, that the statues were sanctified, and that sacrifices were offered to them. This is the picture which some [Muslim] historians give of religious development in Arabia after Abraham dedicated the Kaaba to the worship of God" (30–1). Haykal, however, then cites Herodotus and Diodorus as witnesses "to the antiquity of paganism in the Peninsula and therefore to the fact that the religion of Abraham was not always observed there" (31). Haykal thus finds himself unable to support the traditional Islamic view by means of sound historical evidence. As we have now heard the Islamic views concerning Abraham's role, it is time to hear how Western scholars view it. And as Haykal merely touched upon Muir's analysis, we need to provide a fuller exposition of it.

## William Muir on the Abrahamic Question

Muir opens with an analysis of the Abrahamic tribes according to the Hebrew Bible and the Arabic tradition.[3] He begins by noting that the Arabic tradition is comparatively late, and that all that is ancient is derived from the Jews. The Muslim tradition concerning Abraham is not original, but taken at second hand from the Jews. "Muhammad," Muir writes,

> having claimed to be of the seed of Ishmael, the Jewish Rabbis who were gained over to his cause endeavored to confirm the claim from the genealogies of the Old Testament and of rabbinical tradition . . . Muhammad's paternal line (which he himself declared could not be followed beyond Adnan, that is, about a century before the Christian era) was nevertheless traced up by fabricated steps, eighteen centuries farther, to Ishmael. Both the legends and the ethnological assumptions of Mahometans regarding events prior to the Christian era, being thus directly derived from the Jews, possess no value of their own, and as evidence must be entirely rejected. (cviii)

For Muir, the books of Moses are our only guide and, according to that source the Abrahamic ethnic groups are: (1) Ishmaelites; (2) Keturahites; (3) Edomites; (4) Moabites and Ammonites; and (5) Nahorites. It would be fair to say that the northern and central tracts of Arabia were widely peopled by the Abrahamic tribes. This proposition is strengthened for Muir by indisputable traditional and linguistic evidence. The popular tradition of some of these tribes is that they are descended from Abraham, and this view of themselves was current as far south as Mecca before the time of Muhammad. Now Muir makes a point deserving of careful consideration:

> It is, indeed, improbable that a tradition of this nature should have been handed down from the remote age of the patriarch by an independent train of evidence in any particular tribe, or association of tribes; it is far more likely that it was borrowed from the Jews, and kept alive by occasional communication with them. Still, the bare fact of such a notion gaining even a partial and intermittent currency in any tribe, affords a strong presumption that the tribe was really of Abrahamic descent or connexion; and that the common associations, habits, language, or religious tenets, derived from that origin, naturally fell in with the tradition and rendered easy and natural its adoption. (cxv)

Muir needs, therefore, to address the question of how Abrahamic tradition became blended with what he calls the "legend of the Kaaba." He writes:

> We learn from the Muslim tradition that the earliest inhabitants of Mecca, Medina, and the deserts of Syria, were Amalekites; and that it was an Amalekite tribe which, attracted to Mecca by the well Zamzam, there adopted and nurtured the youthful Ishmael and his forlorn mother.

Muir, continuing, uses strong words:

> The legend is a myth, or rather a travestied plagiarism from Scripture. We may conjecture the facts to have been thus: Amalekite or Idumean tribes were scattered over the north and center of the Peninsula. They formed probably the aboriginal population of Mecca, or settled there in conjunction with immigrants from Yemen, at a very remote period. Subsequently, an Ishmaelitish tribe, either Nabatean or of some collateral stock, was attracted thither also by the wells, and its favorable position for the caravan trade, and acquired great influence. This tribe would carry in its train the patriarchal legend of Abrahamic origin, and engraft it upon the local superstitions, which were either native or imported from Yemen. Hence arose the mongrel

worship of the Kaaba, with its Ishmaelitish legends, of which Muhammad took so great advantage. (cxxv–cxxvi)

It follows from Muir's analysis that some of the Arab tribes may have been acquainted with monotheistic or henotheistic ideas, thus producing what in the Quran and the *hadiths* are referred to as the phenomenon of the *hanif*. But this phenomenon early had become mixed with or syncretized with idolatry, fetishism, the belief in Fate and other forms of polytheism. Muir then advances another cogent proposition, that a decline into total polytheism would eventually have caused the memory of Abraham and his religion to fade and vanish, had it not been for the presence in the neighborhood of the Jews who, in communication with the Arab tribes, revived the knowledge of Abrahamic descent and the nature of the common progenitor's faith. Social interaction with the Jews, settled at many points throughout the Peninsula, would have extended and deepened this knowledge. Circumcision, Muir notes, was received among the Arabs apparently as an Abrahamic rite; and the biblical "story of Abraham, grievously distorted indeed and shorn of its spiritual bearing, but yet possessing a grain of truth, was current at Mecca prior to Islam and, inwrought into the ritual of the Kaaba, was adopted by the whole Arab race [sic]" (cxxix). Of course, Christianity reinforced the Abrahamic origin of monotheism.

## Muir on the Founding of Mecca and the Abrahamic Legend

In 440 CE, Kussai gathered the scattered members of the Quraysh tribe and settled them at Mecca. Its main function became the provision of food and water for the pilgrims. The religious observances of the Kaaba included the *umra* or lesser pilgrimage, the hasty passing to and fro seven times between the little hills of Safa and Marwa near the Kaaba, which may have been performed at any season of the year, but was especially meritorious if performed in the sacred month of Rajab. Before entering the sacred territory, the votary put on the pilgrim garb, and at the conclusion of the ceremonies shaved his head and pared his nails. In addition to the lesser, there was also the greater pilgrimage (*hajj al Akhbar*), involving all the ceremonies of the lesser, but performed only in the holy month Dzul Hijja, and requiring as well, the additional rite of pilgrimage to Arafat, a small mountain composed of granite rocks in a valley ten or twelve miles east of Mecca. The environs of Mecca for several miles around, as noted earlier, were considered sacred, *Haram*. The Four Holy months were also regarded as a part of this religious system. During three consecutive months (the last two of one year and the first of the following) and during the seventh month (Rajab), war was by the mutual consent of the tribes suspended, and a universal truce appears to have prevailed. Pilgrims from all regions of the Peninsula were then free to make their way to Mecca.

Originally, the Meccan calendrical year was, most probably, lunar. This continued until the beginning of the fifth century, when under Jewish influence it was turned, by the insertion of a month at the close of every third year, into a luni-solar calendar.

This examination by Muir of pre-Islamic religion suggests strongly that there was no Abrahamic element in the ceremonies of the Kaaba – and this in the light of the remote antiquity of the Kaaba. Muir cites Herodotus who named one of the chief Arab divinities Alilat, which is strong evidence of the worship, at that early period, of Allat, the Meccan idol. Herodotus alludes also to the Arab veneration of stones. The conspicuous absence of Abrahamic elements in the religion of the desert Arabs of the Peninsula, is further indicated by the wide extent of the worship of the Kaaba. Muslim tradition represents Mecca as the scene, from time immemorial, of yearly pilgrimages from all quarters of Arabia. "The circuit of veneration," Muir estimates, "might be described by the radius of a thousand miles, interrupted only by the sea. So extensive an homage must have had its beginnings in an extremely remote age; and a similar antiquity must be ascribed to the essential concomitants of the Meccan worship – the Kaaba with its Black Stone, the sacred limits, and the holy months. The origin of a superstition [sic] so ancient and universal may naturally be looked for within the Peninsula itself, and not in any foreign country" (ccxii).

The practice of idolatry, fetishism and stone worship was evidently prevalent throughout Arabia even earlier than 200 CE, the time when Muhammad is related to have said that Amr ibn Lohai (the first Khozaite king) dared to change the pure "religion of Ishmael" and set up idols brought from Syria. "Thus," writes Muir, "the religion of Mecca, in its essential points, is connected strictly with forms of superstition [polytheism] native to Arabia, and we may naturally conclude that it grew out of them" (ccxiv).

The central question, then, is whether Muir's historical analysis is in any way reconcilable with the notion of the Abrahamic origin of the Kaaba. The cogent reconciliation proposed by Muir is that the Nabateans or some other mercantile people of Abrahamic stock, attracted to Mecca by its gainful opportunities, brought along with them the Abrahamic legends, which discourse with the ubiquitous Jews had tended to revive and perpetuate. The mingled stock of Abraham and of others who were polytheists, had required a modification of the original Meccan religion that would correspond with their diverse origins. Hence, Abrahamic legends were grafted upon the indigenous worship.

To enable us to understand better how the Abrahamic legend was combined with the indigenous polytheism, Muir reminds us of the historical fact that the Jews were largely settled in northern Arabia where they acquired considerable influence. There were extensive colonies in Yathrib, Khaybar, and in Wadi al-Qura and on the shores of the Gulf. The Jews maintained a steady and friendly relationship with Mecca and the Arab tribes who, having learned about the Jews' religion and their holy books, looked with respect and veneration upon their beliefs and practices. When once the conception of Abraham and Ishmael as the great forefathers of the Arab people was superimposed upon Meccan polytheism, and had received native acceptance, it is understandable how even a purely Jewish tradition would be eagerly welcomed and Jewish legend adopted. "By a summary and procrustean adjustment," writes Muir,

> the story of Palestine became the story of the Hijaz. The precincts of the Kaaba were hallowed as the scene of Hagar's distress, and the sacred well of Zamzam as the source of her relief. It was [then purportedly] Abraham and Ishmael who built the Meccan temple, placed in it the black stone, and established for all mankind the pilgrimage to Arafat. In imitation of him it was that stones were flung by the pilgrims at Satan; and sacrifices were offered at Mina in remembrance of the vicarious sacrifice by Abraham in the stead of his son Ishmael. And thus, although the indigenous rites may have been little if at all altered by the adoption of the Abrahamic legends, they came to be viewed in a totally different light, and to be connected in the Arab imagination with something of the sanctity of Abraham the Friend of God. (ccxvii–ccxviii)

In a highly illuminating footnote, Muir adds:

> It is to this source that we may trace the Arab doctrine of a Supreme Being, to whom their gods and idols were subordinate. The title of *Allah Taa la*, the most High God, was commonly used long before Mahomet to designate this conception. But in some tribes, the idea had become so materialized that a portion of their votive offerings was assigned to the Great God, just as a portion was allotted to their idols . . . The notion of a Supreme Divinity to be represented by no sensible symbol [i.e., as formless, incorporeal and invisible], is clearly not cognate with any of the indigenous forms of Arab superstition [i.e., polytheism]. It was borrowed directly from the Jews, or from some other Abrahamic . . . [ethnic group] among whom contact with the Jews had preserved or revived the knowledge of the "God of Abraham." (ccxviii)

# 4

# Recent and Current Scholarship

It seems to be relatively clear, then, that the religion of the pre-Islamic, northern Arabs of the Hijaz was a form of polytheism. The Arabs worshipped a pantheon of divinities, and at no point, apparently, had their indigenous consciousness produced an original monotheistic intuition. Long before the birth of Muhammad, the two earliest monotheistic religions had taken a firm foothold in the Peninsula, and together contributed to the creation of the third.

Following the Roman destruction of Jerusalem in 70 CE, and owing to the enlargement of the Jewish Diaspora in the Near East and Jewish proselytization, Judaism had become a significant social and cultural factor in the Yemen and in the Hijaz. In the former it had even become the official religion of the last Himyarite King (Yusuf Ashab, called in the Arab tradition, Dhu Nuwas) who is said to have persecuted the Najran Christians, thus inviting Abyssinian intervention. In the Hijaz, as observed earlier, there were Jewish colonies not only in Medina, but in all the oases of the north. It was they, almost exclusively, who were the agriculturalists, craftsmen, and goldsmiths. It will be interesting therefore to listen to recent and contemporary scholars in order to learn whether their findings compel us to change the conception of things we have acquired from earlier scholars. One central issue, as we have seen, is the origin of the so-called Abrahamic element in Islam.

The contemporary scholar, F. E. Peters[1] reminds us that the Quran goes directly from Abraham's "conversion" to monotheism, to God's command to construct the Kaaba, making no mention at all of Hagar or Sarah or of the Bible's elaborate narrative concerning the births of Ishmael and Isaac. It was the much later traditions, as we have learned from Muir, which had access to diverse Jewish and Christian sources, who created the details of how Abraham and Ishmael got from Palestine to Mecca. As Peters observes, there were several Muslim versions of how that occurred, and the historian

Tabari (d. 923 CE) presents a fusion of several of them. Peters' discussion of the Abrahamic question tends to support Muir's analysis. "Neither the Quran nor the Muslim tradition," Peters avers,

> had much sense of what went on among the Israelites after Ishmael, while the Arabs' own long tribal genealogies led back into the past in a direction that had no apparent connection with the Bible. There was a further complication. Their own history told the early Muslims that Muhammad's immediate ancestors at Mecca, the people called Quraysh, were in the first place relative newcomers to Mecca, that they replaced another Arab people; and second, that they were pagans. Thus the appearance in the story of the Jurhum, an Arab people who replaced the sons of Ishmael at Mecca and who introduced paganism into Abraham's sanctuary. (35)

In a collection of essays by well-known scholars in the field, Peters,[2] as editor, provides a highly illuminating introduction. He begins by addressing the question of what we really know of pre-Islamic Mecca. All our literary sources, he reminds us, are Islamic, "and no pre-Islamic author, even the best-informed, seems to have heard of it." The Quran itself mentions the town by name only once (Sura 48, v. 24). As for the Jewish presence in the oases north of Yathrib up through the Wadi al-Qura, it is now better attested, as is the relatively influential position of Jews within the Yathrib settlement, and their connections with the Quraysh in Mecca. As regards Mecca, this town of the Hijaz appears early on to have been a shrine center, probably controlled and administered by the most powerful clans of the Quraysh, the rulers of the settlement. But there appear to have been serious divisions and conflicts among the clans, which most likely had a social-class dimension – richer and stronger against poorer and weaker. Such conflicts, Peters suggests, may have been the social and moral dynamic that first stimulated Muhammad's concerns and reflections.

Though Mecca was a tribal society, it was socially open, accepting new groups through formal alliances or by marriages with Meccan women. There were outsiders in Mecca such as Jews and Christians, which fact, of course, becomes pertinent to the question of influences on Muhammad's inspiration. In addition, there may have been among the populace Abyssinian mercenaries who might have served as a protective military force for the Quraysh.

Peters now sets the stage for the issues discussed by contributors to the volume: was it primarily religion or commerce that accounted for Mecca's apparent salience and relative prosperity? Peters, reflecting on the debate, proposes that religion was unmistakably the main business in Mecca, for without its shrine, even in pre-Islamic times, it would not have had much significance. It became prosperous and rich due to the sacred environs of the Kaaba, with its diverse local deities. Although, as we shall see, the commercial factor as accounting for the prominence of Mecca is seriously challenged by Patricia Crone, some modern scholars, notably W. Montgomery Watt, imagine the "town" to have been the commercial heir to earlier caravan cities such as Petra and Palmyra. Watt, and those who agree with him, therefore posit economic development as the determining factor in Mecca's social and political growth. That is the view, says Peters, of later Muslim sources, and the Quran, too, seems to support such a construct. The Quran employs a certain commercial vocabulary suggesting a familiarity with trade and a condemnation of usury and the "heaping up of gold and silver," which appears to be aimed at a greedy commercialism. Although Peters observes that the quality and extent of trade of pre-Islamic Mecca is still an open question, he does tend to support Crone's critique by concluding that Mecca of that era bore no resemblance to the earlier caravan cities of the Second and First Centuries BCE. Neither the Mediterranean consumers nor the eastern consumers of luxury items were accessible to the Quraysh. Peters agrees, therefore, that Patricia Crone's re-reading of the Arabic sources on Meccan trade has yielded dramatically different results from those of the earlier scholar Henri Lammens. The historical truth appears to be that there was no large-scale trade in Mecca – none, at least, of the kind imagined by W. Montgomery Watt.


## The Religion of Mecca

The best-attested aspect of the religious life of the Arabs of Western Arabia has to do with pilgrimages to the various shrines there. In the earliest Muslim histories of Mecca, Peters observes, we hear of offices being fought over and then enjoyed by the chief families of the Quraysh. There were struggles, apparently, over gains to be derived from control of the pilgrimages to the Kaaba. There was *profit* as well as prestige in these offices: taxes exacted from the pilgrims. They paid for their food and water; and the Quraysh, or the most powerful among them, had a monopoly on providing these necessities. So Peters, coming down again on the side of Patricia Crone's critique, avers that

> here if anywhere lies the kernel of truth about the commercial successes of the Quraysh and the renown of Mecca. Whatever fortune the Quraysh possessed, came from the cult around the Kaaba. This was not what Muslims

later called the *hajj*, whose ceremonies unfolded well outside Mecca, but rather the *Umra*, the 'lesser pilgrimage,' as the Muslims later called it. The *Umra* was a spring festival (the *hajj* took place in the fall) . . . and included the adoption of ritually pure clothing and lifestyle, the performance of sacrifices at prescribed places, and ritual processions around the Kaaba shrine and between the sacred high places of al-Safa and Marwa. (Peters, xxxvii)

Peters calls our attention to another significant fact concerning the peculiarity of the pilgrimages to Mecca: that although many of the pilgrimages of pre-Islamic Arabia had fairs attached to them, during the months of truce, there appears not to have been any fair connected with Mecca. "The close confines of the town," Peters assumes, "may have been too dangerous a place for the hostilely jostling nomads, whereas all the other fair sites were desert places where the Bedouin could camp at a safe distance from one another." For Peters, since there were no fairs in Mecca, and no sound evidence supporting the notion of Mecca as a center of international trade, it is to the pilgrimages that one must look for the source of the relative prosperity of the stronger Quraysh clans, and the relative poverty of the weaker.

## The Kaaba and its Devotees

Scholarly research re-examining earlier descriptions of the shrine, have introduced a few modifications in our conception of it. Peters acknowledges that no one really knows the origin of either the Meccan sacred area (*haram*) or the Kaaba. Muslim sources, as we saw earlier, traced the Kaaba back to Abraham and Ishmael; but modern Western scholarship, unwilling to accept this view, interprets it as an attempt to provide the site with an Islamic legitimacy. The original Kaaba, scholars suggest, was a rude, perhaps circular, enclosure without a roof; it was hardly cube-like, as the term Kaaba implies, though Muslim sources remember no other description of it. And, of course, none of the Muslim historians, having written many generations later, had ever seen the original. What we do know, though, is that however it was shaped, and whatever it was called, the Kaaba underwent reconstruction sometime late in the sixth century, with the wood of an Abyssinian shipwreck washed on to the shores of the Red Sea.

The Quran provides an impressionistic view of how the pagan gods of Mecca were worshipped. The liturgy included the sacrifice of animals and cereals, and the rites, including divination, were performed at the Kaaba. Pilgrimage to Mecca by the surrounding tribes was a popular, seasonal custom, which included ritual processions or circumambulation (*tawaf*) around the Kaaba and between the two hills of al-Safa and Marwa next to the Kaaba. There was prayer in the pagan era, but it is characterized in the Quran as "whistling and clapping of hands" (Sura 8: 35). One form of prayer, antedating Islam, has been preserved by Muslims: when, as pilgrims, they approach the sanctuary, they cry out again and again a formulaic salutation that opens with: "We are here, O Allah, we are here." There was also a form of spiritual retreat to a shrine by pre-Islamic Arabs, referred to in Sura 2: 187, connected, perhaps, with fasting in the hope of gaining favor with its god. The Prophet himself used to go into a kind of retreat on Mount Hira outside Mecca.

## Hanifiya and the Religion of Abraham

As regards pre-Islamic Mecca, there are two traditions. The first is Quranic and states that under divine inspiration Muhammad was restoring the religion of Abraham (Sura 22: 78), beliefs and practices presumably present in Mecca from its patriarchal beginnings. The other tradition suggests that there were already in Mecca, among Muhammad's contemporaries, individuals who may be described as *Hanifs*, Abrahamic monotheists. This concludes Peter's Introduction, and we now turn to several of the volume's essays on the pre-Islamic conditions of the Hijaz.

### G. E. von Grunebaum, "The Nature of Arab Unity Before Islam"

In von Grunebaum's essay, we will recognize Ibn Khaldun's characterization of the condition of pre-Islamic desert Arab–Bedouins, a condition in which no political institution had ever come close to uniting a majority of them, nor was there an unambiguous geographical limitation to take the place of a political structure. There was, of course, a certain commonality of language and culture, but no real state-like political organization. Von Grunebaum thus agrees that the Arabian tribes were in a "war of each against all" in the full Hobbesian sense.

Such Arab states as did exist were dependencies of the two powerful empires of the time, the Byzantine (Eastern Roman) and the Persian of the Sassanids. "This is as true," von Grunebaum writes, "of the Ghassanid and the Lakhmid principalities, to which the sources frequently refer as the 'Arabs of the Romans' and the 'Arabs of the Persians.'" The urban settlements of Mecca, Taif and Yathrib, which enjoyed an autonomous political life, included only a small segment of the Arab population, and far from inspiring a sense of Arab identity, represented a way of life that set them apart from the Bedouins.

Von Grunebaum uses the analogy of ancient Greece to convey the political character of the Arabian Peninsula. The Arabian tribes may be likened to the Greek city-states, which possessed no national unity and even fought each other, but were nonetheless Hellenes. The sentiment that might be called "Arabism" was shared by the tribes, and their perpetual skirmishes appear not to have diminished their sense of identity, in quite the same way in which the incessant, internecine warfare of the Greek city-states left their pan-Hellenic identity intact. In a word, as Ibn Khaldun had observed, there was no common power that served to unite the Arab tribes in one political federation. Indeed, von Grunebaum aptly remarks that any Arab identity that might have existed in pre-Islamic Arabia, was felt rather than named.

It appears that for the overwhelming majority of the Arab clans and tribes, Bedouin and town-dweller alike, there was a strong and persistent aversion to kingship despite the unmistakable fact that only under an approximation to monarchic rule (what Ibn Khaldun called "royal dynasty") did the tribes, under Islam, eventually become effective on the larger political stage. They seem to have regarded those who aspired to positions of power similar to that of kings, as potential tyrants. Although it was "glorious" to lord it over others, it was equally glorious to resist a strong leader and to break out from under the yoke of a *malik*. The chief virtues of Bedouin life were to be free in a close-knit tribe led by a *sayyid*, "spokesman" and leader who becomes such by assuming definite tribal responsibilities, thus gaining social honor and influence rather than prerogatives. The Bedouin outlook was, therefore, a blend of extreme individualism and an equally extreme submergence of the individual in the collective "on whose standing or 'honor,' *ird*, and cohesiveness his own safety and rank" was dependent. Von Grunebaum describes the relation of the desert to the sown in Ibn Khaldun's terms: "Everywhere, the interdependence of nomad and settler was lived as a series of intermittent conflicts and stigmatized by the same fear and mutual contempt" (8). The closer-knit unit within the tribe was the clan – a more intimate and real kinship organization – and the family. Hence, ancestors were throughout the cultural area objects of a veritable cult, as appears to be evident from the criticism of it in the Quran (2: 199; 31: 21; 43: 22–3).

Von Grunebaum recognizes that it was the change in strategy, adopted by Muhammad in Medina (which we shall analyze in detail in a later chapter), that transformed the Arabs of northern Arabia into a massive social movement and something like a state. Von Grunebaum further recognizes that in the absence of Islam the northern Arabs were most unlikely to have achieved the unity of a social movement or state, because the pre-Islamic ideology and tribal structure " . . . could not be overcome through an inherent dialectics, but had to be depreciated by means of a truly comprehensive principle of organization promulgated by higher authority. Where the *malik* failed, the prophet and his *halifa* succeeded. What is true for 'foreign policy' is true for the enforcement of rules regulating inter-Arab relationships; only Islam could hope to render effective the application of the principle that no Arab should be enslaved by another" (15). But there is also truth in the proposition that despite the unifying Islamic influence, Bedouin attitudes persisted and never died, thus disrupting and weakening the Islamic empire not too long after it was founded. Indeed, as von Grunebaum observes, "the intensification of tribal tensions after the conquests, is, in fact, remarkable" (19). The social cause of this remarkable phenomenon is the Bedouin individual's identification with his clan or tribe, not with the "Arabs." The term "Arab" is practically unrepresented in pre-Islamic Arabic poetry. It begins to be used in the work of the Prophet's "court poets" and occurs quite freely in poetical texts of the Umayyad age to designate the Arab nation.

### M. J. Kister, "Al-Hira: Some Notes on its Relations with Arabia"

Kister explores the significance of the rivalry of the Persian and Byzantine empires over the control of the regions of the Arabian Peninsula at the end of the sixth and the beginning of the seventh century. Kister shows that the rivalry is reflected in a number of traditions attributed to the Prophet and recorded in some commentaries of the Quran. Al-Hira is far north of the Hijaz, close to the Euphrates River. Kister cites Qatada (died 117 AH) who provides a description of the sad situation of the Arab population of the Peninsula before they embraced Islam, commenting on Quran, 8: 26: "And remember when you were few and abased in the land and were fearful that the *people* (*al-Nas*) would snatch you away." Qatada describes their sorrowful economic condition and their weakness, stating that they were "confined on the top of a rock between Faris [Persia] and Rum [Byzantium]. The "people" in the Quranic passage are said to refer to Persians and Byzantines. A *hadith* (tradition) reported on the authority of Ibn Ahhas (died 68 AH), states that the Prophet interpreted *al-Nas* (the "people") as referring to the Persians. But whatever the interpretation of the term, says Kister, it seems evident that the early commentators mirror the apprehensions felt by the Arabs of the Peninsula in the face of the two rival empires and the negative impact their rivalry had on the life of the tribes.

The struggles of the two empires, in which the two vassal kingdoms of al-Hira and Ghassan took an active part, was closely watched by the unbelievers and the Muslims in the different stages of their respective contexts. According to the commentaries on 30: 1–2, the sympathies of the unbelievers of Mecca were with Persia whereas the Muslim community inclined towards the Byzantines. The victories of the Byzantines, it is stressed, coincided with the victories of the Prophet. The imperial rivalry, then, has to be taken into account in our search for the fertile soil that nourished the birth of Islam.

## *Joseph Henninger, "Pre-Islamic Bedouin Religion"*

Henninger acknowledges at the outset, that too little documentation is available for highly reliable portraits of the desert-Bedouin's religion. That is the reason for no attempt in the West, prior to the seventeenth century, to publish monograph-length studies of pre-Islamic beliefs and practices. Henninger makes the thoughtful point that in searching for relevant evidence, one must be careful in employing the conceptual dichotomy, nomadic-settled. The dichotomy is not always helpful, he argues, because many of the tribes were partly nomadic, partly settled, and the nomads often maintained a close symbiotic relationship with one or more oases, which also served as religious centers. Henninger makes the claim that pre-Islamic cultic centers were located in oases, but since Mecca was no oasis, either it was an exception to the rule, or the rule requires qualification. Whether and to what extent there were also cultic practices in the desert itself is not known, says Henninger, though evidence for portable sanctuaries does exist.

Henninger proposes that the Bedouins appear never to have been especially zealous in the practice of Islam, which is not surprising in view of the fact that Islam is markedly urban in origin and character. The moral ideal of the pre-Islamic Bedouin was *muruwwa* ("virility"), as we learned earlier, which had little or no religious character. Henninger thus sees some truth in the notion of the "religious indifference" of the Bedouin. This view of Bedouin religion tends to support Max Weber's theoretical-historical insight, that the noble warrior ethic shows no interest in "salvation."

The evidence we do have for certain forms of pre-Islamic beliefs and practices – some of which we touched upon earlier – includes fetishism, the existence of sacred stones, raw and unpolished, and a reverential attitude towards them because, presumably, they possess helpful supernatural qualities. Fetishism, as analyzed originally by E. B. Tyler, takes two forms: either the fetish contains an indwelling spirit; or the object itself, like a charm or rabbit's foot, possesses supernatural powers. That the belief in spirits was prominent in pre-Islamic Bedouin religion, is attested by the persistence in the Quran of a belief in the *jinn*; and the testimony of both pre-Islamic and Islamic literature adequately demonstrates its importance at the beginning of the seventh century. Henninger cites approvingly Julius Wellhausen's observation that such spirits were thought to inhabit or haunt desolate, dingy and dark places in the desert and that they were feared. One had to protect oneself from them, but they were scarcely the objects of a true cult.

There is, however, a problem with the prevalent notion that the belief in the *jinn* originated with the Bedouin. William Foxwell Albright, basing himself on certain facts that had already been established by Th. Nöldeke and M. Lidzbarski, has shown that the word *jinn* is not Arabic, but derived from Aramaic. Aramaic-speaking Christians used the term to designate pagan gods reduced to the status of demons. This suggests that the idea of the *jinn* was introduced into Arabic folklore only late in the pre-Islamic period. Nevertheless there may have existed among the Bedouin an autochthonos pre-Christian animism, which was later reinforced by influences from sedentary Arabs.

Henninger calls attention to another element of pre-Islamic, Bedouin religious experience – a cult of ancestors – that seems to have been indigenous. That this is highly probable may be seen in the extensive diffusion of this cult among Bedouin in more recent times, a fact which cannot be attributed to Islam whose principles are opposed to it. Henninger is careful to explain what he means by a "cult of ancestors," and what meaning it might have had for the participants in it. It has not been sufficiently established, he states, that the dead generally were regarded as powerful, superhuman beings. They appear, rather, as having been deprived of protection, thus needing the charity of the living. That is why sacrifices for the dead seem not to signify a cult of the dead, but rather a continuation of social obligations beyond the grave. On the other hand, certain ancestors, especially eponymous heroes of the tribe, and chiefs and warriors were, apparently, objects of real veneration. "People not only slew animals and made libations by their tombs, but also erected stone structures as they did at the sanctuaries of the local gods" (116). As for astral deities, their importance, Henninger believes, has been exaggerated; they present a chaotic picture rather than a pantheon.

Henninger now turns our attention to the significance of the concept of *Allah*. It is, of course, interesting and of considerable moment that *Allah* was recognized *before* Islam as a god, and if not the only god, then at least a supreme god. The Quran makes it clear that he was recognized at Mecca, though belief in him was certainly more widespread. Earlier scholars attributed the diffusion of this belief solely or primarily to Christian or Judaic influences. But now a growing number of scholars hold that this idea had older roots in Arabia itself. If, for the moment, we assume that *Allah* was indigenous to Arabia, there is still the question of whether it had a nomadic origin. For Henninger, there are indications of a nomadic origin, which he infers from a comparative analysis of the beliefs of nomads in central and northern Arabia and northeastern Africa. Like the supreme being of many other nomads, Allah is a god of the sky and dispenser of rain. Rain, Henninger reminds us, is, after all, essential not only for settled agricultural peoples, but also for nomads, perhaps even more essential for the latter. He explains: "whereas agriculture is possible with artificial systems of irrigation, which lessen the dependence on rain, for the nomads the condition of the pasture lands, vitally important for both animals and people, is much more directly dependent on rain" (118).

"Prayer" is, for the most part, associated with the monotheistic religions and the belief in a personal God. So Henninger, in addressing the question of whether there is evidence of prayer in the pre-Islamic cult, states that prayer seems not to have been very important. More frequently mentioned are sacrifices, bloody ones as well as those involving no shedding of blood (vegetables and cereals). The animals immolated were the camel, the sheep, and the ox; fowl are never mentioned. Other types of sacrificial offerings were libations of milk, which were indigenous, while libations of wine and oil were of foreign origin. Human sacrifices, on the whole rather rare among the Bedouin, may be traced to the influence of the northern Semites. As a rule, such sacrifices ended in a common meal.

As for festivals of springtime and the sacrifices of the firstborn of a herd, there are solid reasons for supposing that the Arabic feast of the month of Rajab, for which originally the firstborn of the herd was sacrificed, and the Jewish Passover have a common origin. "Both are derived from a spring festival common to nomadic Semites, although of course, the Passover was given a new significance" (119).

Pilgrimages, as already mentioned several times, appear to have been a definite component of the Bedouin social and religious experience, as were divination, magic, and sorcery, which have received ample attention from Muslim authors in their descriptions of pre-Islamic religion. The sacrificial cult was often an integral part of the pilgrimage; and as each man was allowed to slaughter his own victim, there is the question whether there was in the cult a specialized role equivalent to the "priest." The "priests" (*Sadin*, pl. *Sadana*) mentioned in the Arabic sources, were not sacrificers, but rather guardians of the sanctuaries. Henninger recognizes the need, however, to touch at least briefly on the question suggested by the linguistic identity of the words *kahin* (soothsayer) in Arabic and *kohen* (priest) in Hebrew. Scholars since the time of Julius Wellhausen have seen in this fact proof of a development from the sorcerer through the soothsayer to the priest. This view, however, was contradicted by W. F. Albright who, on the basis of Ugaritic documents, wrote:

> unfortunately . . . the word *kahin* is isolated in Arabic and may, therefore, like thousands of other cultural words in that language, be considered equally well as a loanword from the older Canaanite *kahin* or from the Aramaic *kahana*, both meaning "priest"; should this be true, we have an indication of a specialization in function among the Arabs and not a supposed magical background of the Israelite priesthood. (120)

One must appreciate the thoroughness with which Henninger has approached the question of the nature of pre-Islamic religion in the Arabian Peninsula.

## Moshe Gil, "Jews of Yathrib"

This article by Moshe Gil, dealing as it does with the "Jews of Yathrib," is especially important not only for our understanding of Jewish–Arab relations in the pre-Islamic era, but also for their relations in Muhammad's Medinan period. As we intend in the later chapter on "Muhammad at Medina" to review how several great Jewish historians have viewed the origin of the Jews of Yathrib, it will be interesting to hear whether Gil, a contemporary scholar, finds it necessary to revise or correct earlier Jewish historians' analyses.

Gil opens by observing that both Talmudic and Islamic traditions are quite unanimous in describing a Jewish population inhabiting the southeastern parts of Palestine (inclusive of Transjordan) and having an extensive common border with the Bedouin tribes. Jericho, Elat and their surroundings formed the northern edge of the Jewish area, which stretched into the Arabian Peninsula, starting from the "valley of villages" (*Wadi al-Qura*) and reaching the city of Yathrib. "The Jewish character of the said area," Gil writes, "can be seen from the Hebrew designation *Darum* used in early Muslim sources for southern Palestine" (146). Relying on the Muslim sources, Gil observes that Muslim traditionalists could think of no earlier settlers in Yathrib than the Jews, who are described as the first inhabitants of the agricultural strips of land in northern Hijaz, in Yathrib and its vicinity. It was the Jews who dug the wells, planted the palm trees, practiced every kind of farming, and who built houses (*atam*), although as we shall see, this word in the context of the Hijaz meant more than mere houses; it meant fortified strongholds.

The Jews are, in a word, the only real historical *settlers* known by Muslim sources. All the concepts and practices of sedentary culture – farming, property, crafts, and so on – were represented by the Jews in contrast to the concepts and practices of the desert Arabs, the Bedouin, the nomads (146). Gil cites the words of Nuaym b. Masud of the B. Ghatfan, who acted for the Muslims during the battle of Khandaq: "The Banu Qurayza [one of the three Jewish tribes of the Medinan area] were people of high lineage and of properties, whereas we were but an Arab tribe who did not possess any palm trees nor vineyards, being people of only sheep and camels" (Waqidi, 480). During the harvesting of dates, the Jews hired the Bedouin who would come with their camels and transport the bunches of dates to the villages for sale, taking half the revenue for themselves. In the Bedouin view, such labor was unpleasant and perhaps even demeaning, as one can surmise from the Prophet's encouraging verse when they had to carry bricks or stones to build the first mosque.

In the earliest period, the Jewish tribes, the B. Nadir and B. Qurayza are described as "kings" (*muluk*) over Yathrib/Medina, ruling the Aws and the Khazraj; and that it was the Jews, standing on guard at the gates of Yathrib, to demand tithes from any person wishing to enter the city. "This general picture," writes Gil,

> seems to have prevailed at the time the Prophet arrived in Medina, Persian suzerainty, based on the Jews of Medina, being strengthened by the victory over Byzantium. This appears to lend credibility to the Muslim traditions which have the *ibn ra's al-jalut*, the son of the exilarch [the spiritual leader of the exilic Jewish community at the time], present in Medina and discussing with the Prophet the matter of the names of the stars in Joseph's dream; those traditions are even aware of his name, Bustanay. The tradition reflects two facts: the connection of the Medinan Jews with the Babylonian center, and their influential position in the Hijaz . . . backed by the world power of the time, Persia. (Ibid.)

In the period before the Prophet and the Medinan Jews became estranged from one another, the Prophet, Gil writes, "always addresses the Medinan Jews as kinsfolk and offspring of the ancient Banu Israil. They spoke a language of their own, which Muslim sources call *ratan*, apparently meaning a non-Arabic tongue, which Tabari says was Persian [but was most probably Aramaic]. The Prophet ordered Zayd b. Thabit [the Prophet's secretary] to teach himself al-Suryania, i.e., Aramaic . . . in order to be able to understand what the Jews were writing" (148). This should be taken to mean that the Jews spoke Arabic as well – for some even excelled in reciting Arabic poetry – but wrote primarily in Aramaic.

Gil now addresses the much-discussed question of whether the Medinan Jews were the offspring of ethnic Jews or of Jewish proselytes. He cites the view of the famous Semiticist, Nöldeke, who argued that if the Jews of Arabia had been the offspring of immigrants, they could not have been so well absorbed by the tribal society of the Arabs. Nöldeke was impressed, in particular, by the Jewish contribution to Arab poetry, which he considered an expression of a real Arabic character without any Jewish elements. Other scholars, such as Winckler, Lammens, and Nau, shared Nöldeke's view. Indeed, Nau states what he regards as four decisive facts, which Gil summarizes: (1) The Jews conducted an intensive campaign to spread Judaism in various places, including Arabia. (2) Almost all the Jews of Medina mentioned during the Prophet's lifetime have Arab names. (3) They needed spiritual leadership from outside, from Palestine or from Babylonia [but so did other Jewish communities of the Diaspora]. (4) The phenomenon of a Jewish kingdom (*Himyar*) is something outside the Jewish norm of the time, unless that royal family was proselytes [which they might have been]. The Jewish historian, D. S. Margoliouth, also expressed far-reaching doubts of the Medinan Jews having been real[?] Jews, preferring to think of them as monotheistic, in his term, *Rahmanists*. This view was based on – among other considerations – the name of God, *Rahman*, as found in the Arabian epigraphic sources. And Gil remarks that "C. C. Torrey seems to have been the only scholar of that generation who was willing to accept the Judaism of the Yathrib Jews as genuine" (151). Torrey's view will receive a full exposition later.

Meanwhile, however, it needs, perhaps, to be said, that the views of Nöldeke, et al., who question the Judaism of the Yathrib Jews, and ask whether they were originally "ethnic" Jews or proselytes, hold, consciously or not, a racial or quasi-racial conception of Judaism. The Jews from biblical times to the Maccabean era and the Pharisaic Revolution, to the time of Muhammad, never considered Judaism a matter of ethnicity. A convert or proselyte to Judaism was a Jew regardless of his or her ethnicity. This continued to be true throughout subsequent Jewish history as well. Indeed, an examination of the Muslim sources concerning the relations between the Jewish tribes and the Arabs, shows that neither "side," so to speak, had any interest, positive or negative, in their respective ethnic backgrounds. The issues and conflicts between them were religious, economic and political in nature; conflicts, as we shall see, that may also be characterized in Ibn

Khaldun's terms, as rooted in the antagonistic encounter between the desert and the sown.

Moshe Gil's research tends to support the non-ethnic criterion of Judaism that prevailed in the period under discussion. Much can be found in the Arab sources, he writes,

> about Arab tribes or clans which were influenced by Judaism, many of them accepting it completely. Suhali informs us, for instance, that besides Qurayza, Nadir and Qaynuqa [the Jewish tribes], there were people of Aws and Khazraj who became Jewish. Some of their women used to make a vow that if their child lived, they would make it a Jew, since they considered the Jews to be people of knowledge and the Book. Yaqubi, after describing Yaman [i.e, Yemen] as an area which became mainly Jewish due to the action of the *tubba* [the royal title of the Himyarite kings], mentions that people of Aws and Khazraj became Jewish as well after they arrived from Yaman, due to their being neighbors of the Jews of Khaybar and Yathrib. People of the B. Harith b.Ka'b, Ghassan and of Judhum, also accepted Judaism. In fact it appears that many more clans in Medina were Jewish. Samhudi mentions many such clans, like B. Qusays, B. Marthad, B. Muawiya, B. Jadhma, B. Naghisa, B. Zaura, B. Hujr, and B. Thalaba. (152)

More of such evidence is available, and as Gil states, "no conclusive evidence is yet available of who these Jewish *mawali*[3] were and whether they stemmed from Arab clans or were the offspring of Jews who settled in the city centuries before Islam. However, the bulk of traditions on Jews preserved in the [Muslim] sources surveyed so far points to proselytes from among the Bedouin" (153).

By means of a fastidious examination of Jewish and Muslim sources, Gil sheds more light on the question of the probable origin of Yathrib's Jews. He writes that

> during the Byzantine period there was a well-known and a well-established category of proselytes, of Bedouin descent, known as the "sons of Jethro." The similarity with the Muslim sources on the matter of the Jewish tribes and clans of the Hijaz and their connections with B. Judhum, the inhabitants of the land of Madyan [i.e., Midian; Jethro was prince and/or priest of Midian. Moses married his daughter, Zipporah], kinsfolk of the Shuaybo-Jethro cannot be ignored . . . A similar parallelism exists concerning the Jewish refugees who fled from the Romans [in 70 or perhaps also in 135 CE] into Arabia. It is apparently these refugees who formed the first layer of the Jewish population in northern Hijaz. During the centuries that followed they

increased in number through Arab tribes who converted, and adopted an agricultural life, taking over not only the Jews' religion and way of life, but also their spoken language, Aramaic. (160–1)

As we shall see, Gil's analysis tends to confirm that of the earlier Jewish historians.

### Fazlur Rahman, "Pre-Foundations of the Muslim Community in Mecca"

Rahman's aim, in his important contribution, in the volume edited by F. E. Peters, is to address the question "of the emergence of the Muslim community in Medina as a separate entity from the Jewish and the Christian communities." Rahman proposes that judging from certain passages of the Quran (e.g., 37: 168–70), it seems evident that some Meccans had desired a new religion of the Judean-Christian type. This was the result of the penetration of the Judeo-Christian ideas into the Arab milieu, and it attests to the existence of a religious ferment among certain individuals and possibly even groups. Although, as the evidence suggests, there may not have been a sizeable population of Jews and Christians in Mecca, one must not assume that they were without influence on that account; for it seems highly probable that some non-Jewish, non-Christian individuals had arrived at the concept of monotheism, and some had become Christian. Moreover, the Quran points frequently to a longing for some kind of Messianism, or a desire for a new prophet – an Arab prophet (35: 42). This, most probably, expresses Muhammad's own strong longing, desire and wish that the Arabs would acquire and possess a prophet of their own, just as did the Jews and the Christians. It is possible that Muhammad's longing was a reflection of a more general such longing, prompted by the presence of Jews and Christians, and their religious ideas. But if the longing took on an ethnic or "national" dimension, in the sense that it became an aim to be striven for politically, then it is more likely that such an aim was late, and came to the fore in Medina, rather than Mecca.

### Uri Rubin, "Hanifiyya and Ka'ba: An Inquiry into the Arabian Background of Din Ibrahim"

Earlier we explored the question of the Abrahamic element in Islam, and the historicity of the claim that Abraham and Ishmael were associated with the founding of the Kaaba. Rubin, continuing to examine the question, claims that Muhammad's attachment to the idea of *din Ibrahim* began already before the *Hijra*, while he was still at Mecca, where there were some older *hunafa* (monotheists or quasi-monotheists) who probably introduced the idea to the young Muhammad.

Rubin mentions as the most notable of these *hanifs*, Zayd b. Amr b. Nufayl, who appears in a report recorded by Ibn Ishaq, mentioning four persons including Zayd, who, resolving to abandon the idolatry of Quraysh, left Mecca in search of the true religion. Zayd is described as the only one who refrained from adopting Judaism or Christianity, and insisted that he worshipped the Lord of Abraham. The monotheistic attitude of Zayd is implied in some poetic verses attributed to him in which he voices his aversion to the worship of the Daughters of Allah and other deities. In other verses he professes his exclusive devotion to Allah.

According to Rubin's extraordinarily interesting findings, Zayd's views led to strife with his fellow tribesmen, and to his being driven out of Mecca by his paternal uncle, al-Khattab, father of Omar, the second Caliph. What Khattab feared, apparently, is that other Meccans might follow Zayd's example and abandon the old *din* of Quraysh. Highly interesting are the traditions reporting on the meeting between Zayd and the young Muhammad which took place before his first revelation. In the earliest versions of these traditions, Rubin informs us, Muhammad offers Zayd a bag of meat that Muhammad had sacrificed to the idols, and of which Zayd refused to partake, explaining that he does not eat what has been offered to idols. Zayd also states on that occasion, that he has been searching for the true religion and has become a follower of the religion of Abraham. Rubin suggests that the motivation for such a tradition was to underscore the virtues of Zayd as an early mentor of Muhammad's. Rubin reminds us, however, that even ideologically motivated traditions may contain a nucleus of historical truth, which in this case prompts the fair inference that Zayd was a monotheistic adherent of *din Ibrahim* while Muhammad was still an idolator. Rubin is on strong ground in this respect, for "such a tradition," he convincingly argues, "could never have been invented, not even for the mere purpose of glorifying Zayd. From this tradition, which Muslim scholars indeed tried to reshape, one must, therefore, conclude that Zayd was indeed a *hanif* who introduced to Muhammad the monotheistic idea of *din Ibrahim*" (283).

There are several traditions indicating that Zayd prayed facing the Kaaba. In one of these he used to say, "I follow the religion of Abraham and I prostrate myself towards the Kaaba which Abraham built." Rubin then advances this cogent proposition: "The observation that the *hanifiyya* [Abrahamic monotheists] at both post-*hijra* Medina and pre-*hijra* Mecca was focused on the veneration of the Kaaba, entails the conclusion that the Abrahamic sacredness of the Kaaba is pre-Islamic in origin" (284). Rubin also calls our attention to this fact: though the chief pre-Islamic deity in the form of an idol was Hubal, whose statue was the only one inside the Kaaba, rituals performed in front of Hubal nevertheless contained an Abrahamic element, notably circumcision. That circumcision was common among the Arabs since pre-Islamic times, is a well established fact, which the Muslim tradition, like the Jewish, connects with Abraham who was the first to be circumcised. This was already known to Joshephus who wrote in his *Antiquities* that the Arabs " . . . circumcise after the thirteenth year, because Ishmael, the founder of the nation, who was born to Abraham of the concubine, was circumcised at that age" (Bk. 1, ch. xii/2).

Rubin provides *new* information showing how the Abrahamic element, in the context of the Kaaba rituals, was syncretized with the polytheistic elements: the casting of arrows before Hubal, for example, was considered to be Abrahamic, which shows that in the Kaaba context, at least, the pre-Islamic form of the Abrahamic religion was not a pure or strict monotheism. As Rubin informs us, the image of Abraham holding these arrows was actually painted inside the Kaaba, and when Mecca was conquered by Muhammad and the Muslims, he ordered it to be erased (286). More, even the view that the sacred area of Mecca, the *haram*, was founded by Abraham may be regarded as pre-Islamic in origin (288). Indeed, it seems to be a fair generalization that the pre-Islamic Arabs were well aware of the tradition according to which they were the descendants of Abraham and Ishmael; even the authority of the Quraysh among the rest of the Arab tribes was based on this tradition. Ibn Ishaq states that the Arabs recognized the Quraysh as the noblest descendants of Ishmael and, therefore, as their leaders. Rubin again makes the point that even reports motivated by apologetics do not necessarily consist solely of untruths. So in light of the rest of the evidence adduced in his essay, he states that "there does not seem to be any serious reason for doubting the authenticity of the reports about the pre-Islamic Abrahamic sacredness of the Kaaba and Quraysh" (289).

Rubin therefore maintains that the tradition of the Kaaba, as the sacred "House of Abraham" is very early. Its origins may be traced back to the *Book of Jubilees*, some of the relevant passages of which were already noticed by the outstanding scholar, S. D. Goitein in his *Ha-islam shel Muhammad*, Jerusalem, 1966 (in Hebrew, pp. 166–7). According to the Jewish conception the proper place for the eternal Abrahamic sanctuary was on Mt. Moriah in Jerusalem, where Solomon had built the Temple (2 Chronicles, 3: 1). This place was said to have been the site of the binding of Isaac Gen. 22: 1). Rubin then makes this enlightening observation:

> The Messianic idea of the building of the "House of Abraham" as formu-
> lated in *Jubilees* could easily have been known in pre-Islamic Arabia through

Abyssinian Christians for whom this book was sacred. Thus the Arabian "monotheistic" adherents of *din Ibrahim* in the vicinity of Mecca and Medina could quite naturally locate their own "House of Abraham" in the most notable sanctuary of the area, the Kaaba. (291)

However, for the majority of the Jews of Arabia, the "House of Abraham" was, of course, not in Mecca. "When Muhammad diverted his *qibla* [the direction faced in prayer] from Jerusalem to Mecca," Rubin writes, "the leaders of the Medinan Jews reportedly told him that if he claimed to be an adherent of *din Ibrahim*, he must return to the former *qibla* (Ibn Hisham, II, 199). This means that for those Jews the *qibla* of the true religion of Abraham was Jerusalem" (291).

## More on Pre-Islamic Religion in the Arabian Peninsula

*Hamilton A. R. Gibb, "Pre-Islamic Monotheism in Arabia"*

The discussion of the Abrahamic phenomenon in pre-Islamic Arabia continues in Hamilton A. R. Gibb's article, "Pre-Islamic Monotheism in Arabia." For Gibb, the search for the "sources" of Muhammad's revelation tends to be inconclusive, in that Jewish scholars seem to forget that the Old Testament was as much a part of the Christian as of Jewish scripture, and that even *haggadic* supplements had long since been taken up into Christian writings; and Christian scholars, who argue for a Christian source, are somewhat embarrassed by Muhammad's rejection of Christological doctrine. Both sides provide good arguments, says Gibb, but neither seems decisive in enabling us to resolve the issue in favor of one side or the other. As for Muslim doctrine, it has never denied a relationship of Islam with Judaism and Christianity and their commonality of origin; but Muslim doctrine does explicitly reject the claim that either side had "influenced" the content of the Quran, since it is considered to be the verbally inspired Word of God, directly communicated to the Prophet by means of Gabriel's mediation. From the Muslim standpoint, then, even if one sees in the Quran parallels with the earlier scriptures, that proves nothing, since both the earlier and the later emanate from the same divine source. Gibb therefore proposes that " . . . if the teaching of the Quran was to be understood by its first hearers, as is rightly assumed by Muslim scholarship, there must have been not only in existence, but widely enough known in Mecca, an Arabic religious vocabulary applicable to the monotheistic content of the Quran" (246). For Gibb, "it is self-evident that these elements of technical religious vocabulary could have

come only from the language of the surrounding monotheistic communities . . ." (Ibid.)

Although Gibb sees in the Quran words and phrases of Syriac/Aramaic
and even of Greek and Persian origin, he acknowledges in a parenthetic
comment, that in the early Medinan Suras of the Quran there is evidence
of direct adoption of Hebrew terms "in certain special contexts" (Ibid.).
But he goes on to argue convincingly that

> It is a far cry from this, however, to infer that pre-Islamic monotheism in
> Arabia was directly connected with the institutionally organized Jewish or
> Christian communities. Such communities certainly existed in Arabia, but
> there is considerable evidence both from Muslim texts and from external
> sources that other monotheistic groups were to be found in Arabia, inde-
> pendently of the organized churches and hence "heretical" in their eyes.
> Such groups may have been offshoots not only of Christianity, but also of
> Judaism, or Judeo-Christian. (297)

The very fact that the Islamic tradition speaks of *hanifs* makes it highly
probable that such individuals or groups existed, though, unfortunately, no
sound, specific evidence of their character is provided by the tradition. For
Gibb, then, the problem of determining the origin of *hanifs* is enormously
complex because "there are many details in the Quran which relate evidently to a prophetic tradition that is purely Arabian, even while it links on
to the Jewish and Christian traditions." It follows, that "in these circumstances, it is absurd to postulate even as a hypothesis, a 'Jewish foundation'
for Islam [referring evidently to C. C. Torrey's *The Jewish Foundations of
Islam*]; the phrase 'Christian environment' [referring to Richard Bell's *The
Origin of Islam in its Christian Environment*] has the merit of being at least
less assertive, and leaves room for an intermediate group or groups" (297).

We shall soon review both Torrey's and Bell's works, but meanwhile it
seems fitting to respond briefly to the above statement of Gibb's. Is it not
equally absurd to deny a Jewish foundation when one recognizes that the
*ultimate* origin of Christianity, *hanifiyya* and Islam can be found nowhere
else but in Judaism? And if we add to this truism the historical fact that
there was a very significant Jewish presence in the Peninsula and in the
Hijaz centuries before Islam, what other origin can one posit for *hanif*
monotheism – especially given its pronounced Abrahamic element – than
Judaism and its living descendants in the historical context with which we
are concerned? Gibb is right to argue that with the evidence presently
available it is impossible to assign causal weightings to the respective influences of Judaism, Christianity, and *hanif* monotheism on Muhammad's

inspiration. Yet, there is, perhaps, one more pertinent point that needs to be made: where the origins of Muhammad's inspiration are concerned, it seems fair to say that the strictness of the monotheistic conception to which he arrived *after* the affair of the "daughters of Allah," was such that it had the greatest affinity with the Jewish view of the Deity as an Almighty, Ethical, Creator-Ruler of the universe who is formless and incorporeal. Moreover, as we have learned from Rubin and other scholars, pre-Islamic, Abrahamic *hanifiyya* was a syncretic phenomenon that retained polytheistic elements. Now if we add to this the Islamic repudiation of Christological dogma, as Gibb himself has noted, then we can, perhaps, agree, that since Judaism and Islam are the strictest forms of monotheism, the latter was most influenced by the former.

In continuing his analysis, Gibb argues against an influential view that Muhammad's message would, in effect, have confronted Meccans with a body of *new* ideas. In making his case, Gibb cites a passage from the Quran in which, he argues, "the existence of pre-Islamic monotheism is most openly acknowledged and its character most clearly presented. This passage is a self-contained section at the end of Sura 53, and is clearly to be dated in the early Meccan period of Muhammad's mission. If we read verses 33 to 56 of Sura 53, and take note of the conception of the Deity and the historical individuals mentioned, we find reference to the Deity as the Unseen, and to the Tablets of Moses *and* Abraham." Gibb makes the cogent point that the situation of the passage, especially verses 33–56, is clear: "Muhammad turns on a Meccan opponent, and pointedly asks if he does not know 'what is in the Scriptures of Moses.' The obvious inference is that the 'Scriptures of Moses' were so familiar in Mecca that one could scarcely imagine any Meccan being ignorant of them. So far from presenting a body of completely new ideas, therefore, the Quranic Revelation was (in its early stages) basically dramatizing and expanding well-known religious teachings" (273).

Gibb now wants to show that the verses in Sura 53 are not a precise reference to the Torah, because the addition, "of Abraham" after the "Tablets of Moses," is neither Jewish nor Christian, but rather a first suggestion of a deviant tradition. For Gibb, the content of these verses appears to have been derived from Christian rather than from Jewish sources. Verse 38, for example, "while reflecting a general scriptural theme, is not found in the Torah. The closest parallel is in St Paul's Epistles (Galatians 6: 5), 'For every man shall bear his own burdens.' So too, does the maxim in verses 39 and 41 reflect another passage from St Paul (I Cor. 3: 8), 'Every man shall receive his own reward according to his own labor . . .'" For Gibb, the central theme of these verses is the "lordship of God, the personal responsibility of the created being, and God's reward and punishment." But Gibb discerns even in these Quranic verses a deliberate or almost deliberate avoidance of the distinctive confessional elements of both Judaism and Christianity, and an emphasis on the basic themes of a monotheistic faith divorced from both rival creeds. Gibb observes in this connection that Muslim tradition links these religious rivalries with the political rivalries of the two imperial powers, and the apparent Jewish support of the Persian empire, and the early Muslim support of the Byzantine. But apart from this political matter, says Gibb, "there could well have been good reason for a native monotheistic movement in Arabia to seek an independent middle course. And such was in fact to become a cardinal element in Islam" (303).

But if there was, as Gibb surmises, an "almost deliberate avoidance" of what was distinctive in Judaism and Christianity, and if the native monotheistic individuals or groups sought an independent middle course, such an attitude on their part pre-supposes enough familiarity with Judaism and Christianity to enable them to seek or steer an independent course. But what was the nature of that middle course? If it was in fact a syncretic phenomenon, retaining polytheistic elements, then it was not a strict monotheism. It seems sensible, therefore, to view Muhammad's inspiration as a *developmental process* in which he moved from a less-than-strict conception of monotheism, as seems to have been the case in Mecca, to a strict conception in Medina. Therefore, if the so-called middle course of the *hanifs* retained polytheistic elements, and the Christological doctrine was rejected by the Quran, it seems to follow that the sole remaining model for Muhammad's strict monotheism was Judaism, from which all polytheistic elements had been expunged.

### W. Montgomery Watt, "Belief in a 'High God' in Pre-Islamic Mecca"

Montgomery Watt, best known for his studies of *Muhammad at Mecca* and *Muhammad at Medina*, opens his contribution by reminding the reader that from the time of Julius Wellhausen it has been accepted by scholars that Quranic evidence points to the existence in Mecca of individuals who, although continuing to worship the pagan deities, regarded Allah as the creator of the world, and a "high god" superior to the other gods. Watt's purpose is not to propound a fresh view of this phenomenon, but merely to show how extensive is the Quranic material portraying Allah as the "High God."

Watt cites several Quranic passages that speak of Allah as the Creator, but which then associate other deities with him. All such passages refer to "some persons" in Mecca (39: 38; 43: 9–15) who place Allah's servants on a level with him. The servants are in some places referred to as "peers" and in other places as "partners" (2: 21f.; 40: 12; 39: 3/4; 10: 18/19). Watt therefore infers that such passages reflect the idea prevalent in Mecca at the time that the pagan deities serve to intercede with the high god; which strongly suggests to Watt, that the story of the so-called "Satanic Verses" (added after 53: 20) is probably true. The story is – as mentioned in an earlier chapter – that after the verses, "Have you considered al-Lat and al-Uzza, and Manat, the third, the other?" Satan inserted the words, "These are the exalted *qharaniq*; their intercession is hoped for (or may be expected)."

Al-Lat or El-Lat, perhaps the Alilat of Herodotus (3: 8) was an idol at Nakhlah, a place east of Mecca. Al-Uzza was an idol of the Kinanah tribe. According to the story originally told by Muslim historians or traditionalists, the Prophet, at the first recital of this Sura, 53: 20 ("And Manat the third idol besides"), added: "These are the exalted females, and truly their intercession may be expected." These words, however, which were received by the Quraysh idolators with delight, were repudiated by Muhammad a few days later as a Satanic suggestion, and replaced by the text as it now stands. Western scholars assume that Muhammad's difficulties in Mecca led him to attempt a compromise with the Quraysh by making the "daughters of Allah" concession, of which he speedily repented.

The word *qharaniq* is often translated as "swan" or "crane." Watt accepts the plausibility of the suggestion that they were Numidian cranes, reputed to fly very high, and so the epithet was appropriate for those who interceded with the high god. For Watt,

> it is clear that the temptation for Muhammad was to acknowledge the pagan goddesses as capable of interceding with God, in accordance with the belief of many of his contemporaries. The Quran sometimes speaks of the deities as angels and criticizes the pagans for giving them female names (53: 27/28). A verse before this (53: 26) speaks of many angels whose intercession is of no avail. The occurrence of these ideas in close proximity to the passage into which the satanic verses were inserted gives strong support to the view that Muhammad's temptation was to interpret Allah as the high god already acknowledged by many in Mecca. (309)

We shall return to this subject in a later review of Tabari's narrative concerning Muhammad's years in Mecca.

*Uri Rubin, "The Kaaba: Aspects of Its Ritual Functions and Position in Pre-Islamic and Early Islamic Times"*

From Uri Rubin's second contribution to this volume edited by F. E. Peters, we gain considerably more understanding of the religious beliefs and practices of that time and place. His analysis requires a diagram – which I shall attempt to duplicate[4] – of the Kaaba and the sacred area surrounding it. (See figure 4.1.)

Rubin cites Ibn Jurayj (died 150 AH/772 CE) who, having been born in Mecca and thus having an excellent knowledge of his hometown, relates that the Kaaba was originally an *arish* into which cattle could burst, and that it remained in this condition till Quraysh built the Kaaba, 15 years before Muhammad's first revelation. The term *arish* has profound ritual significance, for it is the word Arabs used to refer to the Tabernacle built in the Wilderness by the Children of Israel in the time of Moses. The report by

Fig. 4.1.   The Kaaba and its surroundings (this figure has been prepared according to the groundplan of the Haram in C. Snouck Hurgronje, *Mekka*, tr. by J. H. Monaham, Leiden 1970. Scale in meters was calculated according to the map in *National Geographic Magazine*, vol. 154, pp. 584–5).

Ibn Jurayj seems to imply that the Kaaba was originally built and treated as a similarly sacred tabernacle. Due to the danger of frequent floods characteristic of the area, a barrier was built near the Kaaba at a very early period. The barrier eventually proved to be inadequate, and according to Musa b. Uqba (758 CE), it was eventually overflowed, which prompted the Quraysh to turn the Kaaba into a massive building. The "Hijr," regarded as an integral part of the Kaaba, refers to the semi-circular, open-air enclosure situated opposite the northwestern wall of the Kaaba. Rubin cites, in addition, a report from Ma 'mar b. Rashid (770 CE), saying that, "the Kaaba was built in the Jahaliyya [pre-Islamic era] with loose stones (*radm*), without clay. Its height was such that young goats could burst into it. It had no roof, and its clothes [tent material] were merely laid upon it, hanging down. It had two corners, like this ring:⊂" (317).

A few years before Muhammad's first revelation, the ancient *arish* was turned into a permanent roofed structure, the timber for it having been taken from a ship of a Byzantine merchant named Baqum, which had been cast ashore near Jedda. Several reports suggest that the new building of the Kaaba was inspired by certain Christian models. It is known that the interior of the Kaaba was decorated with the images of Jesus and Maria. When Mecca was conquered, the prophet himself ordered that the images of Jesus and Maria be left untouched; and in the days of Atab Abi Rabah (732 CE), these images were still there. *Christian influence appears, therefore, to be indisputable.*

In the pre-Islamic period, it seems that the main function of the entire enclosure containing the Kaaba and the Hijr was to mark the boundaries of a sacred ground in which several idols were worshipped. In the Kaaba itself, however, there appears to have been no statues at all. Although this may at first seem strange, Rubin reminds us that the Kaaba was considered "the sacred house of Allah." Allah was worshipped by the Meccans as the High God, as we have seen, and for him there was no statue. The lesser deities were apparently worshipped outside the Kaaba, in the area of the Hijr, where their statues were located. "The actual worship of the idols in the Hijr," Rubin writes, "consisted of sacrificial slaughter which was performed near the well of Zamzam. It is reported that this well was situated in the place where Quraysh used to slaughter the sacrificial animals" (321). "The term Hijr itself," Rubin explains,

> has a profound ritual significance which is connected with sacrificial slaughter. This term means "inviolable," "sacrosanct," and the basic function of the area to which this term was applied is elucidated in a Muslim tradition relating that Abraham built the Hijr next to the Kaaba as an *arish* made of *arak*

trees, into which goats could burst. It served as a pen (*zarb*) for Ishmael's sheep.

This legend, Rubin avers,

> seems to reflect an authentic reality, namely, that the Hijr, or the area between the ancient *jidar* [barrier against floods] and the Kaaba, served as a pen, or fold for sheep. The same is suggested by the term "*jidar*," which in ancient Hebrew denotes quite often a fold for sheep. (323)
>
> The term "Hijr" [Rubin continues] appears in a similar context in the Quran. Sura 6: 138 deals with cattle and cultivated fields which the pre-Islamic Arabs used to consecrate to their idols by labeling them as *Hijr*, i.e., sacrosanct. In view of this, one may conclude that "Hijr" signifies a fold for sacred animals which were regarded as belonging to the idols. (Ibid.)

In Islamic times the Hijr continued to function as a place of worship, but now was devoted exclusively to the Lord of the Kaaba, Allah. For Muhammad, the area served mainly as a place of prayer. Some traditions report that the Prophet used to pray in the Hijr during the early Meccan period. More specific traditions say that he used to pray opposite the Black Stone, which served, apparently, as his first *qibla*, the direction faced in prayer. For Muslim traditions, the sacredness assigned to the Hijr stems from the idea that the area was the burial place of the noble dead, especially Ishmael.

Rubin now explains the significance of the *Hatim* in the diagram. This area of the Hijr is often referred to in Muslim sources as al-Hatim, which like "Hijr," is applied today to the semi-circular enclosure opposite the northwestern wall of the Kaaba. Originally, however, the term seems to have been applied to the area opposite the front wall of the Kaaba. The term "Hatim," like Hijr, is used in Muslim sources to refer to the residence of sacrosanct animals.

As for the Black Stone, Rubin cites a report indicating that originally it was located on the mountain of Abu Qubays, where it became an object of veneration due to its unusual brightness, suggesting a celestial origin for it. People used to ascend the mountain to stroke the stone, which was originally white, until it eventually blackened. The Quraysh removed the stone from the mountain four years before Muhammad's first revelation. Rubin points out, however, that the real reason for the originally bright, white stone turning black was that it was stained with blood. Rubin also explains the Quraysh's interest in establishing its control over the Kaaba and imparting to it centrality in the pilgrimages. It appears that places such as the mountain of Abu Qubays tended to divert worshippers from the Kaaba, so that the Quraysh did their utmost to make the Kaaba the central place of worship in Mecca. With that aim, they reconstructed the Kaaba, using stones from the surrounding mountains, including Abu Qubays, and the Kaaba thus became a permanent stone building. The same aim is evident, Rubin argues quite convincingly, in the Quraysh's decision to take into its cult all the objects of veneration that had been worshipped at other places in the Meccan vicinity. This appears to have been the reason for transferring the Black Stone from the mountain to the new building of the Kaaba.

Rubin also clarifies how the whole area lying between the two famous hills, Safa and Marwa, might have acquired their religious significance. It was an area abundant with stones of striking qualities, which could become objects of veneration. This is reflected in the names given to the hills, Safa meaning "broad smooth stones," and Marwa meaning "bright glittering stone which may produce fire." Rubin, citing early Muslim traditionalists, relates that when Muhammad conquered Mecca, there were 36 idols, one on the Safa, one on Marwa, and the rest covering the area between them. Describing in detail the nature of the worship between the two hills, Rubin informs us that it consisted of the *tawaf*, circumambulation between the hills, while stroking the statues of the idols; or, according to other reports, striking at the stones of the two hills. The circumambulation was performed by running, during one of its stages, upon crossing the valley between the hills. The original worldly reason for the running appears to have been the fear of flash-floods "which were quite frequent and dangerous in that area" (340–1).

Apparently, the Quraysh came also to regard the circumambulation as a threat to their interests. Seeing themselves devoted primarily to the Kaaba, they objected to this practice. Among the circles of the Quraysh who led the opposition to the practice were the Hums, an organization whose main aim was to preserve the privileged position of the sacred area of Mecca in general, and of the Kaaba in particular. The attempt of the Hums to turn the Kaaba into the sole or primary place of worship was less than entirely successful. Some of the tribes continued to worship certain idols at the Safa and the Marwa.

With the rise of Islam, it was Muhammad himself who, in effect, dashed the Hums' hopes of maintaining the leading position of the Kaaba; for although he had belonged to the organization of the Hums, he nevertheless attended the rites of the Safa and the Marwa during each pilgrimage to Mecca. His first *Umra* from Medina was in 629 CE, and during this pilgrimage he not only made the *tawaf* between the two hills, but also slaughtered sacrificial animals near the Marwa, declaring that this was the place of slaughter, together with the rest of the Meccan area.

Islam adopted the practice of running between the two hills during the *tawaf*, and in order to legitimize the practice, Islam connected it with Abraham who, purportedly, had run in that area in order to escape the devil; alternatively, the practice was connected with Hagar who, according to the legend, had run to and fro, looking for water. Rubin concludes that Muhammad's chief aim in adopting the *tawaf* appears to have been motivated by his desire to make Islam acceptable to all the Arabs, and not just to the Quraysh (343).

We see, then, that the religious source of Muhammad's inspiration is a complex, central issue requiring further analysis. We have just learned from Rubin that the new building of the Kaaba was probably inspired by certain Christian models, and that its interior was decorated with images of Jesus and Mary, which the Prophet ordered to be left untouched. That there was Christian influence of some kind on the Prophet is therefore an undeniable fact. The question is, what kind of influence? For as we have seen in our dialogue with Hamilton Gibb, Muhammad ultimately rejected fundamental elements of christological doctrine. We need, therefore, to dig deeper to learn the nature of the Christian influence upon him. If we may assume that Muhammad derived the ideational substance of his inspiration from one or another of three possible sources, or from all three, those sources would have to be (1) Judaism and the Prophet's Jewish contemporaries; (2) Christianity and his Christian contemporaries; and (3) the quasi-monotheism of Muhammad's contemporary *hanifs*.

If Muhammad had no first-hand knowledge of the Scriptures (in the sense of not having read them), as seems to have been the case, this means that virtually all the information he acquired concerning the Bible had come to him through oral communication with contemporaries. If the affair of the "daughters of Allah" is historical, as is most likely, it suggests that at an early stage in the developing process of his conception of monotheism he had believed that the idea of subordinate deities as intercessors with Allah is compatible with monotheism. By the end of his Medinan career, however, or somewhat earlier, perhaps, it seems clear, as we shall see, that he had definitely arrived at a strict or pure monotheism. How he arrived at that conception, and owing to what influences, is a question worth pursuing. It is an especially interesting question because he reached a strict monotheism by transvaluing virtually all of the pre-Islamic religious institutions and practices: Mecca, the Kaaba and its sacred environs, Allah, circumcision, circumambulation, Ramadan, and more. Such a transvaluation appears to have taken form in his mind late in the Medinan period when, as a rather successful armed prophet, he recognized the need and the possibility of unifying the tribes of the Peninsula by means of an ideology that would resonate with Arab ethnic sentiments. As we review the possible influences on Muhammad's mature conception of monotheism, let us entertain the hypothesis that it became a deliberate ideological strategy on his part to retain selected elements and symbols of the Arabs' religious experience by transvaluing them.

# 5

# Possible Influences on Muhammad's Inspiration

Charles Cutler Torrey opens his *The Jewish Foundations of Islam* by calling attention to the fact that the "Prophet himself declared Islam to be the heir of the old Hebrew revelation – in which term he would include also the New Testament."[1] Moreover, the revelation was "designed and expected by its founder to conquer the world." Muhammad believed, Torrey proposes,

> that the new faith was an old faith and that its evident foundations went far outside Arabia. The first impression gained by a reader of the Quran is that Muhammad had received the material of his new faith and practice mainly from the Jews of the Hijaz. On almost every page are encountered either episodes of Jewish history, or familiar Jewish legends, or details of rabbinical law or usage, or arguments which say, in effect, that Islam is the faith of Abraham and Moses. It is natural to suppose that all this is derived from Israelites; and that these Israelites were Muhammad's own neighbors is the inescapable impression constantly produced by his language . . . (2)

These facts, taken by themselves, would imply that the Prophet's education was thoroughly Jewish. But Torrey recognizes that this was not the case, and that many more facts need to be taken into account, such as the fusion of diverse elements in Islam. What was quite evident to Torrey and what also ought, perhaps, to be evident to us after our review of Arabian poly-theism in the pre-Islamic era, is that Muhammad adopted certain polythe-istic elements of his culture and transvaluated those elements by adapting them to his conception of monotheism. Torrey also recognized in the Quran distinctively Christian elements, so he reviews the early controversy between Jewish and Christian scholars over which influences had prepon-derance in the Prophet's inspiration.

Torrey cites the pioneering study of Abraham Geiger, *was hat Muhammad aus dem Judenthum aufgenommen?* [what did Muhammad take from

Judaism?], published in 1833, which held the field for many years, but which eventually provoked a reaction from Julius Wellhausen, in his *Reste Arabischen Heidentums* [vestiges of Arabian polytheism], 1887, claiming that the primary source of Muhammad's inspiration was Christian. Torrey explains that Wellhausen was influenced by the fact that Muhammad's converts were at first called Sabiens by the Meccans and also known as Mandaeans, a Gnostic sect in southern Babylonia. It appears that Muhammad was stimulated by the report that this ancient community, belonging neither to Judaism nor to Christianity, nevertheless bore a resemblance to both. Although Wellhausen's arguments were remarkably weak, says Torrey, his verdict remained in force, and several distinguished scholars continued to assert that the Christian influence was more potent than the Jewish in starting Muhammad on the course that he followed and in providing him with the essential materials of his new religion.

Torrey reminds us that the two religions had much in common in that day, each continuing to influence the other, so that one can point to certain Quranic passages and say that they reflect Christian doctrine, and then with equal justification say they have close parallels in the Hebrew scriptures. Indeed, one can even find similarities with pagan doctrines. It seems clear, then, that Torrey approaches the question of the respective influences rather objectively and certainly non-dogmatically. He readily acknowledges that Christian doctrines and terms were much more widespread in Arabia in the Prophet's time than scholars of a former generation had realized; and where the Quran is concerned, that certain doctrines such as the resurrection, judgment day, heaven and hell, the merit of certain ascetic practices, and so on, had become common to both religions.

However, Torrey regards it as an undisputable fact, that in the principal cities of the Hijaz, in Muhammad's time, a very large proportion of the population professed Judaism; and he recognizes the substantial adoption of Judaism by native tribes. He cites D. S. Margoliouth and other outstanding Jewish historians – whose works we shall review in due course – to support the fact that Judaism from the time of the Maccabees and the Pharisaic Revolution, was a highly successful proselytizing religion. Indeed, Christian emissaries found the soil everywhere prepared for them by Judaism. Even Wellhausen had acknowledged that the Jewish propagation of its religious ideas was different in quality and in lasting effect from that of any other of the religions of the time. Torrey also cites George Foote Moore's view (*Judaism*, I, 324), that Judaism was "the first great missionary religion of the Mediterranean world."

Margoliouth responded to the extraordinarily successful proselytizing by the Jews as a problem. He somehow came to believe that it is important to determine whether those who were regarded as Jews in Yathrib, were "ethnically" Jewish. He finds it perplexing that the Jews of Yathrib appear to have had the Arab form of tribal organization; the names of their tribes were Arabic, as were, with few exceptions, the names of individual members of whom we happen to hear. Margoliouth also observes that there is no record of any outstanding Jewish antagonist of Muhammad; nor did the supposed Jews of Yathrib produce any outstanding individual whose name the community believed was worth preserving. All this suggested to Margoliouth, that the "Children of Israel" whom Muhammad so often addressed, were "merely" Arab tribes made Israelites by conversion. As I remarked earlier, I find this view bizarre, for it sounds as though Margoliouth, a truly outstanding scholar, has in this instance entertained an ethnic or quasi-racial criterion for Jewishness, rather than purely religious criteria.

Torrey's response to Margoliouth is that all through the Quran we find references to Israelite tribes with their rabbis, their sacred books, their faith and their living contact with the past (27). Even in Mecca, where scholars assume there were few Jews, the Quran takes notice of Jewish scholars (*ahbar*), and rabbis (*rabbanis*), as in 3: 73 and 5: 48, 68. In 26: 197, Muhammad boasts that "the learned (*ulema*) of the Children of Israel had given him encouragement" (34).

For Torrey, it is quite likely that Muhammad was literate and that he could write. For if that had not been true, why would the prosperous widow Khadija have chosen him to take charge of her trading ventures. Muslim scholars prefer to believe that Muhammad was unlettered in order to accentuate the miraculous nature of his having written down the words of God, mediated by Gabriel. But Torrey believes that Muhammad had possessed "the three Rs" from boyhood, and that he did indeed write down the whole of the Quran "with his right hand." Torrey surmises further, that Muhammad must have frequented the Jewish quarter of his native city, learning much about the Children of Israel "whom Allah preferred over the rest of the world" (45: 15 and elsewhere). The Prophet thus learned about their fundamental beliefs, their forms of worship, their legends and the laws and customs by which they regulated their private and communal lives. Without such personal experiences on the part of the young Muhammad, without his seeing with his own eyes the actual example of Jewish communal life, Torrey insists, the aspiring prophet could not have conceived Islam. And though Torrey acknowledges that there are in the Quran at least three passages which seem clearly to be dependent on the New Testament (7: 38; 57: 13; and 19: 1–15), he maintains that it was not from Christians that the Arabian Prophet obtained information about the Gospels, for "it is utterly

impossible to suppose that Muhammad ever had any continuous inter-
course with Christians" (60). Furthermore, Torrey's argument continues,
the name for Jesus in the Quran, Isa, is strange, and he escapes the fate
intended for him and is taken up to heaven (Sura 3: 48); and there is no
mention of the Second Coming, the Christian doctrine which was more
universally held and built upon than any other. Torrey sees this as support
for his view that Muhammad's familiarity with Christian doctrine and his
impression of the Prophet Jesus, were derived not from direct Christian
informants, but rather from "Jewish teaching, very shrewdly given" (81).

For Torrey, then, if one weighs the relative proportions of Jewish and
Christian materials in the Quran, it is indisputable that the materials
obtained from Jewish sources greatly predominate. Moreover, in Quran 7:
156, Muhammad plainly declares his own legislation to be a revision
and improvement of the Hebrew laws. Where religious legislation is concerned, Torrey sees many parallels: the "religion of Abraham," to which
Muhammad so often appeals, he viewed as a pure monotheism, sharply
opposed to idolatry; the first two commandments of the Hebrew Decalogue
were the twin pillars of Islam from the very first, especially the conception
of Allah, the one and only God, without image or likeness; the parallel
between the Muslim *shahada*, "there is no God but Allah," and the Hebrew
*shema* is hardly accidental. Concerning God's unity, Torrey cites Sura 112:
1, and the Islamic warriors' battle-cry, *ahad, ahad*! [one, one!]. Also,
Muhammad began by directing his adherents to face Jerusalem in prayer,
and changed the *qibla* only after his arrival in Medina, when he failed to
receive Jewish support. As for the duty of children to parents (e.g., Sura 46:
14), Muhammad cannot have been ignorant of the fact that this commandment, in particular, was given special weight by the Jews. In both the
Talmud and the oldest *midrashim* (Heb. plural, singular, *midrash*, meaning
exposition and explanation of the underlying significance of a biblical text),
"Honor thy father and mother" and "Honor the Lord" are explicitly yoked
together. In addition, Torrey calls attention to "the great emphasis laid
upon almsgiving by the Jewish teachers, from Daniel (4: 24) and the Book
of Tobit (4: 7–11, 16f.), is faithfully reproduced in the Quran and the
Muslim tradition (57: 7–12, and other passages). The Quran and the *hadith*
thus repeat the Jewish doctrine, that almsgiving atones for sin." Torrey
makes his case, then, by calling attention to Muhammad's probable encounters with Jews even in Mecca, and by showing Quranic parallels to Jewish
scriptures, and to Talmudic and Midrashic teachings.

In pursuing the issue of the relative weights of Jewish and Christian
influences on Muhammad's inspiration, it seems to be a logical next step to
listen to several major Jewish historians who have discussed the Jewish

presence in Arabia. Our exposition of their views will be followed by a review of Richard Bell's well-known study, *The Origin of Islam in its Christian Environment*.

## Jewish Historians on the Jews of Arabia

Heinrich Graetz, the father of Jewish history, views it as historically plausible that Jewish fugitives had escaped to Arabia as early as the time of the destruction of the First Temple by Nebuchadnezzar in 586 BCE. It is a historical fact, however, that the Roman destruction of the Second Temple in 70 CE prompted a Jewish group to establish itself in northern Arabia.[2] From these fugitives there emerged three Jewish tribes, the B. Nadir, the B. Qurayza and the B. Bahdal, the first two of which were apparently descended from Aaron and therefore called themselves *kohanim* (Al-Kahinani), that is, priests. Another Jewish clan, the B. Qaynuqa, also settled in northern Arabia. All of these groups settled in Yathrib, situated in a fruitful area where they cultivated palm trees and practiced diverse forms of agriculture. As the fierce Bedouin tribes often attacked the settlements of the Jews, they built themselves strongholds on the elevated places in the city and the surrounding country, where they sought to protect themselves and preserve their autonomy. Originally, they were the dominant group in the district, but in about the year 300, they were forced to share power with two Arab tribes, the Aws and the Khazraj, that had settled in the vicinity. These Arab newcomers to the area sometimes stood in friendly relations, and at other times in hostile relations with the Jews.

North of Yathrib was the district of Khaybar, entirely inhabited by Jews who, following the destruction of the First Temple, are said to have wandered from Judea as far as Khaybar, attracted by its abundance of palms and grain. The Jews of Khaybar who were also periodically menaced by the Bedouin, constructed a line of fortified castles on a rocky formation difficult of access. Wadi-al-Qura (the valley of villages), a fertile plain a day's journey from Khaybar, was also inhabited exclusively by Jews.

Graetz now addresses the phenomenon touched upon earlier, the saliently Arabic character of these Jews of northern Arabia. Their language was closely related to Arabic, and their customs, except those of their religion, were not substantially different from those of the sons of Arabia. The primary difference between the Jews and the Bedouin, apart from religion, was that the Jews led a sedentary existence, practicing agriculture and cattle-breeding. Graetz calls attention to another important aspect of the Jews' relations with the Bedouin tribes. A Jewish group, out of security and political considerations, would ally itself with an Arab tribe, and thereby find itself in opposition to its co-religionists who had entered into a different alliance. This meant that there was no unwavering solidarity among the Jewish groups, a condition, as we shall see, that led to fatal consequences for them.

The Jews shared with the Bedouin Arabs the virtues of manliness, courage, and poetry, speaking with elegance the Arabic language, and adorning their poetry with sonorous rhymes. Graetz points out that whereas few northern Arabs before the seventh century were familiar with the art of writing, it was universally understood and practiced by the Jews who, reportedly, made use of the square, or so-called Assyrian characters. As the few Arabs who succeeded in learning to write generally employed the Hebrew characters, it would appear that they first acquired the art of writing from the Jews. Virtually every Jew in Arabia was able to read the scriptures, which probably is the reason the Arabs referred to the Jews as the "nation of writing" (*Ahl ul Kitab*).

Graetz, now addressing the nature of the Judaism of the Jews of the Hijaz, states that they had absorbed the chief tenets of the religion, which had been transmitted by the Tannaim, the earliest teachers of the rabbinic faith, and also by the Amoraim, the post-Mishnaic teachers. Supporting this view is the evidence that these Jews strictly observed the dietary laws, the festivals and the fast of Yom Kippur (Day of Atonement), which they called *Ashura*. They honored the Sabbath with such rigor that their sword remained in its scabbard on that day. In addition, they daily awaited the coming of the Messiah, a fact, as we shall see, that led to Muhammad's invitation to Yathrib-Medina. The Jews of the Hijaz faced Jerusalem in prayer and also appear to have been in communication with the Jews of Palestine, and willingly subordinated themselves to the religious authorities in Tiberius from whom they received religious instruction and interpretation of the Bible. Graetz avers that the Arabian Jews might even have been in touch with the Babylonian academics. Yathrib itself was no backwater where Jewish learning was concerned; it possessed rabbis, or teachers of the Law, a fact also mentioned in the Muslim tradition. Graetz does say, however, that the direct knowledge of the Bible that these Arabian Jews possessed was not considerable. They were acquainted with it primarily through the medium of Aggadic exegesis, and for them the history of the past fused so completely with the Aggadic additions, that they seldom made the distinction.

Given the relative freedom and autonomy of the Jews of the pre-Islamic Hijaz, they practiced their religion without fear and, doubtless, communicated the articles of their faith to their pagan neighbors. The Arab mind was open to intellectual promptings, says Graetz, and was delighted with the subject matter and narratives of the Bible. Hence, the Jewish religious ideas, by degree, became familiar and current in Arabia. Moreover,

> the Arabian Jews made their neighbors acquainted with a calendar-system, without which the latter were completely at sea in the arrangements of their seasons; learned Jews from Yathrib taught the Arabs to insert another month in their lunar year, which was far in arrear of the solar year. The Arabs adopted the nineteen-years cycle of the Jews (*c*. 420 *CE*), and called the inter-calary month Nasi, doubtless from the circumstance that the Jews were accustomed to receive their calendar for the festivals from their Nasi (patri-arch). (III, 59–60)

The Jews even succeeded in instructing the Arabs with regard to their historical origin, by teaching them their genealogy from the Pentateuch, thus proving their kinship with them as William Muir, we recall, had also argued. It was under Jewish instruction that the Arabs of the Hijaz came to derive their origin from Ishmael, and they readily accorded the Jews recognition of a common descent from Abraham. From this it followed that significant numbers of Arabs gained an affection for Judaism, embracing it through conversion. The tribal and clan structure of the Arabs meant that when a chieftain became a Jew, his whole clan at once followed. It is explicitly recorded about several Arabian tribes that they were converted to Judaism. Graetz mentions as examples the B. Qinana, a clan related to the Quraysh, and several other families or clans of the Aws and Khazraj tribes of Yathrib (vol. III, 61).

Graetz now proceeds to relate the events that enabled the Aws and the Khazraj to achieve dominance in Yathrib. In the early part of the sixth century, the Jewish religion had made so many converts in southern Arabia, notably in Yemen, that the last Himyarite King, dhu-Nuwas, became a Jew. Rivalry between the south Arabian converts to the two newly introduced monotheistic religions led to active hostility. Apparently dhu-Nuwas, representing a nationalistic spirit, associated the native Christians with the hated rule of the Christian Abyssinians; and to him is ascribed a massacre of the Christians of Najran in October, 523 CE. According to Arabic tradition, Daws dhu-Thalaban survived and implored the Emperor Justin I for aid, the emperor at the time being regarded as the protector of Christians everywhere. He wrote to the Negus of Abyssinia, the Christian power nearest the scene of the trouble. The Negus is said to have sent 70,000 men across the Red Sea to Arabia. This campaign therefore falls within the network of the international politics of that age. Byzantium was seeking through Abyssinia to bring the Arabian tribes under her influence and use them against Persia. The Abyssinians were victorious in 523 and again in 525. The commander on the latter occasion was Abrahah (variant of Abraham). According to the Muslim historian, Tabari, dhu-Nuwas was defeated in battle and, setting spurs to his steed, plunged into the waves of the sea and was never seen again.

The Christian Abyssinian rulers were intent upon colonizing the land and creating a rival to pagan Mecca, the center of pilgrimage in the north that was a source of considerable income to the Quraysh. The Abyssinian overlords were successful in establishing a southern, religious shrine that drew large numbers to the detriment of the Hijaz sanctuary. The memory of this economic–religious rivalry has been preserved in the local tradition in which two Arabian pagans, attached to the cult of the Kaaba, polluted a cathedral on the eve of a festival, provoking Abrahah to launch a punitive expedition against Mecca. This event is said to have occurred in the year of the birth of the Prophet, 570 or 571, a year called the year of the elephant, after the elephant that accompanied Abrahah on his northward campaign and which greatly impressed the Arabs of the Hijaz, who had never seen elephants before. According to tradition, Abrahah's army was destroyed by a smallpox epidemic.

The earlier victory of the Abyssinians over dhu-Nuwas meant that plundering and killing raged in Himyara. The Abyssinians were so enraged at the Jews of Himyara that they massacred thousands in revenge for the Christian martyrs of Najran. Thus ended the short-lived, Jewish kingdom of Himyara.

The foregoing background is necessary for an understanding of how and why the Jews of Yathrib fell into strife with the neighboring Arab tribes. The Jews of Yathrib, owing to the close relationship they had had with the King of Himyara, whose power had extended over the province, ruled the Arab tribes with a Jewish chief as governor. The Aws and the Khazraj envied and hated the privileged position of the Jews, and seized the opportunity to rebel when the Jews could no longer rely on assistance from Himyara. An Arabian chief of the Ghassanids named Harith, attached to the Byzantine court, was commissioned to lead his troops toward Yathrib. But in order to avoid alerting the Jews to his mission, Harith gave out that he was heading to Himyara, and merely encamping near Yathrib, where he invited the Jewish chiefs to visit him. Many accepted the invitation, expecting to be welcomed with a prince's usual generosity. But as they entered the tent of the Ghassanid prince, they were murdered, one by one. Thereupon, Harith announced to the Arabs of Yathrib, that he had liberated them from their enemies' chiefs, and that now they should be able to deal effectively with the rest. But the Arabs of Yathrib, to avoid an open engagement with the Jews, also resorted to a stratagem. They invited the other Jewish chiefs to a banquet where all of them were murdered. Now leaderless, the Yathrib Jews were overrun and forced to give up their strongholds (*c*. 530–5 CE). In an effort to adapt themselves to the new insecurity of their lives, the Jews gradually placed themselves under the protection of one or another of the Arab tribes and thus became clients or dependents (*mawali*) of either the Aws or the Khazraj, who, themselves were at each other's throats, vying for hegemony in the area.

Towards the end of the sixth century the Yathrib Jews had nearly recovered from the blows dealt them by their Arab neighbors. The Aws and the Khazraj had exhausted themselves in bloody feuds which had lasted twenty years, thus giving the Jews respite in which they could regain some of their previous importance in Yathrib society. Their sense of insecurity, however, was still there, owing not only to the memory of their recent history, but also to their awareness of the fact that they had earlier taken sides in the Aws-Khazraj conflict and were, therefore, divided against themselves. This situation naturally heightened their yearning for the coming of the Messiah, an article of faith with which their Arab neighbors had become familiar. This was the state of affairs in Yathrib-Medina when the Prophet of Mecca received an invitation to immigrate to Medina. Those who invited him, thinking that perhaps the Meccan Prophet was the Messianic figure whom the Jews awaited, hastened to win him over in the hope that he would successfully mediate between the Aws and the Khazraj and put an end to their bloody confrontations.

Simon Dubnov,[3] the other "father" of Jewish history, providing pretty much the same historical analysis, is in essential agreement with Graetz. Salo W. Baron, who may be regarded as one of the leading Jewish historians of the twentieth century, also goes over some of the same ground covered by the pioneers Graetz and Dubnov, but provides more details about Jewish–Arab relations in the pre-Islamic Hijaz.[4]

## Baron on Pre-Islamic, Arab–Jewish Relations in Arabia

Basing himself on more recent investigations than those relied on by Graetz and Dubnov, Baron avers that up to the sixth century, Jewish tribes tended to dominate social and economic life in Yathrib-Medina. The later Arabic literature mentions about twenty Jewish tribes, but those that stand out as being the most prominent are the B. Nadir, B. Qurayza, and B. Qaynuqa, who between them occupied at one time 59 strongholds and practically the entire fertile area. This means in Ibn Khaldun's terms, that the Jews of the Hijaz represented the "sown," the sedentary, agricultural societies of the area, a fact the significance of which becomes central in a later analysis of their fate under Muhammad.

Baron regards it as most likely that it was the Jewish settlers who had changed the city's ancient Egyptian name, Yathrib (Athribis), also recorded in Greek sources, to the Hebrew–Aramaic "Medina," meaning city. The Jewish settlement of Khaybar, about sixty miles north of Medina, took its name from the Hebrew word *heber*, meaning "association" or "league" of communities. Other settlements verifiable as Jewish or predominantly Jewish, were Dedan, Al-Hijr, Teima, Ablaq, central Arabian Yamama, Taif, and perhaps even Mecca. Baron cites Werner Caskel who described the Jews as the primary representatives of Nabatean culture in the Hijaz after 300 CE "These were the beginnings," wrote Caskel, "of the Jewish population, which later occupied all the oases in the northwest including Medina" (Baron, vol. III, 65).

These were flourishing settlements which – as particular cases confirming Ibn Khaldun's general sociological theory – attracted irresistibly the Bedouins from all over the Peninsula. The Bedouins not only regarded these agriculturally prosperous oases as fit objects for raids, but also – for some at least – enviable sources of economic security. Gradually, several Arab tribes drifted into Medina, and by the sixth century, prevailed over the settled Jewish communities. Baron, like Graetz, views these Jews as descended from Arab proselytes. He cites a Muslim source stating that the new Arab arrivals " . . . were prevented by the Jews from entering their fort as long as they professed another religion, and only when they embraced Judaism were they admitted."

So Baron views the Jews of northern Arabia as cultivating their particular blend of Arab–Jewish culture. In Ibn Khaldun's terms, again, it was these Jews of the northern Hijaz who also fostered advances in the technical and economic aspects of the oases. The Jews of Yathrib, Khaybar, and Teima appear to have pioneered in introducing advanced methods of irrigation and cultivation of the soil. They also developed new arts and crafts, ranging from metal work to dyeing and the making of fine jewelry; in economic relations, they also taught the neighboring tribes more effective methods of exchanging goods and money. Most of the agricultural terms and names of tools recorded in pre-Islamic poetry or the Quran are Aramaic, the spoken language of the Jews and, indeed, the lingua franca of the region; and the Arabic traditions themselves attribute to the Jews the introduction of the honey-bee and many new fruits, including the date. The palm tree, the long glorified symbol of Judaism, now became the object of adulation in Arabic poetry as well. A Jewish woman, as we learned earlier, was reported to have brought the first vine to Taif near Mecca.

Even more interesting is the fact that by their irrigation system, the observance of their dietary laws, and especially by building their strongholds on hills rather than in the fever-infested valleys, the Jews pioneered in resisting the deadly, contagious diseases of the area. These Jewish farmers and craftsmen had long recognized not only the "war of each against all" raging among the Bedouin tribes themselves; they also recognized what Ibn Khaldun later proposed, that the Bedouin conditions of economic life were such, that it was second nature for them to raid the settled communities for plunder. This explains the strongholds on hills which the Jews built to stave off raids, and to introduce refinements in the amenities of life, which certainly appeared to the Bedouins as an enviably luxurious way of life. So although Baron would not go the whole length of Sidney Smith's assertion, that there were thriving cities in northern Arabia, he would say that " . . . during the few generations of Jewish control, the focal northern areas were raised almost to the high level of the southern [Arabian] civilization, which had long earned for Himyara and its vicinity the Roman designation of *Arabia Felix* [Arabia, the fruitful, happy and fortunate]" (vol. III, 71).

These Jews were also cultural pioneers in the region, for they were a "people of the Book," as Muhammad later called them and the Christians; it was these Jews who communicated to their Arab neighbors the chief elements of their religious and ethical outlook. The Arabs, captivated as they were by excellence in poetry, by the narrative content of a good poem, and by effective story telling, used to gather in Jewish and Christian inns, and, while sipping a glass of wine, would listen with rapt attention to the recitation of the exploits of biblical heroes. Baron agrees that the stories were naturally adorned with the embroideries of post-biblical Aggadah (legend). In the minds of the Arab audience and, most likely, of the Jewish listeners as well, the biblical and legendary elements soon became indistinguishable ingredients of a new cultural entity. In that way, the Jewish settlers introduced to the Bedouins the rudiments of the Hebrew Bible and the monotheistic idea.

Baron recognizes, of course, that besides the Jews there were Christians in the vicinity and also Judeo-Christian sectarians of several kinds. He also notes that these Jews had direct intellectual contacts with the centers of Jewish life in Babylonia and Palestine, though the contacts do appear to be few in number. The several distinguished poets among them seem to have been more Arabian than Jewish, judging from a total of some 200 stanzas that have come down to us.

D. S. Margoliouth is apparently alone, among the Jewish historians, in looking most searchingly at these Jewish tribes.[5] In his review of the Mishna, the Talmud, and later rabbinic writings, he sees no record of the existence of either Jewish colonies in the Hijaz or of a Jewish kingdom in south Arabia. And in his review of the available epigraphic evidence in which the name Yathrib appears, it seems to have been a pagan, not a Jewish settlement at some time BCE. On the other hand, the Muslim *tradition* seems definitely to have known of Jews who inhabited Medina in the Prophet's time; and that tradition has preserved the names of the three Jewish tribes with which we have become familiar: the B. Nadir, the B. Qurayza and the B. Qaynuqa. The Quran states that these Jews possessed copies of the Law, had rabbis, and observed the Sabbath and the food taboos. For Margoliouth, however, as noted earlier, there is still a puzzling and perplexing problem, since neither the tribes nor the individuals showed any signs of typically Jewish respect for the Hebrew Bible by naming their children after outstanding biblical personalities, or the patriarchs or the prophets. And when we hear of conversational encounters between Muhammad and the Jews, their names are either identical with those common among the Arabs, or, if they are unusual, have nothing Jewish about them. After such considerations, Margoliouth concludes that the Jews of Medina were most probably Arabs who had embraced Judaism (61).

Margoliouth now addresses the *hanif* phenomenon. He agrees that there may have existed a form of Arabic monotheism or quasi-monotheism, such as that which Muhammad's biographers report, and which certain inscriptions suggest. Margoliouth cites the well-known inscription made up of two broken stones described by Glaser and afterwards by Winckler that, however, does not quite settle the matter for Margoliouth. His reason is that its phraseology is very different from Hebrew or Jewish usage. The *Rahman* is there styled as the *Rahman* who is in heaven and Israel and their god, lord of Yahud (i.e., the Jews). Moreover, Glaser later admitted the possibility that he may not have copied the inscription accurately, and this admission seriously vitiates the evidence. For Margoliouth, therefore, the inscription may be trusted as far as *Rahman*, but no further. Margoliouth also cites a British museum inscription exhibiting the name *Rahman* for the deity, which evidently contains doctrines approximating Muhammad's early conception of monotheism including the "association" of lesser deities with the high god. So Margoliouth offers this proposition:

Was Muhammad's theology not, as the Quran so emphatically represents it, a fresh start in Arabia traceable, as the tradition suggests, to contact of the Prophet with Jews and Christians on his travels, or at Mecca, but merely the

introduction into North Arabia of a system which had possibly for some centuries been, if not actually dominant, yet at least current in the South? Was
the Judaism even of the King dhu Nuwas monotheism of this type, roughly
identified with Judaism by those whose acquaintance with both systems was
superficial, just as Muhammad's doctrine was at an early period called
Sabiism owing to its resembling that cult in certain ceremonies? (68)

In those terms, "The Quranic technicality *shirk*, association of other deities
with Allah, whose source had previously eluded us, is here traced to its
home" (Ibid.).

Margoliouth is therefore inclined to regard the term Judaism as applied
to the Medinan Jewish tribes as indicating some form of monotheism,
which, for the want of a better term, should be called Rahmanism, " . . .
such as is found in the southern part of the Peninsula, which may indeed
have taken its leading ideas from Judaism, but was by no means identical
therewith" (71). But does this mean, for Margoliouth, that Judaism itself
had no influence on the formation of Muhammad's doctrine? "Judaism,"
Margoliouth writes:

> cannot indeed be removed from the doctrines of Muhammad himself, since
> the Quran consists largely of material taken from either the Old Testament
> or the Jewish oral traditions; . . . (71)

Margoliouth, having thus challenged the nature of the religion professed
by the Jewish tribes of Medina, nevertheless concludes his analysis with
this statement:

> The origin of Islam from Judaism is far more than a hypothesis; for even if
> we regard Christianity as a coalescence of Judaism and Hellenism, and
> suppose the first to have influenced the beginnings of Islam, the Hellenic ele-
> ments, which percolated were so few as to be negligible. If we regard Islam
> as based on the Sabianism of Harran, that, too, appears to have been an
> Abrahamic system, and not far removed from Judaism; and even the
> monotheism of South Arabia, of which we as yet know so little, cannot well
> have been unconnected with the religion of the Israelites . . . (82)

# 6

# The Jews of Arabia: A Recent Re-Examination

In one of the most recent re-examinations of the issues concerning the Jews of the Hijaz, Gordon Newby's summary of research findings[1] tends to confirm the analyses we have reviewed by the major Jewish historians. At the time of the birth of Muhammad in 570 CE, the Jewish communities were in a state of decline, economically and politically, while the Arab tribes around Mecca had become dominant. Arabs replaced Jews in the profitable and powerful posts as tax collectors for the Persian Empire, and Jews everywhere in the Hijaz were losing control over the best land and water. Yet throughout Arabia, and in the Hijaz in particular, Judaism was a vigorous and flourishing Diaspora culture. Jews played significant roles in all areas of Arab society, as merchants, farmers, poets, and warriors, and even as Bedouin. Jews lived not only in castles, as we learned earlier, but in tents as well. They spoke Arabic as well as Hebrew and Aramaic, and they communicated with the chief Jewish religious centers in Babylonia and Palestine. And, of course, like other Diaspora communities, they had developed their own distinctive beliefs and practices, including a serious interest in Jewish mystical traditions and in eschatological visions.

The evidence Newby reviewed confirms the proposition that the Jews had migrated to Arabia in Roman times, where they continued to practice agriculture, but also served as merchants, craftsmen, and scholars. The same pattern is evident in the Hijaz where Jews became fully integrated into the economic life of the Peninsula. Living in towns *and* villages, they worked as sailors, scribes, warriors, sculptors, farmers, and wine merchants. Newby addresses the relevant question of whether tribes in pre-Islamic and early Islamic Arabia were as cohesive as some early scholars had supposed. He cites recent studies showing that, as a rule, tribal subgroups operated as independent units, often at odds with the other subgroups of the tribe. He notes that Arab historical writings concerning the pre-Islamic era have tried to portray tribes as if they were the product of descent from a single ancestor. This fictional emphasis on common descent masked the fact that tribes were often formed by the association of individuals and groups with common interests and geography. Though some Western scholars have recognized that fact, others have accepted the fictional account which, in the case of the Jews, has led to the mistaken view that they could not have been Bedouin because they were not Arab.

Pursuing this issue, Newby turns to Yathrib/Medina that yields the greatest amount of information about Jewish social groupings, information with which we are now familiar. The city was a definite unit with a population divided into Arab and Jewish factions. The Arab tribes were the Aus and the Khazraj, while the three tribes most scholars regard as Jewish were the B. Qurayza, the B. Nadir, and the B. Quaynuqa. Newby cites Michael Lecker's groundbreaking study showing, among other things, that the process of expelling Jews from their lands had predated the Hijra (when Muhammad moved from Mecca to Medina), and that this was accomplished by relatively small groups moving into positions of advantage. Common to such groups was their struggle for power regardless of their tribal affiliations. Medina and other such urban centers in the northern part of Arabia were amalgamations of villages, strongholds, castles, and other types of dwellings. Some individuals and groups came together out of mutual interest and protection, as did the reported 300 goldsmiths living in Zuhra, not all of whom were Jewish; and some prominent families had their fortified castles in the heart of Medina. Wadi al-Qurra, the Valley of Villages, exhibits a similar settlement pattern in which groups, not necessarily of the same ethnic background, merged into a larger urban unit. The pattern of urban settlement, at least to a certain extent, appears to have cut across ethnic affiliations. Newby reminds us that this phenomenon is quite relevant to the conflict between Muhammad and the Jews of Medina, where "the 'fiction' of tribal identifications obscures the real complexity of Medinese life" (52). Newby is referring here to what we learned earlier about the Jewish clans, subgroups, and tribes who were divided against themselves, some siding with the Aus, others with the Khazraj.

Another important finding to which Newby alerts us is that social groups in urban centers of Arabia were not isolated from the rural areas. One must not regard "rural"–"urban" as a rigid dichotomy, for there was a steady commercial interaction between the settled and the nomadic population, with some of the pastoralists settling in the towns and gradually assimilating urban culture. In one case, at least, such assimilation meant becoming Jewish. The B. Hishna b. Ukarima b. Awf asked to settle in Tayma. The town was dominated by a strong Jewish population insisting that the Arabs adopt Judaism before settling, and they are reported to have agreed, and later moved to Medina.

Newby also observes – as we learned earlier from other sources – that some of the Aus and Khazraj converted to Judaism or were converted by their mothers who "used to make a vow that if their child lived they would make it a Jew (*tahawwadathu*), since they considered the Jews to be people of knowledge and the book (*ilmin wa-kitabin*)." This resulted in a large number of Jewish clans in Medina, and meant that being Jewish did not necessarily imply affiliation with a particular clan or tribe.

This brings us to the question raised earlier in our discussion of Margoliouth's view. Newby addresses the question of whether and to what extent the conversions were made on "religious" or on "social" or "economic" grounds. The question that has often been asked, is whether the Arabian Jews were "really Jewish." Newby replies cogently:

> From the evidence that the tribes and individuals retained their Judaism after conversion, in the instance cited above, after they had moved from Tayma to Medina, and by the fact that the converts were regarded as Jews by other Jews and non-Jews in the Hijaz, we have to assume that they were indeed "real" Jews as Judaism was understood in that context. From another perspective, we see that the process of conversion to Judaism in Arabia in the pre-Islamic period is paralleled by the patterns of conversion to Islam during Muhammad's lifetime. Whole tribes became Muslim in connection with political and military submission to Muhammad and, apparently, in proportion to his increasing strength and influence. While it has been argued in the Muslim case also that the conversions were not as "sincere" as individual conversions, particularly in light of the apparent apostasies after the death of Muhammad, such an argument seems to derive from a Western overemphasis on the centrality of individual autonomy coupled with Muslim revisions of the history of that same period. What group conversions do underscore is the social and economic aspects of converting from one religious group to another without denying the spiritual and aesthetic qualities. (53)

In pre-Islamic Arabia, conversion to Judaism as well as conversion to Monophysite or Nestorian Christianity, meant a radical break with the old social and spiritual order and the adoption of a new political and social matrix. When, for example, Muhammad turned his back on his ancestral religion, the Quraysh called it *Saba*, implying not only a departure from the old but also the creation of an active antagonism between the old and the new. Newby gives the additional example of Dhu Nuwas who, when he acceded to the throne, was joined by all of Himyar in his Judaism, which represented political opposition to the Ethiopian forces. For Newby, then, the conversion of large groups to Judaism indicates that Judaism was the dominant social force in Arabia in the fifth and sixth centuries.

Newby's review of the evidence tends also to confirm the view that, whatever the origin of the Arabian Jews, they expressed their interest in correct Jewish practice. They remained in touch with the Babylonian rabbis, consulting them on issues of attire and kosher food. Jewish women and, perhaps men too, wore veils outside to protect themselves from the windblown sand, a custom borrowed from the Arabs and allowed by the rabbis. The nomadic existence of some of the Jewish groups dwelling in tents meant that they had to be exempted from some of the requirements incumbent on those residing in fixed abodes. Especially interesting in this regard is the fact that some Jewish groups were pastoral nomads around the time of the rise of Islam, and that there were Jewish Bedouin in the Hijaz as late as the sixteenth century CE. But the Jews we hear about in the historical and literary texts possessed a political and economic importance for those who wrote about the rise of Islam. This means that the Jews we learn most about are urban, literate, and influential, many of whom opposed Muhammad and emerging Islam. However, we know of several Jewish literary figures who distinguished themselves as outstanding poets in the Arabic language, reflecting the values and pastoral ideals of the pre-Islamic Bedouin, as a noble desert wanderer. The best known of such pre-Islamic Jewish poets is Samawal b. Adiya, who lived in the sixth century CE in a castle, in the Jewish city of Tayma. His father was a *cohen*, a descendant of the priests and a member of a powerful Jewish group in Arabia. Samawal is remembered for his loyalty to Amru al-Qays, who had deposited his family's heirloom armaments with him while on a trip to the Byzantine emperor. According to Arab legend, Amru al-Qays was poisoned by the emperor's agents while returning to Arabia, thus leaving the armaments in the possession of Samawal and Amru al-Qays' daughter, Hind. According to some sources, Samawal's mother was from the Ghassanids, the Arab tribe that served as a client of the Byzantines, protecting the settled communities from the incursions of the Bedouin Arabs. The implacable enemy of the Ghassanids and of Amru al-Qays, the Lakhmid King of Hira, sent al-Harith b. Zalim to Samawal's castle demanding that he turn over the armor and Hind to him. Samawal refused, even after al-Harith had somehow captured Samawal's son, and carried out his threat to kill him before his father's eyes. Thus Samawal's name became immortalized among the Arabs for the fidelity and honor he had demonstrated, even in the face of great personal tragedy. The fact that there is nothing particularly Jewish about this poem, and that it runs counter to paramount Jewish ideals of preserving life, has led some scholars to question the reliability of such poems and even the existence of as-Samawal, although most scholars accept the genuineness of most of the corpus of pre-Islamic poetry.

It is from the Islamic texts and especially the Quran, preserving, as they do, the controversies between Muhammad and the Jews, that we learn much about the beliefs of the Jews of the Hijaz. Newby singles out two terms that seem to designate a specific community of beliefs and practices. The terms are *rabbaniyyun* and *ahbar*, the first of which occurs three times in the Quran: 3: 79; 5: 44; 5: 63; while the second occurs four times: 5: 44; 5: 63; 9: 31; and 9: 34. Muslim commentators are in agreement that *rabbaniyyun* refers to the rabbis among the Jews. As for the term *ahbar*, too little is understood about it to warrant comment. However, from the Quranic evidence and that of the *Hadiths* or traditions, we would expect the existence of a rabbinic body in Arabia and in the Hijaz in particular, with whom Muhammad had contact. Newby, relying on David Halperin and Steven Wasserstrom, provides a discussion too detailed to summarize adequately, illuminating the nature of Arabian–Jewish eschatological speculation. It is highly likely that at least one important element of Arabian–Jewish thought was a concern with Apocalypticism. But this was hardly unique, since Apocalypticism and Messianism had become a major part of the thinking of Jews in both Palestine and the Diaspora in the years of Roman domination of the eastern Mediterranean. It was not only the destruction of the Second Temple, but also tragedies like the virtual elimination of the large Egyptian Jewish communities during the Egyptian revolt (114–17 CE), that persuaded many that the Messianic age was near and deliverance would soon come. Hence, it is quite understandable why Jews are represented in Islamic texts as predicting the imminence of a prophet or a messiah.

Newby also reminds us that by Muhammad's time not only were eschatological expectations at a high pitch, but so also were Jewish forms of mysticism, several features of which David Halperin identifies with Jewish *merkabah* mysticism. Gershom Scholem, in his famous study, *Major Trends in Jewish Mysticism*, averred that "we know that in the period of the Second Temple an esoteric doctrine was already taught in Pharisaic circles. The first chapter of Genesis, the story of Creation (*Maaseh Bereshith*), and the first chapter of Ezekiel, the vision of God's throne-chariot (the *Merkabah*), were the favorite subjects of discussion and interpretation which it was apparently considered inadvisable to make public."[2] As Newby explains, the presence of this form of mysticism in the Jewish communities of Arabia helps us grasp some of the accusations leveled against Jews in Islamic texts. In the pseudepighaphic Jewish literature, Enoch, of the generation of the Flood, was taken up to heaven so as not to be destroyed, as a sign of God's mercy that one pious man would be saved. When elevated into heaven he was transformed into the powerful angel, Metatron, who was taught by God all the secrets, and given guardianship over the treasures of God and who indeed, became a lesser god of sorts (3 Enoch 48c, verses 1–4).

Newby then turns our attention to early Muslim sources relating that a Jewish boy, Ibn Sayyad, who lived at the time of Muhammad, claimed to be the Apostle of God. In an early tradition, Muhammad said to him, "Do you bear witness that I am the Apostle of God?" to which Ibn Sayyad replied, "Do you bear witness that I am the Apostle of God?" In some versions, Muhammad does not reply and in others he is noncommittal. In one variant, Ibn Sayyad admits that Muhammad is an Apostle to the Gentiles, while in others his answers to Muhammad's question indicate that he possesses the right knowledge to substantiate his claim to apostleship. "Included in that knowledge," writes Newby, "is information gathered from the practice of mystical contemplation in which Ibn Sayyad saw the throne of God in the middle of water surrounded by the *hayyot*, the Living Creatures of the book of Ezekiel who are identified as bearers of God's throne. Ibn Sayyad's vision was induced by wrapping himself with a cloak and murmuring incantations in Hebrew . . ." (Newby, 62). In this mystical tradition, the mystic returned as a messenger from the heavenly realm to relate his experiences as a cautionary warning to his fellow Jews. What Newby next has to say is quite important for an understanding of the circumstances that made it possible for Muhammad to receive an invitation to Medina, and to serve in the role of judge, umpire, magistrate, arbitrator, and prophet. "From the Arabian Jewish perspective," writes Newby,

> Muhammad fitted the pattern of the Jewish mystic. He wrapped himself in a mantle, recited mantic prose, brought a message from the heavenly realms, and toured heaven himself. Interestingly, Ibn Sayyad practiced his mystical exercises in a palm-grove where Muhammad spied on him. This feature of *merkabah* mystic practice seems to be alluded to in the story of al-Walid b. al-Mughira's characterization of Muhammad's speech as sweet and his "source" a palm tree whose branches are fruitful. These traditions seem to imply that Muhammad was perceived by some of his contemporaries as fitting in with the Jewish mystical practice represented by Ibn Sayyad. Later Muslims transformed Ibn Sayyad into the anti-Messiah, while interpreting Muhammad's role as quasi-messianic. These traditions still, however, preserve Muhammad and Ibn Sayyad as reflexes of one another. (63)

Clearly, the circulation of Jewish materials for use as the basis of Quran commentary was present in Muhammad's lifetime. Muhammad, Abu Bakr, and Umar are reported to have made several trips to the Bet Midrash in Medina; and Muhammad's amanuensis, Zayd b. Thabit, who was quite central where Quranic materials were concerned, is reported to have gone so far, at Muhammad's request, as to learn *al-yahudiyyah* in a Bet Midrash in order to read Jewish material.

Turning our attention again to the economic life of the Arabian Jews, although they followed a wide range of occupations, as we have seen, it was trade and agriculture that had first sustained the Jews when they came into Arabia, and those professions continued to sustain most of them right up to Islamic times. The city of Medina and most of the other Jewish communities in the Hijaz, were basically agricultural communities, unlike Mecca, which was based on religious pilgrimages and, perhaps, on trade, but to a much lesser extent, if we take Patricia Crone's research into account. The evidence Newby cites concerning agriculture confirms what we have learned from the early Western and Jewish scholars. The chief crop was dates, which required considerable knowledge, skill, and intensive effort to grow and maintain. The Jews had brought Nabataean techniques of artificial irrigation to the oases of Western Arabia, and they employed the techniques of manual pollination of the date flowers to ensure a good yield. Dates, as we have seen, were a major source of nourishment in the Arabian diet, and provided the fruit for a fermented drink. Wine made by Jews was regarded by most in pre-Islamic Arabia as the best available. In Medina, Tayma, and Khaybar the Jews were predominant in the date fields; and one of the sources of conflict between the Arab tribes of the B. Aus and the B. Khazraj of Medina and the Jews, was the control the Jews exercised over those fields. Newby agrees with the proposition that when Muhammad arrived in Medina, displacement of the Jews provided a source of revenue for the new community. However, the nonagricultural Muslims had a limited ability to derive benefit from an agricultural technology in which they were not trained. Such practical realities were the basis for Muhammad's treaty with the defeated Jews of Khaybar, in which he consented to their remaining on their lands in return for 50 percent of the yield.

Newby notes that the Jews played a similarly key role in the trade and markets of the Hijaz, which meant that market day for the week was Friday, the time before Shabbat, the Jewish Sabbath. This day, called *aruba* in the old Arabic sources, was a time not only for making purchases before the holiday, but also for legal cases to be decided and for entertainment. This institution probably influenced the selection of Friday as Islam's day of congregational prayer. Hence, preaching, prayer, and the recitation of the Quran, which formed the core of the Muslim Friday congregational worship, grew out of the social practices associated with the Jewish market on the eve of the Sabbath. In this setting, judges for the legal disputes could be drawn from any group in the community. In Medina, Muhammad served as a judge, but his role was not merely to render wise decision, but also to mediate between the contending parties and to effect a settlement. Thus, Newby concludes, "on the eve of the rise of Muhammad and Islam, political and economic circumstances had reduced the Jews of the Hijaz to a marginal role in the society. Their legacy remained, however, in the profound influence they had on the ideas of Muhammad and Islam" (77).

# 7

# Richard Bell's Origin of Islam in its Christian Environment

Bell opens his classic study with the suggestion that the triumph of Islam in the seventh century CE, can best be understood as a victory over what he calls a "degenerate Christianity," a Christianity plagued by sectarian conflict and the alliance of the Church with the State. This alliance was so tight that the bishops and other high dignitaries of the Church became, in effect, State officials. This was so much the case, that the acceptance of Christianity was regarded as acceptance of subservience to the Roman Empire of the East. This fact has definite significance for Bell, when trying to understand the social conditions of Arabia before and during the time of Muhammad. For it helps to explain the alacrity with which even Christian Arabs accepted an Arabian prophet. The Church–State alliance also played a part in forming Muhammad's conception of religion. For Christianity appeared to him to be not merely a religion, but a State as well, which might explain why, beginning in the Medinan period, Islam became political in the full sense: the pursuit of power and hegemony became an essential element of the Prophet's theory and practice.

For Bell, then, the Church–State alliance of the Byzantine empire, which came to be perceived by the people as a highly oppressive, foreign institution, was one important reason for Christianity's loss of appeal. Another manifestation of Christianity's "degeneration" at the time was its having been torn by internal strife and schism. It was weak in moral and religious insight when called on to meet the challenge of Islam; dogma took the place of reflection where religious questions were concerned. As the power of the State was available to the worldly, ambitious, prideful prelates, they were only too ready to employ State power against doctrinal opponents. As a consequence of the doctrinal quarrels, the Eastern Church became irreparably divided, and the Christian Empire correspondingly vulnerable to dismemberment by Muhammad's warriors. The main result of the sectarian, metaphysical exercises was that when Islam arrived in Syria and

Egypt fully armed, it found a Church divided by embittered feelings, thus making Christians more eager to defeat Christian "heretics" than to unite against a common foe. Moreover, there was wide and deep discontent among the indigenous peoples who resented the Church–State alliance, which sought to force them into the acceptance of a hated doctrine, and a hated, heavy tax, in addition.

Bell, thus showing how Christianity had become a negative stimulus for the peoples of Syria and Egypt, proceeds to explore positive Christian influences on Islam. "Some things in the Quran and in Islam," he writes, "which appear especially Jewish, may really have come through nominally Christian channels." Noteworthy, however, is what Bell has to say in the balance of this passage:

> But even with that allowance there is no doubt about the large influence exer-cised by Judaism. There were Jews in Arabia long before Muhammad's time. In Medina they were numerous, and the fact that many of these Medinan Jews seem to have been proselytes rather than Jews by race [sic], shows that Judaism as a religion had some attraction for Arabs . . . We know that for some time after the Prophet and his followers emigrated to Medina, and even for some time before, he was in close and friendly relations with the Jews of that place.
>
> It is therefore not with any desire to deprecate the influence of Judaism that I intend to devote myself mainly to the question of the relation between Christianity and Islam.[1] (14)

Bell agrees with Harnack, that the absence of any pre-Islamic transla-tions of the Bible into Arabic is strong proof that Christianity had not struck roots among the Arabs in early times. This is also borne out by the fact that even in a later period there is no evidence of a Christian church using Arabic in its services. The language of Christianity in the East was Aramaic (or Syriac). The influence of Christianity on Arabia, Bell sees as emanating principally from three centers: Syria in the northwest, Mesopotamia in the northeast, and Abyssinia in the west, the last of these exercising some of its influence across the Red Sea, but mainly by way of Yemen in the south, which was for a time ruled by an Abyssinian dynasty.

Any student of the Quran will easily recognize the presence in it of Jewish and Christian elements; but Bell recognizes that it is not at all easy to determine which came through Jewish channels, and which through Christian. Given this difficulty, it is important to appreciate that the Prophet had fused distinct elements into a new synthesis. We have to allow, says Bell, for considerable originality in Muhammad, not the originality which produces something absolutely new, but the originality of a strong mind, working upon very imperfect information of outside things, yet finding expression for ideas and aspirations which were dimly present in other minds. He claimed to be an Arab Prophet, and he was. We shall see him consciously borrowing – he is quite frank about it. But to begin with, the materials which he uses, though they may remind us ever and again of Jewish and Christian phrases and ideas, are in reality Arab materials. They may have been originally derived from outside Arabia, but they had by Muhammad's time become part of the Arab mind . . . As regards Christianity, his own direct knowledge of it was to begin with . . . just such knowledge as we might expect in a caravan trader who had been to Syria and seen Christian churches, and perhaps Christian services. (69)

Bell views Muhammad's project as having been a rational and practical one from the very start. His understanding, drawn from both Jewish and Christian sources, was that a prophet is sent to his own people. His central aim in Mecca is to persuade his fellow tribesmen to recognize the true God and to show thankfulness for His bounties. It is when that appeal is rejected that the Prophet warns of punishment on Judgment Day.

Bell now proceeds to illustrate what he regards as Muhammad's syncretic reinterpretation of Jewish and/or Christian ideas. In some passages of the Quran, Muhammad employs the metaphor of embryo, describing its formation in the womb in some detail, which suggests that the process made a deep impression on his mind. This, for Bell, is an example of Muhammad's independence of direct biblical influence at the outset of his career. Bell cites Sura 96, generally regarded as one of the earliest Meccan Suras, where God is spoken of as the Creator of man. But the Quranic account differs from the biblical account of creation. In the Quran, God is said to have created man from *alaq*, and when one compares other passages, it becomes clear that *alaq* denotes the first stage in the formation of the embryo in the womb. Only at a later period, when Muhammad had become more familiar with some of the contents of the Hebrew Bible, the so-called Old Testament, did he refer to the creation of man from clay. After examining several other Quranic passages that have a biblical ring about them – especially those concerning the poor, the orphan and the prisoner – Bell argues that none of them is, apparently, so close to the Bible as to suggest direct borrowing. It is Bell's strong impression, then, that Muhammad, while growing up in Mecca, had personally felt the abuses, injustices, and cruelties that prevailed there. Muhammad's moral conscience, Bell argues, was no doubt formed by that Jewish and Christian atmosphere that had penetrated Arabia. The Quranic passages in question, reflecting his own experience of denigration by the wealthy and powerful of the Quraysh, are a repudiation of what they stood for; he had sought to win them over, found them not only unsympathetic but hostile, and turned away from them.

Bell, referring to the early stage of Muhammad's career in Mecca, proposes that " . . . the religion of the one God implied the possession of a Holy Scripture. Even if he had never been out of Mecca, Muhammad could not have been ignorant of the possession by Christians of a Book which was believed to have been directly revealed. For . . . that was common knowledge among the Arabs. What that Book contained was not so generally known and was certainly in my opinion not known to Muhammad. But the existence of the Book itself he must have known about" (92). Bell's proposition regarding Muhammad's independence of thought, is not, however, a denial that there was a great deal of direct influence exerted upon him by Judaism and Christianity, and that much of the Quran is directly dependent upon the Bible and stories associated with it. Bell, therefore, tends to agree that the influence was of "cardinal importance, but it was in the course of his mission rather than before it began that it was exerted" (100).

Eventually, Muhammad learned about material which admirably suited his aim of impressing upon the recalcitrant, hard-hearted Meccans the consequences of their unbelief, material that one may refer to generally as Apocalyptic – Judgment Day, the End of the World, the pains of Hell and the Joys of Heaven for the Believers. Where did he learn of these Apocalyptic concepts? This material, Bell writes, was, of course, originally Jewish

> . . . and it might have been cherished in Jewish circles in Arabia. The mainstream of Judaism, however, practically dropped Apocalyptic after the Fall of Jerusalem in the first century AD. It was by the Christian Church rather than by Judaism that the Apocalyptic books were preserved, and it was in popular rather than official Christianity that Apocalyptic was really alive – as it lives in popular Christianity to this day. Will it be far wrong to surmise that Muhammad got his information from some Christian (perhaps Abyssinian) slave in Mecca, and that he gave the material form in his qurans? (109)

But Bell again emphasizes that although the origin of so much of the material in the Quran is undoubtedly Jewish, there is no evidence suggesting that his sources were texts. On the contrary, the best explanation would be that Muhammad had by now got in touch with Jews and is relating stories he had learned orally from them. It is a fact, after all, that much of the Jewish legendary material, such as is found in the Talmudic literature, is associated with Old Testament stories. Bell reminds us, however, that much of such legendary material was also current among Christians. Some of the names of the prophets mentioned in the Quran also suggest that they have come not directly from Scripture, but rather as mediated through Greek or Syriac before reaching Muhammad. Examples are: *Ilyas* for Elijah, *Yunus* for Jonah, even *Firaun* for Pharaoh. Among his narratives of the signs of God, there are those that are connected not with the Old Testament or with Jews, but with Christianity. Examples are the stories of the Virgin Mary and the Birth of Jesus. These, however, like the materials of Jewish origin, are conveyed not as they are found in the New Testament, but more in the form in which they appear in Apocryphal Gospels (110). The image of the Prophet that emerges from this analysis, is " . . . a brooding religious genius and man of great native mental power, but very limited knowledge, striving to find out what others more enlightened than his own Arab people knew, which might be of use to him in his own enterprise . . ." (111).

Another piece of evidence indicating that Muhammad most probably had no firsthand acquaintance with the Bible, and that he relied on stories related to him orally, is his inclusion in the Quran a version of the legend of the seven sleepers, references to the story of Alexander the Great, and the legend of Moses and al-Khidr, stories which were never associated with the Bible, but which were prevalent all over the East. Bell surmises that a chance informant might have told Muhammad these stories as somehow connected with that massive religion surrounding Arabia.

Bell now addresses the *Rahman* phenomenon. Muhammad's way of referring to the God he worshipped, shows some change or development. Bell supposes that it was most probably under the influence of the information Muhammad was receiving about monotheism as it prevailed among non-Arabs, that he introduced the word *ar-Rahman*, which he employed for a time almost as a proper name for God. Bell, like Margoliouth, cites the fact that the name is found in South Arabian inscriptions, and may have come through that channel – or may have been a native Arabic formation from the root *rhm*. But the word and the concept, like the kindred word *rahma*, meaning "mercy," comes ultimately from Hebrew and Aramaic; and the prominence that this idea begins to assume in Muhammad's ideological development is due to outside influence (116).

Bell provides a convincing explanation for the choice and prominence of the *Rahman* name and idea. As there was no term for God in Arabic quite free from polytheistic associations, Muhammad begins by using *rabb*, "Lord," in some combinations such as "my Lord," "thy Lord," or "Lord of this house." Then he uses "*Allah*," but with hesitation, probably because it was already combined with the belief in associated and subordinate deities. Then *ar-Rahman* appears alongside it. Too many names, however, had its disadvantages, in that they might lead to polytheistic ideas again. Muhammad appears to have solved the difficulty by settling on *Allah* as the name for the Deity – most probably because this name was best known in the Hijaz as an Arabian deity. Just as he retains and reinterprets several other elements of the old faith that naturally resonated with the Arabian ethnic sentiment – the Kaaba, the centrality of Mecca, Ramadan, pilgrimages, and more. Nevertheless, the concept of *rahma* had a lasting effect, as greater emphasis than earlier was now laid on the mercy of God.

Tracing in this way Muhammad's theological development, Bell proposes that he became more and more interested in the stories of biblical prophets. He discovers Moses who begins to stand out from the rest because it was to him that "the Book" was given. This suggests that at this point in Muhammad's career he came into direct contact with Jews, most probably early in his Medinan period. Bell notes that in Muhammad's stories of the prophets, he seems to be preoccupied with the question of what happens to the believers when the calamity falls upon the unbelievers. In even the shortest reference to a prophet at this stage, he does not fail to mention that he and those who have responded to his message, were saved from the destruction that had overtaken the others. It is in that context that the Christian word for salvation, *purqana*, belongs. "Remembering the meaning of the Arabic root," Bell writes, "it is easy to see how he [Muhammad] associates it with the separation of the believers from the unbelievers when the catastrophe fell. *Furqan* is deliverance from the judgment" (122).

Bell now engages in an exercise that we might appropriately describe as *Verstehensoziologie* in Max Weber's sense, an attempt to grasp how profoundly Muhammad might have been influenced by the Moses narrative. "Moses then," Bell writes,

> was a prophet who proclaimed the true religion. Some rejected him but some believed. The believers he led out from among the unbelieving people. The Book was given to him; "we [i.e., Allah] gave Moses the Book and the Furqan." This community which had followed Moses becomes a conquering people and destroys the unbelieving inhabitants of the land. It is not to underestimate Muhammad's knowledge to suggest that he may have assumed that it was the same unbelievers who had rejected Moses who were thus punished. There, in my opinion, is the suggestion of the Hijra – the exodus from Mecca – and the organization of a fighting community of believers in Medina, who were to be the means by whose hands the calamity which Muhammad had so long proclaimed, was to be brought upon the unbelieving Meccans. (124)

Bell recognizes that Muhammad had hardly settled in Medina when, as we see from the Quran, he began to prepare for war, a new strategy and orientation that came as a surprise to his own followers. Within two years came the great event, the encounter at Badr, a turning point in Muhammad's career. It enhanced his prestige and gave him power. But inwardly, Bell believes, it was of equal consequence. The victory of 300 Muslims over thrice that number was a "miracle," due to the angels which had been sent down to assist the prophet and his band. The battle of Badr, in Muhammad's mind, was the Calamity upon the unbelieving Meccans; and it was the *Furqan*, the deliverance out of that calamity, for the believers. That Muhammad perceived it as a miracle is strongly suggested in the Quran, where it is referred to as an *aya* or "sign." Muhammad now feels assured that he is a prophet like Moses, a giver of laws and the leader of a militant, theocratic community. For Bell, then, it seems quite clear that

> Islam as it finally took shape belongs to Medina and not to Mecca. The same . . . is true of the Quran itself. "The Book" sent down from heaven and revealed to him as required has now taken concrete shape in his mind . . . it is now that he re-edits the early passages and introduces material having to do with the regulation and guidance of the community . . . By the crowning mercy of Badr he has become convinced that he stands in a quite special relation to God. He is a prophet as Moses was a prophet. (125)

In Medina, Muhammad approached the Jewish tribes, thinking, apparently, that they were the Bani Israil to whom Moses had brought the Book. At that stage of the Prophet's education, Bell believes, he might just as readily have applied that term to the Christians as well. But the evidence shows that it was with Jews that he had actually made contact. That in Medina he was eager to learn from them is shown by his adoption of some of their practices such as the fast of the Day of Atonement and by his instructing his followers to pray facing Jerusalem. It is, most probably, at this time that he begins to acquire more and more accurate and detailed information regarding the Torah. Having discovered that Moses came after Noah, he soon makes the discovery which in time he would turn into the ideological foundation of the new faith – he discovers *Abraham* and his place in the succession of prophets between Noah and Moses. What Bell next observes is directly pertinent to the question whether the role Muslim scholars have traditionally assigned to Abraham and Ishmael is historical. The fact, Bell observes,

> that Ishmael is not closely conjoined with Abraham is proof that Muhammad had not, when this passage was revealed, learned of that connection. It soon

became of great importance to him. Ishmael was the reputed ancestor of the Arabs, and having discovered that he was the son of Abraham, the prophet of the Arabs knew how to make use of the fact that Abraham came in time before Moses. It brought the Arabs and himself into the race [sic] of the people of God, and into the line of descent in which the prophetic office was appointed to be, as stated in Sura 57: 26: "We [in the Quran, God often speaks in the first-person plural] appointed the prophetic office and the Book to be among their descendents."

And in a highly illuminating observation, Bell continues:

> The priority of Abraham to Moses and also to Jesus, enabled him [Muhammad] at Medina, when his hopes for the Jews failed, to fall back upon a man of God, independent alike of Jews and Christians, whom he can associate with the Kaaba and the new Arab faith. (130)

Muhammad's logic in this regard was impeccable. If in the Scriptures Abraham is stated to be prior to both Moses and Jesus, then it is certain that Abraham cannot be called a follower of either. Indeed, it is evident from Sura 2: 134 that Muhammad was quite annoyed that the existence of the biblical individual, Abraham, had been concealed from him. But once Muhammad discovers Abraham and reflects on how to assign him a role independent of both Judaism and Christianity, Abraham takes his place at the head of the list of prophets, "a sign that Islam is finally to stand on its own basis . . ." (130).

That was the thought-process, for Bell, by which Muhammad turned Abraham and Ishmael into the original Muslims. They could be made into the precursors of Islam, associated as they were with Arabia, because they represented in his mind the pure religion, which was eternal (*din qayyim*), and free from the corruptions which occasionally crept into it. That is what Muhammad meant, Bell believes, by *hanif*. In Sura 30: 29, the phrase "as a true convert," is literally "as a *hanif*."

Before going on with Bell's analysis we need to observe that his conception of how Muhammad discovered Abraham and his connection with Ishmael, tends to contradict the notion that Muhammad learned about Abraham from the Abrahamic *hanifs*. The fact that Muhammad acquired this information in Medina and perhaps even late in Medina – since he was annoyed that this information had been "concealed" from him – raises the likelihood that he acquired it from the Jews.

After learning about Abraham, Muhammad places the "prophets" in this sequence: Adam, Noah, the family of Abraham, and the family of

Imran [i.e., Amram, father of Moses]. But as Bell notes, the historical contexts of biblical individuals is still quite unclear: "probably, the family of Imran is here meant to include both Moses and Jesus. For Muhammad confused Mary (Arabic, *Maryam*), the mother of Jesus with Miryam the sister of Moses . . ." (132).

Turning his attention to Muhammad's attitude towards Christians, Bell suggests that it was only after the Hijra, and, indeed, late in the Medinan period, that the prophet had any *direct* relations with them. He had very little understanding of Christian teaching or what the Christian church was, and never did acquire intimate knowledge of these matters. In tracing the development of Muhammad's attention to geographical–cultural areas, Bell proposes that the Prophet first centered on Mecca, then on Arabia as a whole, and then gradually and even then rarely, on events outside Arabia. Bell's scrutiny of the Quran with the aim of determining when Muhammad learned about the two earlier monotheistic religions, suggests that it was only after the Hijra that he recognized the distinction between Jews and Christians. Before his discovery of Abraham, he most probably believed that the Jews with whom he had come in contact, were members of the great revealed religion, of which Moses was the founder. There is no indication that Muhammad knew of Jesus as a prophet in the same sense. Sura 19 may be the earliest mention of Jesus who had received the Book.

For Bell, it appears that it was soon after the Hijra that Jesus, in Muhammad's conception of these matters, took his place alongside Moses as one of the great prophets; and it was in this period when the *Injil* or Evangel, which was given to Jesus, assumed its place alongside the *Taurat* (Torah), which had been given to Moses. Bell avers that of the actual contents of the New Testament Muhammad seems never to have gained much knowledge. There are phrases throughout the Quran that remind one of phrases in the New Testament and the Christian liturgies. Sura I is made up almost entirely of phrases that might be used in either Jewish or Christian prayers. "But if they [the phrases]," Bell writes, "are directly borrowed and do not belong to the Judeo-Christian atmosphere diffused in Arabia, *they are Jewish rather than Christian*" (140, italics added). Bell notes, further, that Muhammad appears not to have known many of the New Testament parables which, one may suppose, he would have eagerly incorporated in the Quran, had he known them. Muhammad probably had no desire to learn the contents of the New Testament, Bell surmises, since at that stage of his career he had already set himself up as one who was independent of those who had preceded him. The information he acquired after this period came from the Christian communities bordering Arabia and arose out of his political relations with them.

As Bell addresses other questions concerning the relative influences of the earlier monotheisms, he turns to the *qibla*, or the direction to be faced in prayer. He notes that this was almost certainly Jewish in suggestion, for although there is a Muslim tradition to the effect that already in Mecca the Prophet had stood so as to face both the Kaaba and Jerusalem, this is a harmonizing account. There is really no trace of a *qibla*, Bell concludes, until Muhammad comes in contact with the Jews at Medina; he does so under the impression that this was the *qibla* of all the people of the Book. It is only after his relations with the Jews have disappointed him, and after he had resolved to establish an independent position, that he changed the *qibla* to the direction of the Kaaba, thus making his community one that avoided following either Jews or Christians in matters on which they differed. The same motive is apparent in his choice of Friday as the day of special service instead of either the Jewish or Christian Sabbath. Similarly, in the call to prayer, he avoided both the wooden clapper of the Christians and the ram's horn of the Jews, choosing the human voice instead.

The *Zakat*, however, was retained despite its Jewish origin. In Mecca the word simply meant alms-giving, which never became an institution; in Medina, however, in imitation, of the "Jewish law of tithes, it became a prescribed tax for the support of the poor of the community" (145). As for the Fast of Ramadan, it was instituted in recognition of the victory at Badr; but it was suggested by Jewish practice, since there does not appear to have been any prescribed fast in the Meccan period. As for the Muslim prohibition of wine, Bell doubts that it resulted from Christian influence, and proposes instead that it emerged out of the Prophet's developing conception of the Arabs as a people, since what he forbade was not the native *nabidh* made from dates, but *khamr*, an import, and not a native product at all. Also, given the need for a minimal sobriety in battle, experience, as Bell observes, may have impressed upon the Prophet the need to restrict the use of wine.

As Bell takes up the question of the influences on what became the Muslim pilgrimage, one sees how the ceremonies were adopted from pre-Islamic custom, but with the changes necessary to remove the superficial idolatrous features. As for the mass of legal enactments which the Quran contains, many of them were evidently inspired by Jewish practice; but as most of them were formulated in Medina, the principle that the Prophet's people were to be neither Jewish nor Christian, undoubtedly played a part in the divergence from Jewish practice. During the Meccan period Muhammad's attitude toward the people of the Book, which most probably included both Jews and Christians, was consistently friendly. Even in Medina, following his adoption of a more independent stance, he seems at first merely to have thought of establishing his own community on an equal basis with them. That seems to be the meaning of Sura 3: 57, where we hear "O people of the Book! Come ye to a just judgment between us and you – that we worship not aught but God, and that we join no other god with Him . . ." Bell views this as addressed specifically to the Jews, but sees no reason, based on Sura 2: 59, why Christians would have been excluded from this invitation: "Verily, those who believe (Muslims), and they who follow the Jewish religion, and the Christians, and the Sabeites – whoever of these believeth in God and the last day, and doeth that which is right, shall have their reward with their Lord . . ." Later, however, as Muhammad's power began to spread in Arabia, his attitude towards the Christians changed, precluding not only alliances but even peaceful accommodation with them.

Judging from Sura 4: 154ff., Muhammad had learned that Christians believed in a living Christ whom "God had taken up to Himself." But beyond that information, Bell believes, the Prophet had no real knowledge of Christian sectarian ideas; and, of course, as his power in Arabia increased, it had to come in conflict with Christian power and doctrine. Just as Muhammad had previously accused the Jews, so now he also charges the Christians with corrupting their scriptures, with altering the teaching delivered to them. He makes this charge because he still believes that the message of the *Taurat* (Torah) and the *Injil* (New Testament) must have been the same as his own. It followed that insofar as Christian beliefs differed from his teaching, they must have corrupted the Evangel. In Sura 5: 70ff., we hear the gist of Muhammad's critique of Christianity:

Infidels now are they who say, "God is the messiah, Son of Mary"; for the messiah said, "O children of Israel! Worship God, my Lord and your Lord." Whoever shall join other gods with God, God shall forbid him the Garden, and his abode shall be the Fire; and the wicked shall have no helpers.

They surely are Infidels who say, "God is the third of three": for there is no God but one God: and if they refrain not from what they say, a grievous chastisement shall light on such of them as are Infidels . . .

The messiah, Son of Mary, is but an Apostle; other Apostles have flourished before him; and his mother was just a person: they both ate food.

So the relationship with the Christians ended just as it had with the Jews – in war (159). The strict and absolute monotheism at which the Prophet had arrived meant that no real compromise with Christian doctrine and power was possible. As Bell remarks, Islam was now the only "true religion and acceptance of it meant the acceptance of the Prophet's divinely inspired authority. The example of Moses had implanted in his mind the idea of a conquering religious people" (160).

Although Muhammad thus broke both with Jews and Christians, they are, on the whole, treated more favorably in the Quran than the idolators; idolatry was to be totally rooted out. Theologically, that is what Islamic law, as it subsequently developed, demands. Wherever Muslim power extends, idolators have the choice of Islam or death – or enslavement, "so that they may have time to consider the acceptance of Islam" (178). As for the people of the Book, they are not to be coerced into changing their religion; they were, however, to be fought and reduced to subjection. Under the Caliphates, as a rule, if they agreed to pay tribute (*Jizya*) and accepted Muslim hegemony, they were to be tolerated in their religion. That is how the Christians were treated under Muslim rule. For Bell, it seems clear that in Arabia the vast majority of the Christian Arabs went over to Islam with little hesitation or regret and did so in a relatively short period. This suggests that the adherence of the nominally Christian tribes to Christianity had never been very deep. "Indeed," Bell observes, "what interest could the abstruse questions of christology, about which the Eastern Church had been kept in ferment for centuries, have had for them?" (183) In sharp contrast to the Christian preoccupation at the time with trinitarian and christological disputes, Islam offered the rather simple idea of a God of power and moral will, concerned with human destiny and justice.

# 8

# W. Montgomery Watt's Muhammad

Watt opens with an observation with which we have become familiar: that in the total phenomenon of Islam, the desert had a role of first importance. Mecca and Medina were islands in a sea of desert, but in close economic relations with the nomads. The nomad, however, was more dependent on the settled communities, in that central to his way of life was raiding oases and caravans. Robbery, in the nomad's eyes, was no crime. The Bedouin's fighting prowess is such, that often the settled, agricultural peoples are willing to pay a desert tribe for the protection of their homesteads and herds, and for the safe passage of their caravans. Watt notes that the chief crop of the oases was dates, while in the mountains, as at Taif, cereals were important; and that Yathrib-Medina was a large, flourishing oasis, with several Jewish colonies, while in Mecca, in contrast, there was no agriculture.

## Watt's Muhammad at Mecca

That leads Watt to make a claim concerning Mecca, which has become quite controversial. Mecca, Watt stated in 1953, was a commercial city in the time of Muhammad. Watt attributed the growth of the city as a trading center to the existence of a *haram* or sanctuary area, to which men came without fear of molestation. Due to its favorable geographical location, Watt argued, at the crossroads of routes from Yemen to Syria and from Abyssinia to Iraq, Mecca became a central trading center in the Hijaz. To Mecca, therefore, nomads came, purportedly, for goods brought from the four points of the compass by caravan. By the end of the sixth century CE, the Meccans, Watt argued, had gained control of most of the trade from Yemen to Syria – an important trade route by which the West got Indian luxury goods as well as South Arabian frankincense. Taif was a rival of Mecca in commercial affairs, "but Mecca clearly had the strong position" (Watt, p. 3).[1] Watt goes even farther, claiming that Mecca was more than a mere trading center, it was a financial center. The rulers of Mecca in Muhammad's time were, above all, "financiers, skilful in the manipulation of credit, shrewd in their speculations, and interested in any potentialities of lucrative investment from Aden to Gaza or Damascus. In the financial net that they had woven, not merely were all the inhabitants of Mecca caught, but many notable of the surrounding tribes also. The Quran appeared not in the atmosphere of the desert, but in that of high finance" (Ibid.).

An economic system of the kind described by Watt, implies a correspondingly complex politics. So Watt makes the further claim that within the commercial context of Mecca there was an ongoing struggle for power among several of the most influential groups of the Quraysh. Taking note of the two major empires, the Byzantine and the Persian, and a third, much weaker, the Abyssinian, Watt proposes that given the prolonged heavy fighting between the two great empires, the Meccan leaders benefited from the neutral stance they had maintained toward the conflict. As Watt presents this scenario, he acknowledges more than once that there is much in his " . . . account of Meccan politics that is conjectural" (16).

Watt nevertheless continues to build on this conception of Mecca as a financial center, in his search for the social conditions that might have accounted for Muhammad's critique of his fellow tribesmen. Watt discerns certain individualistic tendencies in the commercial life of Mecca that weakened tribal and clan solidarity. Looking for a new phenomenon that might be pertinent to Muhammad's inspiration, Watt posits business partnerships that had cut across clan relationships. The new phenomenon, for Watt, was the emergence of a "sense of unity based on common material interests" (19). "If we are to look for an economic change," he writes, "correlated with the rise of Islam, then it is here that we must look . . . In the rise of Mecca to wealth and power we have a movement from a nomadic economy to a mercantile and capitalist economy" (Ibid.).

In thus unfolding his central thesis, Watt presents the moral ideals of the desert Arabs, which included, in addition to manliness and bravery in battle, generosity, hospitality, loyalty, and fidelity, the last two of which Watt considers most directly relevant to his thesis. The individual, according to these Arabian ideals, ought to act with the tribe even when he has disagreed with the decision of its leaders. The Arabian conception of honor meant, above all, that one remained loyal to one's kin. Hence, for Watt, it was the undermining and, in practice, the repudiation of the time-honored moral ideals of the desert Arabs that became the negative stimulus, so to speak, for Muhammad's inspiration.

Before we go on with our exposition of Watt's work on Muhammad at Mecca, we have to pause to consider the most trenchant criticism of Watt's conjectural construction of Meccan socio-economic life. Patricia Crone,[2] in an impressively painstaking work, succeeds in challenging the notion that has become prevalent since the time of Watt's book, that Meccan trade and the resulting changes in social structure and social psychology, were the ultimate cause of the rise of Islam. According to Watt, as we have seen, it was the Quraysh's transition to a mercantile economy that undermined the traditional order in Mecca, generating a social and moral malaise to which Muhammad's preaching was the response. To this thesis Crone raises several cogent objections: (1) There was no apparent deterioration of the traditional, tribal values of caring for kin and protecting the weak. The protection that Muhammad himself is said to have enjoyed from his own kin, first as an orphan and then as a prophet, would indicate that the clan and tribal organization remained intact. (2) There was no *general* malaise in Mecca, religious, social, political, or moral. The reason the Meccans are regarded as morally defective in the Muslim sources is *not* that their traditional way of life has broken down, but that it functioned too well, the Meccans preferring their polytheistic way of life to Islam. (3) Watt fails to account for the fact that it was in Medina rather than in Mecca that Muhammad's message was accepted. In Mecca he was only a would-be prophet! It was outside Mecca, first in Medina and then elsewhere in Arabia that there was a receptivity to his monotheism. (4) The tribal disunity and feuds, to which Muhammad offered a solution, were a constant in Arabian history, not a result of change. It was only the solution that was new. "The novelty of the solution," Crone writes,

> lay in the idea of divinely validated state structures; and it was Muhammad's state, not his supposed blueprint for social reform, which had such powerful effect on the rest of Arabia. There is no feeling in Muhammad's biography of burning questions and long-debated issues finally resolved. Instead, there is a strong sense of ethnogenesis . . . that the Arabs have been in the Peninsula for a long time, in fact since Abraham, and that they had finally been united in a state. Muhammad was neither a social reformer nor a resolver of spiritual doubts. *He was the creator of a people.* (237, italics added)

Islam, Crone continues, originated in a tribal society, and this must be the starting point of any attempt to explain its emergence. The fact that Islam originated in a tribal society suggests, to Crone, definite parallels between Moses and Muhammad, and between Yahweh and Allah. In both cases the Deities endorsed and enabled tribal characteristics such as militantism and ethnic pride. What was it that Allah, in particular, had to offer, she asks? What he had to offer was a program of Arab state formation and *conquest*: the creation of an *Ummah*, the initiation of *jihad*. Muhammad was a prophet with a political mission; his monotheism amounted to a political program.

The fact that Muhammad had begun by denouncing the beliefs and practices of his own tribe had this political significance: he had thus asserted that his God was incompatible with tribal divisions as they existed. His God – unlike that of the Christians – was One, universal, and ancestral, the ancestor of the Arabs. It followed that one God requires one nation. It was around Allah and Allah alone that the Arabs should be organized. All the ancestral deities of polytheism that allowed for and sanctioned the current tribal divisions, were *false*! Muhammad was thus a political agitator already in Mecca, and it was as such that he offended the Meccans, and offered his message to other tribes. And it was as such, and not merely as an otherworldly arbitrator, that he was accepted at Medina.

Crone claims that there had already existed in pre-Islamic Arabia some sense of unity, and that the unity was ethnic and cultural – a kind of pan-Arabian feeling despite the tribal divisions and conflicts. Crone proposes quite convincingly, that "Muhammad's success evidently had something to do with the fact that he preached [in Medina] both state formation and conquest: without conquest, first in Arabia and next in the Fertile Crescent, the unification of Arabia would not have been achieved" (243).

As Crone proceeds with her argument, it further challenges the Watt thesis: "And there is no shred of evidence," she writes,

> that commercial interests contributed to the decision, on the part of the ruling elite, to adopt a policy of conquest; on the contrary, the sources present conquest as an alternative to trade, the reward of conquest being an effortless life as rulers of the earth as opposed to one as plodding merchants. Nor is there any evidence that the collapse of Meccan trade caused an "economic recession" that contributed to the enthusiasm with which the tribesmen at large adopted this policy . . . Tribal states *must* conquer to survive, and the predatory tribesmen who make up their members are in general more inclined to fight than to abstain. (Ibid.)

In sum, Crone concludes this portion of her rebuttal, "Muhammad had to conquer, his followers liked to conquer, and his deity told him to conquer: do we need more?" (244) Crone also makes an insightful observation about what she calls the interminable debate whether the conquerors were motivated more by religious enthusiasm than by material interests or the other way around: " . . . holy war was not a cover for material interests; on the contrary, it was an open proclamation of them . . . Muhammad's God thus elevated tribal militancy and rapaciousness into supreme religious virtues: the material interests were those inherent in tribal society . . ." (245).

As we proceed with our exposition of Watt's *Muhammad at Mecca*, we need, in light of Crone's critique, to address this question: Is Watt's thesis fundamentally vitiated by her critique, or are there salvageable elements in it? For Watt, it was so-called Meccan commercialism that had weakened tribal and clan solidarity and given rise to individualism. Material interests were prevailing over kinship relations. In an attempt to support his view, Watt claims that the Quran implies an increasing awareness of the difference between rich and poor, the rich showing less concern for the poor even among their own kin; the references to orphans, presumably, also implying that they were ill-treated by their own relatives who served as guardians. So for Watt, the early passages of the Quran are no more than a "premonition of the real remedy for this situation, namely, that a new basis for social solidarity is to be found in religion" (73). The rise of Islam is "somehow connected with the change from a nomadic to a mercantile economy" (79).

To support this notion, Watt has to try to determine which individuals or strata of Meccan society were most responsive to Muhammad's call. After surveying the various Meccan clans, with the aim of learning who were the earliest converts to Islam, Watt summarizes the results. Muhammad's followers in Mecca were young men, the majority of whom were under 40 at the time of the Hijra; they had been converted eight or more years previously. As Watt proceeds with his sociological analysis, we begin to detect its weaknesses. He claims that "it was not a movement of 'down-and-outs,' of the scum[?] of the population, of 'hangers-on' with no strong tribal affiliations who had drifted into Mecca. It drew its support not from the bottom layers of the social scale, but from those about the middle who, becoming conscious of the disparity between them and those at the top, were beginning to feel that they were underprivileged. It was not so much a struggle between 'haves' and 'have nots' as between 'haves' and 'nearly hads'" (96).

Watt's construction is highly problematic, for it appears to be entirely conjectural, contradicting what Ibn Hisham has to say on the subject. His very heading reads, "The Polytheists Persecute the Muslims of the *Lower Classes*," and under that heading he explicitly mentions *slaves* among the early persecuted converts, stating that before Abu Bakr migrated to Medina, he had freed six slaves in Islam, Bilal being the seventh (143–4). And later, under the heading, "The Apostle Offers Himself to the Tribes," Ibn Hisham states that "when the Apostle returned to Mecca, his people opposed him more bitterly than ever, apart from the ". . . few *lower-class people* who believed in him" (194). So when Watt asserts that Muhammad's support in Mecca came not from the bottom layers of the society, but from "those about the middle," we have to say that he does so without showing why we should accept his assessment rather than Ibn Hisham's.

There is, moreover, something problematic about the logic of his analysis. The thinking of the Prophet and his early followers, Watt writes, " . . . must have been primarily on the religious plane, and it was on the religious plane that men were summoned to Islam; conscious thoughts about economics or politics can have played hardly any part in conversion. Yet, when this has been said, we can go on to admit that Muhammad and the wiser among his followers must have been alive to the social and political implications of his message, and that, in directing the affairs of the Muslims, such considerations certainly weighed with them" (99). But if Muhammad's followers in Mecca were, as Watt claims, from the "middle" layers of the social scale, what were the social and political implications of the Prophet's message for them? That they were suffering from the "relative deprivation" of, in Watt's words, the "nearly hads"? Watt not only fails to provide supporting evidence for his notion that the "middle" layers or "nearly hads" were the most responsive to Muhammad's message, he also employs a puzzling logic. For would it not make more sense even within Watt's theoretical framework, to follow Ibn Hisham, and argue that it was the lower strata who suffered most from the commercialism and individualism which, Watt surmises, prevailed in Mecca at the time?

### The Daughters of Allah or the So-Called Satanic Verses

Watt appears to be on no firmer ground in his interpretation of the significance of idolatry in the "Daughters of Allah" affair. He cites the long passage of Tabari's relating that when Muhammad summoned his tribe to accept the guidance and the light revealed to him, they almost hearkened to him until he mentioned their *idols*. Then there came some of the Quraysh from Taif, owners of property, and rebutted him with vehemence and roused their supporters against him. So most of the people who had followed the Prophet now turned back and left him, except for a few. As the passage continues it suggests that persecution of Muhammad's followers increased, and that he advised them to flee to the land of the Abyssinians, which they did, and where the new Muslims were left in peace thanks to the just rule of a good king, Negus. Interpreting this event, Watt notes that the first active opposition to Muhammad is said to be due to the mention of *idols* on his part; and that some Quraysh with *property* were the leaders of the opposition to Muhammad. Watt, however, fails to consider that the Prophet's mention of "idols" spoke to the Quraysh's control of the Kaaba and the pilgrimages; and that the "property" of the Quraysh in question here was in fact their control of the means of pilgrimaging. Since, however, Watt's central thesis is that the Quraysh's source of wealth, power and prestige lay in their monopoly-hold of the caravan trade, he resists the plain meaning of the passage, that it was precisely Muhammad's threat to Meccan idolatry that most likely intensified the opposition to him.

If we now return to Patricia Crone and consider her findings, we can see clearly why Watt's notion of Mecca as a commercial center with a financial–commercial elite, is misleading. Crone writes that Meccan trade was a trade in leather above all:

> This is as far as we can go. We thus have a problem on our hands. It is not likely that the inhabitants of a remote and barren valley should have founded a commercial empire of international dimensions on the basis of hides and skins. (Crone, 99)
>
> It would . . . be hard to present the Quraysh as large-scale suppliers of perfume to the Byzantine and Persian empires. The Byzantine empire had a perfume industry of its own, centered in Alexandria . . . [And] the empire produced enough to export some of it to the Arabs themselves. Thus the Jews of Medina are said to have imported perfume from Syria to Medina in the time of the prophet . . . (Crone, 96)

Crone's research, incidentally, tends to confirm Ibn Hisham's description of the contents of a Quraysh caravan: it carried dry raisins and leather (Ibn Hisham, p. 287). It is, then, a near certainty that the primary source of the Quraysh's wealth was their control of the Kaaba and its sacred environs. If the Quraysh had a monopoly hold on anything, it was on the essential provisions required by the pilgrims – food, water, and prescribed clothing.

## More on the "Daughters of Allah" Affair

As this is a subject of dispute, we should explore it at some length. In A. Guillaume's translation of Ibn Hisham's work, he inserts Tabari's words wherever he deems it appropriate to do so. This is my paraphrase of what Tabari had to say on the subject of the "Daughters of Allah."

> Now the Apostle was anxious for the welfare of his people, wishing to attract them as far as he could. When he saw that his people turned their backs on

him and he was pained by their estrangement from what he had brought them from God, he longed that there should come to him from God a message that would reconcile his people to him. Because of his love for his people and his anxiety over them, it would delight him if the obstacle that made his task so difficult could be removed; so he meditated on the project and longed for it, and it was dear to him. Then God sent down, "By the star when it sets, your comrade errs not and is not deceived, he speaks not from his own desire," and when he reached His words, "Have you thought of al-Lat, and al-Uzza and Manat the third, the other," Satan, when Muhammad was meditating upon it, and desiring to bring it (reconciliation) to his people, put upon Muhammad's tongue "These are the exalted Gharaniq whose intercession is approved." When the Quraysh heard of this, they were delighted and pleased; and the Prophet's followers believed that this revelation was true, never suspecting that it was a mistake.

The news reached the Prophet's companions who had fled to Abyssinia, that the Quraysh had accepted Islam, so some of them started to return to Mecca. But then Gabriel appeared to the Prophet and said, "What have you done, Muhammad? You have read to these people something I did not bring you from God, and you have said what He did not say to you."

The Apostle was now bitterly grieved and greatly in fear of God, so He comforted Muhammad and sent down a new revelation annulling what Satan had provoked and establishing His authentic verses. God relieved the Prophet's grief in Sura 22: 51: "We have not sent any apostle or prophet before Thee, among whose desires Satan injected not some *wrong* desire, but God shall bring to nought that which Satan had suggested. Thus shall God affirm His revelations, for God is knowing, Wise! That he may make that which Satan hath injected, a trial to those in whose hearts is a disease; and whose hearts are hardened . . ."

That is the way God relieved the Prophet of his grief and annulled what Satan had suggested, replacing the earlier mistaken revelation with the genuine one, Sura 53:19–27: "Do you see Al-Lat and Al-Uzza and Manat the third idol besides? What? Shall ye have male progeny and God female? This was indeed an unfair partition! These are mere names: ye and your fathers named them thus: God hath not sent down any warranty in their regard . . ." and so on.

Watt, in another context,[3] assesses the truth of the story and provides a convincing explanation of how it happened. He writes:

The story of the "satanic verses" (Tabari, 1192–6) shows the persistence of some confusion between Allah conceived monotheistically and Allah as "high god." The truth of the story cannot be doubted, since it is inconceivable that any Muslim would invent such a story, and it is inconceivable that a Muslim scholar would accept such a story from a non-Muslim. It also seems to be vouched for by a verse from the Quran. (22: 52)

Many Muslims reject the story as unworthy of Muhammad, but there is nothing unworthy of him in holding that his knowledge and understanding of "his Lord" developed during the early years of his prophethood as the revelations multiplied

The point to be emphasized here is that Muhammad did not immediately appreciate that there was a contradiction between this permission for intercession and a genuine monotheism. (Watt-Tabari, xxxiv)

It seems to be quite reasonable to posit, as Watt does, a *process* in Muhammad's conception of monotheism – a process culminating in a strict monotheism, but having been less than strict at an earlier stage of his intellectual development. And yet, despite the fact that the story was related by respected Muslim biographers, there are Muslim scholars who regard the story as a fabrication. To take but one example, there is the view of Haykal, that the story's "incoherence is evident upon the least scrutiny. It contradicts the infallibility of every prophet in conveying the message of the Lord."[4] It is Haykal's view, apparently, that genuine prophets, though they are human, do not err. Haykal rejects, in particular, William Muir's argument for the story's veracity. Muir pointed out that the Muslims who had fled to Abyssinia to escape persecution by the Quraysh, had hardly been there three months when they decided to return to Mecca. What prompted them to return so soon? Muir argues, in reply, that had they not heard of a reconciliation between Muhammad and the Quraysh, nothing would have caused them to return so quickly. And, Muir reasons, how could there be a reconciliation between Muhammad and the Quraysh without a determined effort to that effect on the part of Muhammad? The few Muslims who had remained in Mecca were still weak and incapable of protecting themselves against the torments that the Quraysh had been inflicting upon them. Why, then, would the Quraysh have taken the initiative in seeking reconciliation? It followed for Muir that it was the Prophet who initiated the effort at reconciliation with the offer of a concession. To this argument and to the Muslim narrators of the "tale," Haykal replies by citing Ibn Ishaq's allegation that the story was invented by the *zindiqs*, forgers, who had sought thereby to spread doubt about the message of Muhammad and to question his candidness in conveying the message of God.

For Haykal, the Muslim arguments defending the truth of the story are even less convincing than Muir's. Haykal, citing Sura 22: 51, contends that " . . . these verses are utterly devoid of relation to the story of the goddesses. Moreover, they clearly affirm that God will abrogate all that the devil may bring forth, that Satan's work is only a lure to those who are sick of mind and hard of heart, and that God, the all-wise and all-knowing, would keep His Scripture absolutely pure and true" (Haykal, 110). Haykal is right to say that God, according to the Quran, did in fact abrogate all that Satan had sought to bring forth. But that is not the question. What is in question is whether a prophet, however great he might be, can err. If Haykal can agree that to err is human, and that Muhammad was human, then it is possible to conceive of a process, as Watt has proposed, in which the prophet's inspiration culminated in a genuine monotheism, but that in an earlier phase of that process there was less clarity in his mind as to what a strict monotheism meant.

Watt, in his *Muhammad at Mecca*, writes that from the story of the "daughters of Allah" one can deduce two facts: that at one time Muhammad must have publicly recited those verses as part of the Quran, for it is " . . . unthinkable that the story could have been invented later by Muslims or foisted upon them by non-Muslims. Secondly, at some later time Muhammad announced that the verses were not really part of the Quran and should be replaced by others of a vastly different import" (103). This suggests that early in his career in Mecca, he encountered no exclusive worship or veneration of God, and, therefore, that he was at first prepared to make the kind of concession implied by the acceptance of the goddesses as intercessors. We do not know for sure, after all, the nature of Waraqa's religion, since some Muslim scholars had referred to him as a *hanif*, while others described him as a Christian. There is, then, no reason, from a realistic standpoint to rule out the process of development in Muhammad's conception.

In the light of Patricia Crone's findings, we need to continue our critical dialogue with Watt over his central thesis, that Muhammad's general message was a repudiation of the corrosive egoism of Meccan capitalism that was presumably eating away at the traditional tribal and clan solidarity. If we accept Watt's proposition, that the well-spring of Muhammad's original inspiration was primarily religious, and that, accordingly, the motive of his apparent acceptance of the goddesses was also religious, then it is not clear why we would need Watt's thesis of the vested commercial interests of the Quraysh to explain why they opposed Muhammad's change of mind and his refusal to accept the goddesses. Watt, however, insists on the relevance of the "daughters of Allah" affair to his original thesis. For

Watt, the most likely explanation of the opposition is that the leading men of the Quraysh, who were especially interested in the commerce of Taif, had brought Taif's commercial activities within the financial orbit of Meccan finances. Hence, "the removal of recognition from the shrine of al-Lat [the goddess] must somehow or other have threatened their enterprises and stirred their anger against Muhammad" (107). If we take notice of the phrase "must somehow or other," we can see that Watt had no clear idea of how the rescinding of Muhammad's recognition of the goddesses threatened the interests of the so-called commercial–financial elite of Mecca, whose wealth was, presumably, derived from large-scale caravan trade.

Watt thus fails to consider an alternative hypothesis, that the subsequent abrogation of the earlier legitimization of the goddesses was a threat to the Meccan elite's control of the shrine as a pilgrimage center, and a lucrative source of income. As we have learned from Patricia Crone's work, the notion of Mecca as a center at the crossroads of large-scale caravan trade, is doubtful in the extreme. Watt, however, remains wedded to his thesis, that though Muhammad's motives were primarily religious, his teachings ". . . impinged upon economic matters, and in this respect it could perhaps be regarded as . . . opposition to unscrupulous capitalism" (120). Indeed, Watt explicitly rejects the alternative hypothesis: "It is sometimes suggested," he writes, "that the strongest motive underlying the opposition [of the Quraysh elite to Muhammad] was the fear that, if Mecca adopted Islam and abandoned idolatry, the nomads would cease to come to the sanctuary and Meccan trade [?] would be ruined" (134). But this formulation of the alternative hypothesis is not quite accurate. What it should say is that the motive of the opposition to Muhammad was the fear that the Meccan pilgrimage enterprise would be ruined. It is ironic that although Watt frequently states his belief that Muhammad's motivation was primarily religious, he (Watt) nevertheless refuses to take seriously the view that Muhammad's message was perceived by the Quraysh elite as a threat to their control of a *religious* institution, albeit a profitable one.

Watt maintains that the chief reason for opposition was almost certainly that the Quraysh leaders discerned in Muhammad's claim to be a prophet, definite political implications. "The old Arab tradition," he writes, "was that rule in the tribe or clan should go to him who had most wisdom, prudence and judgment. If the Meccans believed Muhammad's warning, and then wanted to know how to order their affairs in the light of it, who would be the best person to counsel them if not Muhammad?" (134–5). But Watt locates those political implications where his thesis has led him. The leaders of the Quraysh, he writes, "were sufficiently far-sighted to recognize the opposition between the ethics of the Quran and the mercantile capitalism which was their life" (135). In the very next sentence Watt states, "there was no whisper of the forbidding of usury till long after the Hijra," which, one would think, should have given him pause where his central thesis is concerned. Instead, however, he follows this sentence with: "But from the very first there was criticism of their individualistic attitude to wealth" (135). This assertion also seems to be questionable, since one finds in the Quran precious little criticism of wealth.

Unrelenting, then, in the defense of his original thesis, Watt concludes this work with the statement that "the great achievement of the Meccan period of Muhammad's career was the founding of a new religion . . . Islam" (151). But since Watt allows in the end that Muhammad's conception of the new religion only received its *full* development after the Hijra, there are good grounds for questioning whether it is historically sound to say that it was in Mecca that Muhammad founded *the* new religion called Islam. What Watt overlooks in this statement is the centrality of Muhammad's Medinan experience for the successful founding of Islam. Indeed, the Medinan experience may be described as the *conditio sine qua non* of Muhammad's success – the condition without which Islam might never have become a world religion. We shall defend the cogency of this thesis by means of a sociological argument.

## A Sociological Argument

As we reflect on history, we see that religious, political, and other organizations often begin with a single leader and a small band of followers. Some of these organizations remain demographically small, but manage somehow to remain in existence for years or even generations. Other such small groups disappear quite soon after they have been formed. A third category of small groups refers to the situation in which a group begins to grow dramatically in numbers and becomes, in short order, a massive social movement, spreading like wildfire. How, then, does one explain the historical fact that some religious sects are short-lived, disappearing not too long after they have emerged, while other sects take off and become world-historical movements, lasting for hundreds or even thousands of years?

Speaking in general terms, one might say that when a sect becomes a world-historical movement, it owes its growth to four commonsensical factors. The first is deep and widespread *discontent*. In order for a social movement to emerge from a sect, large numbers of people in any given context must be highly dissatisfied with the conditions of their existence. The second factor we may call *ideology*, a set of ideas that appeals to the discontented. Such ideologies usually try to explain the cause of the people's discontent, while providing a vision of a better future that the ideology promises to create. The third factor is leadership, or *charismatic* leadership, to borrow Max Weber's concept.[5] Leaders of groups that become mass movements possess striking qualities of some kind. Charisma, meaning literally "gift of grace," is the term Weber used to characterize self-appointed leaders who are followed by those who are in a state of discontent or distress, and who follow the leader because he appears to be extraordinarily qualified. The founders of the world religions, prophets and political and military heroes are the archetypes of the charismatic leader. The fourth factor we may call *organization*, which includes strategy and tactics. It is all four factors taken together that account for the successful emergence and durability of a world-girdling movement.

If we now ask how these general concepts may be applied to the particular case of Muhammad at Mecca, we have to say something like the following. At Mecca there appears not to have been the deep and widespread discontent that constitutes the fertile soil from which social movements rise and from which they draw their nourishment. Not to belabor the obvious, it appears that in Muhammad's Mecca there was not only no massive discontent, there was so little that after thirteen years of preaching, Muhammad made only 200 converts who, far from being representative of a general discontent, were a minuscule and despised minority that had to flee from persecution.

This fact strongly suggests that the religious-ideological message that Muhammad had promulgated in Mecca in the course of thirteen years, failed to appeal to the vast majority of Meccans, or even to the majority of the members of his own tribe. It appears that Muhammad's ideological message found no resonance in the sentiments of the people as a whole.

As for charisma, one would have to say that at Mecca, Muhammad had very little or none. Indeed, recognizing his cause to be lost in his native town, and greeted with jeers and contempt during his futile propagandist visit to al-Taif, he encouraged his 200 followers to escape quietly to Medina, he himself following soon afterward.

Finally, there is the factor called *organization*, including strategy and tactics. In Mecca, it appears that Muhammad relied exclusively on preaching and warning. In Medina, however, for reasons we hope to make clear, he changed his strategy. It is almost as if Muhammad in Medina, having reflected on his Meccan experience, anticipated an insight that Machiavelli put forward in his *Prince*: The innovating prince who relies on persuasion alone will always come to grief. The prince, however, who controls the means of forcing the issue is seldom endangered. "That is why armed prophets have conquered, and unarmed prophets have come to grief" (VI, 52). Machiavelli provides another relevant insight. Outstanding historical individuals, with their extraordinary prowess, had received nothing from fortune except *opportunity*. Fortune provided the material, as it were, but they gave the material its form; for "without opportunity" writes Machiavelli, "their prowess would have been extinguished, and without such prowess the opportunity would have come in vain" (VI, 50). One can say, therefore, that had Muhammad remained in Mecca, his extraordinary prowess would have been extinguished for the lack of opportunity. Our thesis, therefore, is that it was in Medina that Muhammad received the opportunity to bring his prowess to fruition.

As we now proceed to review Watt's treatment of Muhammad's prophetic career at Medina, we shall see whether he acknowledges, at least implicitly, the soundness of this sociological argument.

### Watt's Muhammad at Medina

Watt opens by suggesting that at first Muhammad thought of himself as sent to his own tribe, the Quraysh, but gradually came to see his mission as a wider one.[6] Before the Hijra, the Prophet had summoned some members of the nomadic tribes to believe in Allah, in addition to negotiating with some people of Medina. With the Hijra the notion of an *Ummah* or community with a religious basis became prominent. The most urgent problem facing the Medinans at the time was tribal strife, a condition prevalent throughout Arabia. Hence, the whole of Muhammad's work in Medina may be regarded as building a religious foundation for a *Pax Islamica*. The Medinan clans that joined with the Emigrants to form the new community had already had confederates both among the Jewish tribes of Medina and among the surrounding nomads. Watt suggests that in the early years of the Medinan period Muhammad seems to have contracted alliances with neighborhood tribes on a purely secular basis. Gradually, however, as the Islamic sphere grew wider and stronger, he began to demand, as conditions of alliance, belief in Allah and recognition of himself as Prophet.

Watt now calls attention to the salience of the material dimension of the alliances Muhammad had contracted in the early Medinan period. "It is important to realize," he writes,

> that when Muhammad began to demand acceptance of Islam from some
> would-be allies, he did not cease to make alliances with other groups without

any religious demand. No demand was made of the Meccans when he marched into their city in triumph, and many of them took part in the battle of Hunayn without being Muslims. The survey of tribes in this chapter has shown or suggested that, even up to the time of his death and after, there were many alliances with non-Muslims. This was normally so with distant and powerful tribes. Though such allies were merely secular allies, they belonged in a sense to the *Pax Islamica* in view of current Arab ideas about alliances; they shared in its benefits and helped to maintain it. (144)

As the new *Ummah* expanded as a political system, Muhammad had to give thought to its economic basis. For as tribes entered into these alliances and stopped raiding one another, it was no longer possible for a tribe in need to gain its subsistence by attacking its neighbor. New sources of subsistence and gain had to be found. For a time, Watt surmises, Muhammad may have looked to increased trade as a solution. Watt acknowledges, however, that although there was some trade between Medina and Syria, so little is said about it in the sources as to indicate that it can hardly have been important. Moreover, even an enlargement of trade would have been inadequate for the multitude that now looked to Muhammad as leader. Besides, there was the danger Watt had attributed to trade in his original thesis: that it would foster the false attitude that had been the fault of the pagan Meccans. So Muhammad, rejecting trade for the reason Watt supposes, turned to the remaining option: *booty* from non-Muslims. "It was doubtless love of booty," Watt writes, "that made many men come to Medina and attach themselves to Muhammad. In a sense this was the solution Muhammad chose . . ." (145). But even the raiding of caravans for booty had its limits. As the Muslim population expanded and became well-off, non-Muslims within easy reach decreased, the traditional form of raiding became inadequate. If the whole of Arabia were to become Muslim, only the northern frontier would be available for raiding. Watt describes it as a great, statesmanlike insight on Muhammad's part, to have recognized the need to expand northward.

Watt now addresses the question of the relative weights of material and religious motives in Muhammad's own outlook and in that of his followers. For Watt, understanding the motives of the seventh century Bedouin conversions to Islam requires that one rid oneself of the Western idea that politics and religion are separate phenomena. We must not think of such conversions as emotional in William James' sense. In the history of the Near East from earliest times to the time of Muhammad, says Watt, religion and politics have been closely linked to one another. Islam under Muhammad was the ideology of a political system. Watt wants to make the point that the system attracted Bedouin men for various reasons, not the least of which was booty. Addressing the question of why Muhammad was invited to Medina, Watt recognizes that the violent encounters and the uneasy truce between the Aws and the Khazraj created an opening for the Prophet as arbitrator. The fact that Muhammad was an outsider seemed to promise that he would be truly non-partisan in his mediation.

Watt now turns his attention to the Jews of Medina, where he sees Muhammad's early modeling of Islam on Judaism as an attempt at reconciliation with the Jews. Watt recounts the break with the Jews, which became an opportunity for the physical attack upon them, resulting in their expulsion and destruction. How does Watt explain the harshness of Muhammad's policy towards the Jews? "To suggest that Muhammad was unaware of the wealth of the Jews," Watt writes, "would be a serious underestimating of his intelligence. To make this the sole reason, however, for his attacks on the Jews is to be unduly materialistic. The wealth of the Jews was certainly of great benefit to him and considerably eased his financial position, and the prospect of financial betterment may have influenced the timing of his attacks on the Jews. But the fundamental reason for the quarrel was theological on both sides" (220). Watt had earlier assured us that in Islam the religious or theological cannot be separated from the political. But now in a rather equivocating treatment of Muhammad's policy, Watt wants us to believe that the quarrel was "theological on both sides." It was indeed theological on the part of the Jews, for they had nothing material to gain from their quarrel with Muhammad; while he, in contrast, had much to gain, materially, by turning the quarrel into a deadly one for the Jews. What Watt's interpretation overlooks, as we shall see more clearly in a later discussion, is the valid Ibn Khaldunian thesis regarding the almost natural antagonism between the desert and the sown, and that it is the Bedouins who look upon the wealthy communities of the oases as an alluring, nay, irresistible source of sustenance and more. Muhammad and his tribal followers at Medina were the Bedouins, while the Jews represented the sown.

Watt, in chapter 8, referring us back to his central thesis in his *Muhammad at Mecca*, states that the proclamation of a new religion,

was at bottom due to the transition from a nomadic to a settled economy with a resulting decline in tribal solidarity and its replacement by individualism. Individualism fostered selfishness . . . [which] knew very well how to twist nomadic ideals and practices to the private advantage of those who found themselves with a measure of power. There was a corresponding growth of *discontent* among those who found themselves at a disadvantage in the struggle for wealth and power. (261, italics added)

I have underscored the word "discontent" because that is the very concept that I have designated in my sociological argument as a fundamental factor in the transformation of a sect into a mass movement. The problem with Watt's use of this concept in *his* thesis is his failure to recognize that the so-called "discontent" in Mecca, as we have observed, could not have been very wide or deep in the light of the unimpressive success Muhammad had in Mecca after thirteen years of preaching and warning.

Watt writes in his concluding remarks that it was through Muhammad that the Arab world received an ideological framework "within which the resolution of its social tensions became possible. The provision of such a framework involved both insight into the fundamental causes of the social malaise of the time, and the genius to express this insight in a form which would stir the hearer to the depths of his being" (334–5).

This conclusion of Watt's is remarkable for its generality, and formulated so as to lend credence to the thesis he has held since his *Muhammad at Mecca*. It is formulated in that manner, apparently, in order to give the impression that his Meccan thesis somehow explains Muhammad's success in Medina. But the truth is that Muhammad's success in Medina requires attention to the historically specific circumstances of Medina at the time.

# 9

# Muhammad at Medina: William Muir's Analysis

To understand why Muhammad decided to leave Mecca, one has to grasp the extent to which he felt repulsed and dispirited there. On top of being rejected by his own people, his personal situation had worsened considerably with the death first of Khadija and then five weeks later, of his protector Abu Talib. He resolves to make a final attempt at success with the Banu Thaqif at Taif (620 CE), but fails there too. But his efforts there tell us something about the self-understanding he had reached by that time. In Muir's words: "There is something lofty and heroic in this journey of Muhammad to Taif; a solitary man, despised and rejected by his own people, going boldly forth in the name of God – like Jonah to Nineveh – and summoning an idolatrous city to repentance and to the support of his mission. It sheds a strong light on the intensity of his own belief in the divine origin of his calling."[1]

Meanwhile, he is betrothed to Aisha and is encouraged at the pilgrimage of March 620, upon meeting a party from Yathrib-Medina. For Muir there can be no doubt that Medina was more hospitable to Muhammad and better prepared for his message due to the strong influence there of Judaism and Christianity. Muir refers to the presence of the Jewish tribes and their divided support for the Aws and the Khazraj, whose strife frequently stained with blood the city and its environs. Muir then cites Ibn Ishaq to the effect that "when the Jews used to contend with the idolators at Medina, they would say: a prophet, the messiah, is about to come, his time draws near. We shall follow him, and then we shall slay all idolators. So when Muhammad addressed the pilgrims of Medina at Mina, they spoke to one another saying: surely that is the same prophet whom the Jews are wont to threaten us with. Wherefore let us make haste and be the first to join him" (vol. II, 211).

Muir sees historical truth in this event and statement, though exaggerated and distorted. There was close and constant communication between the Jews and Arabs of Medina, and the expectation of a messiah, so essential an element of the Jewish outlook, was bound to be known by their Arab neighbors. Moreover, the idolators were bound also to be at least somewhat influenced by the Jewish criticism of their beliefs. There was also the Christian influence in Medina, a city much closer geographically to the Christian tribes of Southern Syria. And in light of the violent tribal conflicts of the Aws and Khazraj, it seemed to many Medinans that a mediator and judge was urgently needed. The bloody battle of Buath, a few years earlier, had left those two tribes in a stalemate and temporary truce. There was no Common Power, in Hobbes' sense, that could put an end to the sanguinary, internal war, and both the Arabs and the Jews lived in fear and uncertainty. Medina was ready for an umpire; and since many Medinans had heard of Muhammad's claims, there was a certain receptivity to him there that existed nowhere else. The receptivity was further enhanced by the fact that Muhammad was descended from a distinguished woman of Khazraj birth, espoused by Hashim, so that a favorable interest in Muhammad within that tribe was thus gained. Furthermore, the Jews of Medina had heard that Muhammad was a zealous supporter of their monotheism.

Given such receptivity, the Prophet sends Musab to Medina to instruct the few converts. At the second pledge at Aqaba, Muhammad begins by reciting appropriate passages from the Quran and inviting all present to the service of Allah; he concludes by saying that he would be content if the strangers pledged themselves to defend him as they did and would their own wives and children. As the Meccans renew persecution, Muhammad commands his followers to begin to immigrate to Medina, a process that continues for about two months. The Quraysh are stunned by this sudden turn of events – by areas of the small city entirely deserted and the doors of the houses left deliberately locked. Muhammad and Abu Bakr escape to the cave of Thaur, and then head for Medina June 20, 622 CE, the so-called Hijra, or move to Medina. Soon afterward he begins his close association with the Jews.

## Muhammad and the Jewish Tribes of Medina

In the beginning, Muhammad not only fully acknowledged the divine origin of the religion of the Jews, but largely based his own claims on their Scriptures and on what he heard from their learned men. Indeed, he strongly desired a unification with them, perhaps even in one *Ummah*. All of his feasts, fasts, and ceremonies were modeled on Jewish custom, and Jerusalem was his *qibla*, as we have seen. It was towards Jerusalem that the

Prophet and his followers turned five times a day, prostrating themselves in prayer. At this time, Muhammad was ready to go far, short of abandoning his claim to the prophetic calling, in order to win the Jews over to his cause. His desire to enter into a close union with the Jews expressed itself in a formal agreement shortly after reaching Medina. He brought them into a treaty of mutual obligation, drawn up in writing, between the Emigrants and the men of Medina, in which he confirmed the security of the Jews in the practice of their religion and the *possession of their property*.

According to Ibn Ishaq, the contract, made in the name of God, was between the Emigrants and the believers of Yathrib, and whoever else joined them in striving for the faith. The provisions of the agreement stipulated that the several clans of the Emigrants would defray the price of bloodshed and ransom their prisoners, and the Medinan clans would do the same. Anyone who seeks to undermine the unity of this alliance, shall be opposed by all signatories to the contract. No believer shall be put to death for killing an infidel; nor shall any infidel be supported against a Believer. Those among the Jews who join the alliance, shall receive aid and relief when needed; they shall not be injured, nor shall any enemy be aided against them. No unbeliever (i.e., those of Medina who had not submitted to Muhammad's claims, but who were, nonetheless, brought indirectly into the contract) shall give aid to the Quraysh of Mecca, either in their persons or their property. Whoever kills a Believer wrongfully shall be liable to retaliation; the Muslims shall join as one man against the murderer. The curse of God, and his wrath in the day of judgment, shall rest on the man that shall aid or shelter him.

As the contract turns more specifically to the Jews, it states that they shall contribute their share along with the Muslims in case of war against a common enemy. The Jews shall maintain their religion, the Muslims theirs. The Jews shall be responsible for their expenditures, the Muslims for theirs. Each, if attacked, shall come to the aid of the other. Medina shall be sacred and inviolable for all who join this treaty. New questions and doubts, likely to produce evil and danger, shall be referred for decision to God and Muhammad his prophet. War and peace shall be made in common (vol. III, 33–4).

For a while relations between the Jews and Muhammad had remained cordial. But, as Muir observes, it soon became evident to the Jews that Judaism could not go hand in hand with Islam. The reasons appear to be the following: Although Muhammad rested his claims on the prophecies of the Jewish Scriptures, he did not profess to be the messiah, for the messiah, he said, had already come in the person of Jesus, and had been rejected. Muhammad now stated openly that he was not only a prophet, but a greater prophet as foretold in the Jewish Book; the Jews know this, he alleged, but out of jealousy and spite reject him as they did their own messiah. Given this openly declared position, a Jewish acceptance of it would be tantamount to abandoning Judaism. Such an option being out of the question for the Jews, a growing antagonism with the Prophet was unavoidable.

There were, however, a few Jewish converts to Islam, and Muhammad employed them to great effect. As Muir describes the situation, "They were constantly referred to as 'witnesses.' They bore evidence that the Prophet's career answered to every mark predicted in their Books; and asserted that their brethren, actuated by jealousy and mortified that the gift of prophecy should pass over from their nation to another people, had concealed the passages . . . favorable to his claims" (III, 35–6). It was such individuals with allegations of that kind that enabled Muhammad to rebut the Jewish criticisms of his claims. The Jews persisted, however, with substantive scriptural questions which he found annoyingly difficult and embarrassing. In Muhammad's eyes, this "stiff-necked" people, to whose corroboration he had earlier appealed again and again, had now become a living witness against him. What made this state of affairs especially threatening from his standpoint, was the strong sympathy that existed between the clans of Medina and the Jewish tribes, who had stood by them in times of trouble and had shed their blood in defense of those clans.

Muhammad resolved, therefore, to rid himself of what he came to regard as a dangerous adversary; and his resolve is reflected in the allegations he makes in the Quran (Sura 2) against the Jewish forefathers. His break with the Jews explains his decision to change the *qibla* and to secede, so to speak, from Jewish religious institutions. The Kaaba now became the *qibla* of Islam. "The Jews," Muir cogently observes,

> knowing full well the motives which led to this alteration, were mortified and still further estranged. Muhammad had cut . . . the last link binding him ostensibly to their creed. They charged him with fickleness, and the worshipping towards an idolatrous temple. These charges he endeavored to meet in the Quran; but it was the victory at Badr, one or two months after, and the subsequent hostilities against the Jews, which furnished the only effective means for silencing their objections. (III, 44–5)

Not too long after Muhammad had arrived in Yathrib, he observed the Fast of Atonement; but now that he is furious with the Jews and estranged from them, he substitutes the Fast of Ramadan.

Muir avers that Muhammad had contemplated punitive measures against the Quraysh from the day of his flight from Mecca and his arrival in Yathrib. But no opportunity had as yet presented itself, since the Medinans were pledged to defend the Prophet from attack, not to join him in aggressive actions against the Quraysh. But now we hear of expeditions against Quraysh caravans led by one of Muhammad's uncles, the power-fully built and high-spirited Hamza; but his raids were not particularly suc-cessful. Nor were those led by Muhammad in person in the summer and autumn of 623 CE. The next significant event is the affair of Nakhla, where Muhammad's men attack a caravan of the Quraysh in the sacred months, killing one man and carrying off two as captives. Muhammad at first disclaims responsibility for the attack, but then promulgates a revelation approving it (Sura 2: 217). The Muslim writers attach much significance to this event. Ibn Hisham, for example, wrote that "this was the first booty that the Muslims obtained; the first captives they seized; and the first life they took." The hostility of Muhammad and his followers toward their countrymen grows. Soon we hear of a divine command to fight the Quraysh and paradise is promised to the slain.

## The Battle of Badr

The campaign of Badr was the first occasion on which the Medinans joined the Emigrants in large numbers. Muhammad sends scouts for intelligence of Abu Sufyan's approach, who, warned of Muhammad's intentions, sends to Mecca for reinforcements. Muhammad gives the command for the cam-paign, and marches from Medina. Abu Sufyan, discovering traces of Muhammad's scouts, quickens his pace and escapes. At Mecca there is alarm, and the Quraysh resolve to march to the rescue of the caravan. They set out and soon meet Abu Sufyan's messenger. They debate whether to return or to go forward, and they resolve to advance to Badr. Muhammad receives intelligence of the march of the Quraysh army. In a Quraysh or Meccan council of war, the march is enthusiastically approved. But the Muslims are more implacable than the Quraysh.

We can now begin to grasp the causal weight of the Islamic promise of paradise for the slain and the extent to which that promise was internalized as a motivating force by the Muslim warriors. We also see how the new faith overrode kinship. "It is remarkable," Muir comments, "how entirely absent from the minds of the Muslims was any trace of compunction at the prospect of entering into mortal combat with their kinsmen" (III, 94).

Muhammad learns from the Quraysh water-carriers the proximity and strength of the enemy. The caravan escapes, while Muhammad takes up a position at Badr. Fierce combat breaks out by the reservoir, and three

Quraysh, according to custom, challenge the Muslims to single combat. The Muslim army puts the Quraysh to flight, and kills some of Muhammad's chief opponents, notably Abu Jakl. The booty is gathered together, contention over its division is decided by a revelation, and the enemy's dead are cast into a pit. This victory at Badr is interpreted as a divine intervention in favor of Islam, and it seems almost certain, Muir avers, that Muhammad would have found it difficult to maintain his position at Medina in the face of any reverse or failure. The victory provided Muhammad with new and effective ideological ammunition, for he attributed the entire success to the miraculous assistance of God, an argument made easier by the fact that the Muslims were vastly outnumbered in this battle. Muhammad's reputation now stood or fell by his success in the field.

In the year following the battle of Badr, there was an early movement against the Jews and others who disputed Muhammad's claims and denied the authenticity of his revelations. To prepare us for the upcoming war against the Jews, Muir writes in a footnote:

> I must again draw attention to the importance of bearing in mind, at this stage of the history, that [Muslim] tradition in respect to these Jews is *exclusively one-sided*. They were *all* (with the exception of the few gained over to Islam, and therefore lost as witnesses) either expatriated or exterminated. They are reproached in the severest terms in the Quran; every Muslim, therefore, believes it a merit and a privilege to cast abuse upon them. It would be vain to expect impartial evidence from such a source. (III, 130)

Muhammad began his campaign against the Jews by authorizing first the assassination of Asma, daughter of Marwan, and then the deliberate murder of Abu Afaq who lived in the suburbs of Medina and who had reached the great age, it was said, of twice three-score years, and known for his opposition to the new religion. He had composed some stinging verses which annoyed the Muslims; so the Prophet indicated his wish for the murder of this man by saying to his followers, "who will rid me of this pestilent fellow?" A convert fell upon the aged man as he slept outside his house, and dispatching him with one blow of his sword, escaped unrecognized (III, 133). The Jews are alarmed, and the B. Qainuqa are threatened by Muhammad, due to an incident with a Muslim woman in the market place of the Qainuqa, where a silly man, unperceived, pinned the lower back hem of her skirt to the upper dress. When she got up, the exposure provoked laughter and she screamed with shame. A Muslim then slew the offending Jew, whose brothers, in their turn, fell upon and killed the Muslim in revenge. This became the pretext for Muhammad's siege of their fortified dwelling that lasted fifteen days before the defenders gave in. We learn from Ibn Hisham that Muhammad wanted to put them all to death, but a powerful Muslim, Ibn Ubayy, interceded on behalf of his allies. The Prophet began to turn away without answering him, whereupon Ibn Ubayy seized the top of Muhammad's breast plate. His face became dark with rage and he shouted, "Let me go." "No, by Allah!" came the answer. "I shall not let you go until you deal kindly with my allies: 400 men who have always defended me against all-comers. Will you slay them all in the space of a morning? By Allah, in your place I would fear a reversal of fortune!" This was a threat and Ibn Ubayy was still powerful. So Muhammad yielded and spared the lives of the Qainuqa on condition they left Medina within three days, leaving their goods for the victor. The spoil was mainly armor and goldsmith's tools, for that was the chief occupation of the tribe. Apparently, they possessed no agricultural property, nor any fields. So Muhammad takes the spoil and lets them go. This experience, as we shall see, taught Muhammad a valuable lesson about the inherent vulnerability of even strongly fortified positions.

In the battle of Uhud, the next battle of significance, the Quraysh waver, but Khalid saves the day. The Prophet's Medinan army is routed, and Muhammad himself is wounded. But by this time Muhammad has become a military strategist. For it was evident, writes Muir, "that the destruction of the whole [Medinan] force was only averted by the foresight of Muhammad in keeping a secure place of refuge in the rear" (III, 177). Although Muhammad's prestige was affected by the defeat, he presented a line of argument to lessen its ill effect: that the setback at Uhud was necessary to separate the true believers from those who were infidels, at heart.

> Some of you were for this world and some of you for the next. Then, in order to make trial of you, He turned you to flight from them – yet hath He now forgiven you; for all-bounteous is God to the faithful –
>
> When ye came up the height and took no heed of anyone, while the Prophet in your rear was calling you *to the fight*! God hath rewarded you with trouble upon trouble, that ye might *learn* not to be chagrined at your loss of booty, or what befell you! (Sura 3: 140ff.)

It was usually after setbacks or when he was in urgent need of funds, that Muhammad turned his attention to the Jews. One of his followers, Amr, had murdered two men, and Muhammad, apparently, thought it right that the Jewish tribe, Banu Nadir, should help him defray the cost of compensation, the blood price. It was asserted that a member of the B. Nadir had plotted to climb upon the roof under which the Prophet sat during the conversation about the blood price, and roll down large stones upon him. "But," Muir comments, "as his own followers saw nothing to excite suspicion, and as the chapter in the Quran specially devoted to the subject does not hint at any such perfidy, the charge is open to grave suspicion" (III, 209). The B. Nadir, refusing to share the cost of the blood price, are besieged, and their date trees are burned. "The Jews," Muir writes, "remonstrated against this as barbarous and cruel; so Muhammad felt that his reputation demanded a special order from the Almighty, which was produced accordingly, sanctioning the destruction of his enemy's palm trees" (III, 213). The Banu Nadir submit to the order of expatriation, and their fields are divided among the Emigrants.

Muhammad had up to that time trusted Jewish "secretaries" with the transcription of dispatches that had to be written in the Hebrew or Syriac languages. But now, to rid himself of such dependence, he sends his adopted son, Zayd to learn Hebrew and Syriac to qualify him for secretarial duties.

It is at about this time that the battle of the Trench or *ditch* took place. At the earlier battle of *Uhud*, we recall, the Quraysh, reacting against Muslim raids from Medina, sent a force against Muhammad and defeated the Muslims on the slopes of Uhud. As the Quraysh failed to follow up their advantage by continuing to Medina – perhaps because they felt not strong enough – the Muslims suffered a slight setback, but not a disastrous defeat. Muhammad compensated his followers by attacking and driving out another of the Jewish tribes – the B. Nadir – just as he had after the battle of Badr. The Quraysh, however, had not yet given up the struggle. In the spring of 627 a Meccan army of some 10,000 men advanced to Medina and laid siege to the city. As we learned earlier, the defeat of the Muslims seemed almost certain until a Persian convert suggested the expedience of digging a ditch around the town, which proved to be sufficient to stymie the forty-day siege and compel the Quraysh army to withdraw. We see, then, that whether it was victory or a slight reversal in the fortunes of the Muslims, Muhammad used the occasion for an assault upon the Medinan Jews.

Soon after the battle of the Trench, Abu Sufyan, a leader of the Quraysh's opposition to Muhammad, succeeded in persuading the Jewish tribe of Qurayza to detach itself from the alliance with Muhammad (Sura 33: 26). The Prophet, alarmed, now recognizes that his previous treatment of the Jewish tribes might drive the Qurayza to desperate measures. He attacks and they surrender at the discretion of the Banu Aws, who intercede on behalf of their ancient allies, pleading that their lives be spared. The Aws requested that this Jewish tribe, the Qurayza, be shown the same consideration that earlier, at the intervention of the Khazraj, had been shown to the B. Nadir, who were allowed to emigrate with all the property they could carry away. "Are you content, then," replied Muhammad, "that their fate be decided by one of yourselves?" They said yes, and Muhammad nominated Saad Ibn Muadz to serve as judge. He was urged by his fellow Aws tribesmen to spare their Jewish allies, but his answer was not encouraging. He demanded an oath that his sentence would be carried out, and then he pronounced it: all the men were to be slain, the women and children sold into slavery and their property divided among the Muslims.

The next day Muhammad had ditches dug in the market place of Medina, while the Jewish men were led out in groups, beheaded, one by one, on the edge of the ditch and thrown in (Ibn Hisham, 461f). One woman, who had thrown a millstone from the battlements, was put to death. From Muir we learn that Aisha, Muhammad's young wife, related ". . . that this woman, whose heart, perhaps was sustained by the faith in the God of her fathers, went smiling and fearlessly to her fate. Aisha said that she could never get the image of this woman out of her mind" (Muir, III, 277). Ibn Hisham states that "the number of beheaded men was six or seven hundred, though some put the figure as high as eight or nine hundred" (466). Muir, however, states that the number of weapons enumerated among the spoil suggests that even 900 seems to be a moderate estimate of the male victims. "That the massacre," he writes, "was savage and cruel, to a barbarous and inhuman degree, it does not require any comment to prove. The ostensible grounds upon which Muhammad proceeded were *purely political*, for as yet he did not profess to force men to join Islam, or to punish them for not embracing it" (Muir, III, 282). In the abridgment[2] of his four-volume study, Muir adds this comment:

> The massacre of the Banu Qurayza was a barbarous deed which cannot be justified by any reason of political necessity. There was, no doubt, a sufficient cause for attacking them, and even for severely punishing the leaders who had joined the enemy at so critical a moment. Muhammad might also have been justified in making them quit altogether a neighborhood in which they formed a dangerous nucleus of disaffection at home, and an encouragement for attack from abroad. But the indiscriminate slaughter of the whole tribe cannot be recognized otherwise than as an act of monstrous cruelty, which casts an indelible blot upon the Prophet's name.
>
> The sanguinary fate of the Qurayza removed the last remnant of open opposition, political or religious, from the neighborhood of Medina. It did not, indeed, at the moment escape hostile criticism; but it struck terror into the heart of every disloyal citizen. The Prophet was invested with a halo so supernatural, and to his enemies so dreadful, that no one dared outwardly to signify dissent. (Muir, Abridgment, pp. 151–2)

## Current Research on the Massacre of the B. Qurayza

In an article entitled, "On Arabs of the Banu Kilab Executed Together with the Jewish Banu Qurayza,"[3] Michael Lecker calls attention to a unique record that illuminates an aspect of history otherwise unknown to us. As the title of the article states, the record concerns a clan of Arab proselytes whose men were executed by Muhammad together with the Banu Qurayza. Lecker makes the significant observation that the massacre was unprecedented in the Arabian Peninsula – a novelty. Prior to Islam, the annihilation of an adversary was never an aim of war. When, after their victory in the battle of Buath on the eve of Islam, the Aws killed many of the defeated Khazraj, someone allegedly shouted: "O Company of the Aws, be gentle and do not destroy your brothers, because having them as neighbors is better than having foxes as neighbors." This is a genuine reflection, says Lecker, of pre-Islamic attitudes and practices.

## The Conquest of Khaybar

On his return from Hudabiyya in the spring of 628, where Muhammad had negotiated a treaty with the Quraysh, he promised those who had accompanied him in that pilgrimage the early prospect of rich and extensive plunder. But the summer passed without any action, and his followers became restless. Muhammad was, most likely, waiting for some act on the part of the Jews of Khaybar that he could describe as a provocation. It was the fertile lands and villages of Khaybar that he had hoped to turn over to his followers. As no such provocation occurred to serve as a pretext for attack, he resolved in the autumn of 628 on a "sudden and unprovoked invasion of their territory" (Muir, vol. IV, 61).

The army marched from Medina, 1600 strong, about the same number that had accompanied him on his pilgrimage to Hudabiyya. The army was reinforced by a cavalry, estimated at one or two hundred. It is clear that Muhammad and many other Medinans looked upon Khaybar as the juiciest plum available. As Muir observes, many of the other inhabitants of Medina and the surrounding Bedouin tribes that had ignored Muhammad's earlier summons, were eager to join this expedition, but were not permitted, and their disappointment was great at being left behind.

The distance of 100 miles or so, was accomplished in three forced marches. So quick was their movement and the surprise so complete, that the cultivators of Khaybar, coming out to their fields in early morning, suddenly found themselves confronted by a huge army, and rushed back to the city in dismay. The rich valley of Khaybar consisted of numerous villages and strongholds overlooking date groves and fields of corn. The rapid approach of Muhammad's forces precluded any timely aid from the Banu Ghatafan, as Ibn Hisham explains:

> In his march from Medina to Khaybar Muhammad halted in a wadi between Khaybar and Ghatafan so as to prevent the men of the latter from reinforcing Khaybar, for they sided with Khaybar. When the men of Ghatafan heard of Muhammad's assault on Khaybar they marched out to help the Jews, but after a day's journey, hearing a rumor that their camps have been attacked in their absence, they went back on their tracks and left the way to Khaybar open to Muhammad. (Ibn Hisham, p. 511)

Before any general defense could be organized in Khaybar, their forts were attacked, one by one, and overcome. From the villages in the valleys of Natah and Schickk, which Muhammad defeated with little loss, he proceeded to the region of Kutayba. There, however, the Jews had had time to rally around their chief, Kinana, and to prepare for the assault. They posted themselves in front of the citadel, and resolved on a desperate struggle. After several failed attempts to dislodge them, Muhammad planned a major offensive. A great black flag was placed in the hand of Ali, the Prophet's cousin, and Muhammad's troops advanced. At that moment a warrior stepped forth out of the Jewish line of defense and challenged his adversaries to single combat – which was the customary way that battles began. The first Muslim who answered the challenge, aimed a blow at the Jewish warrior with deadly force, but the sword recoiled upon himself and he fell fatally wounded. The Jew named Marhab repeated his challenge, and then Ali advanced, saying that his mother had named him *the Lion*, and he will demonstrate that the name is well deserved. The two combatants closed in upon each other and Ali cleft the head of Marhab in two. Marhab's brother renewed the challenge, and was also slain. In the battle that ensued between the two forces, the Muslim victory was decisive, the Jews losing 93 men and the Muslims nineteen.

After the defeat, the fortress of Qamuss surrendered on condition that its families would be free to leave the country but yield all their property to the conqueror. With the rest, Kinana, Chief of the Jews of Khaybar, came forward with his cousin. Muhammad accused them both of keeping back a portion of their wealth, especially the treasures of the Banu Nadir, which Kinana had obtained as a dowry when marrying the daughter of the chief of that tribe. "Where are the vessels of gold," Muhammad asked, "which you used to lend to the people of Mecca? If you conceal anything from me,"

Muhammad continued, "and I should discover it, then your lives and the lives of your families will be at my disposal." Kinana and his cousin agreed, but a traitorous Jew divulged to Muhammad where a part of the wealth was hidden. Kinana was then subjected to cruel torture – fire was placed on his chest until he almost expired – with the aim of forcing him to confess where the rest of the treasure was concealed; and hearing no such confession, Muhammad gave the command, and the two chiefs were beheaded.

The torture and bloodshed had hardly ended, Muir observes, when Muhammad sent Bilal to fetch Safia, the wife of Kinana, whose beauty was well known at Medina. She was brought across the battlefield strewn with the dead, and past the corpses of Kinana and his cousin. When Safia's companion saw the headless trunks, she screamed wildly, beating her face and casting dust upon her head. Muhammad then placed his mantle around Safia, thus signifying that she was to be his own, and the marriage was consummated at Khaybar. In a footnote, Muir explains why Safia's beauty was, most probably, well known at Medina: " . . . (1) she was the daughter of a chief who had long lived in Medina, and was well known there; and (2) because Muhammad, immediately upon Kinana's execution, sent for her and cast his mantle over her. Indeed, he is not free from the suspicion of being influenced in the destruction of Kinana by the desire of obtaining his wife" (IV, 68).

The remaining fortresses capitulated and were thus saved from being sacked; but like the rest of Khaybar were subjected to a tax of half their produce. Evidently, Muhammad agreed to this arrangement because he recognized that the Jews of Khaybar possessed the agricultural skills which his followers lacked. There was more to gain from leaving the Jewish farmers in place, and exacting from them 50 percent of their yield, than from expelling or killing them. That seems to be the substance of Ibn Hisham's account: "when the people of Khaybar surrendered, . . . they asked the Prophet to employ them on the property with half share in the produce, saying, 'We know more about it than you and we are better farmers'" (Ibn, Hisham, 511–12).

The plunder of Khaybar was richer than any of Muhammad's previous preys – enormous stores of dates, oil, honey and barley, flocks of sheep and herds of camels, and a large treasure of jewels. A fifth of the whole was, as usual, set apart for the use of the Prophet, and for distribution at will among his family and the poor. The remaining four-fifths were sold and the proceeds, according to the prescribed rule, were divided into 1800 shares, one for every foot soldier and three for a horseman. The villages and lands were also divided, but on a different principle: one half for Muhammad, which was treated as a kind of crown domain; the other half divided into 1800 portions and allotted by the same rule as the personal booty. Clearly, a large and permanent source of revenue was thus secured for all those who had remained loyal to the Prophet. Muir recognizes, of course, that

> even in those portions of Khaybar which were gained by storm, it was found expedient, in the absence of other [i.e., Arab] cultivators, to leave the Jewish inhabitants in possession on the condition already specified, of surrendering half the produce . . . This arrangement continued until the Caliphate of Omar, when, there being no scarcity of Muslim husbandmen, the Jews were expatriated and entire possession taken of their lands. (IV, 75)

After returning from Khaybar, Muhammad undertook several expeditions which showed that his influence was fast expanding and bringing him gradually into relations even with distant tribes. His mind now turns to Mecca. The time had come, he believed, to return to his country and people. He plans a lesser pilgrimage, takes precautionary measures before entering Mecca, enters and performs the circuit of the Kaaba, and sizes up the situation. He discerns the growth of his reputation, the declining power and spirit of the Quraysh, the war-weariness of the Meccans, and the growth of advocates of compromise and peace. And among the Quraysh there no longer seemed to be leaders of marked ability or commanding influence. It was time for a bold and rapid stroke that would bring Mecca too into his militant polity. In January 630, the murder of a Muslim by a Meccan in a private quarrel, provided the pretext for the final attack and the conquest of Mecca. With the capture of Mecca and the submission of the Quraysh to the Umma of Islam, the mission of the Prophet during his lifetime was virtually completed; and in the year of life that remained to him, he appears to have engaged in no notable activity.

For Muir, it seems clear that Muhammad had acquired in Mecca a vivid sense of a special mission and had developed an authentic belief in the one God, with its corresponding denunciation of polytheism. At Medina, however, one sees the salience of worldly motives, though mixed with religious interests. In the name of the Almighty, he wielded the sword against all who opposed him.

# 10

# Muhammad and the Jews

Basing himself on several well-known inscriptions, and on the work of Werner Caskel, Barakat Ahmad[1] is inclined to agree that the evidence points to a Jewish population that eventually occupied all the oases in the northwest of the Peninsula, including Yathrib–Medina, which, having been rich in underground water, provided the Jews with a land where they could apply their farming experience. Ahmad agrees with the Jewish historians whom we cited earlier – Graetz, Baron, and others – that it was the Jews who introduced in the Hijaz, palms, a variety of fruit trees and rice, as well as advanced methods of irrigation and cultivation; they also introduced diverse arts and crafts, ranging from metal work to dyeing, to the making of fine jewelry.

Ahmad also agrees that these Jews appear to have become Arabianized, judging from their tribal and personal names. He therefore addresses the question of whether the term Judaism ought to be applied to these Jews of the Hijaz. He cites two Jewish scholars with opposing views. H. G. Reissner, for example, calls it inappropriate to call these tribes "Jews":

> Less than a hundred years prior to Muhammad's birth, the Talmud had been completed in Babylon. At that time, there was complete agreement, *intra muros et extra*, as to who was a Jew and what constitutes the essence of Judaism. A Jew was a follower of the Mosaic Law as interpreted by the teachers of the Law in accordance with the principles laid down in the Talmud . . . Whoever did not conform . . . was discounted. If [however] he was Israelite by descent, he could not be deprived of his birthright, viz., to be called Ben Israel, as in Arabia . . .[2]

Israel Friedlaender, disagreeing with Reissner, states that his examination of the Gaonate documents have shown that there was, in fact, contact of Arab Jews with the Gaonate, Jewish religious leadership, in Babylon:

> It is characteristic of the central position of the Gaonate in Jewish life that . . . it was able to exert its influence over the distant half-mythical Jews

in free Arabia and shape their professional and civil life. It shows at the same time that the Arabian Jews, however far removed from Jewish learning, recognized the authority of the Talmud and were not in any way guilty of those anti-Talmudic sentiments which Graetz is prone to ascribe to their forefathers.[3]

Ahmad, proceeding with the assumption that the tribes and clans in question were certainly regarded as Jewish, describes their situation as he understands it from Muslim sources as well. They owned almost 60 *atam* (sing. *utum*), which formed a prominent feature of Yathrib, and were, in fact, forts stocked with provisions and water and strong enough to withstand attacks and big enough to endure long sieges. The forts also contained schools, synagogues and council halls. In Ibn Khaldun's terms, the Jews represented the sedentary culture in the Hijaz. They lived in forts in recognition of the Hobbesian nature of their environs, and their potential vulnerability to those whom Ibn Khaldun characterized as "savage Bedouin."

Ahmad now refers to Khaybar (with which we are now quite familiar) as the second most important Jewish settlement, about 90 miles north of Medina, and located on a very high mountainous plateau entirely composed of lava deposits and malarial swamps. There the Jews cultivated grapes, vegetables and grain, and raised sheep, cattle, camels, horses, and donkeys. They also had palm groves; and they traded with Syria, benefiting from the caravan trade between Arabia, Syria and Iraq. In addition, the Khaybar Jews were known for crafting metal tools and weapons, such as battering rams and catapults. There were several groups of forts, many built on hilltops, in what appeared to be impregnable positions. According to al-Yaqubi, thousands of people lived in these forts. It hardly needs to be said, then, that the Khaybar Jews lived in strongholds out of the same security considerations as those of the Medinan Jews.

Ahmad now reviews briefly the pre-Islamic history of the Hijaz, the arrival of certain Arab tribes from the south who settled or camped on land that had not been brought under cultivation. They apparently accepted the economically dominant position of the Jews and entered into a relationship with them that was of *jiwar* (neighbor) or of *hilf* (confederation). *Hilf* is a compact between separate tribes with the aim of establishing long-term peace between them. The compact is made for common defense, common responsibility for debts to third parties, for revenge and for common use of pasturage. Towards the middle of the sixth century the relationship between the two parties changed owing to the revolt led by Malik b. al-Ajlan against the Jewish overlords, a revolt prompted by the tribute they had been paying. It appears, then, that the Medinan Jews had lost their position of dominance some time before the birth of the Prophet.

After the middle of the sixth century, the Jewish tribes of Medina appear definitely to have become weaker. The fact that even before the battle of Buath (the battles between the Arab tribes, the Aws and the Khazraj, fought some years before the migration of the Prophet) the Banu-Nadir and Banu-Qurayza had given hostages to the Khazraj, suggests that they were fully aware of their weaker position. Hence, at the battle of Buath, both Jewish tribes helped the Aws against the Khazraj even at the cost of the lives of some of their hostages. The Jewish support made it possible for the Aws to gain victory at Buath. Though the Aws seemed to have gained the upper hand, they and the Khazraj and everyone else in Medina knew that this was only a temporary truce and that the deadly quarrel can break out again at any moment.

We get close to the historical truth, then, by recognizing that the Arab tribes in Medina and its vicinity, and indeed, throughout the northern Peninsula were – when Muhammad arrived in Medina – in a condition which Ibn Khaldun had described in proto-Hobbesian terms as a "war of each against all." Though no formal peace was made after the battle of Buath (c. 615 CE), the warring clans and tribes were too exhausted to continue an active struggle. During this uneasy truce, the Jewish tribes regained some of their former influence. This was the state of affairs in Medina that made possible the invitation to Muhammad to move to Medina, and to serve as an arbitrator seeking to arrange that the warring tribes should settle their dispute by peaceful means. His ultimate aim, at first, was to put an end to the conflicts both among the Arabs and between the Arabs and the Jews, and to create a new community based on his new religious message. His efforts at creating the first stage of such a unity resulted in a formal document, *Sahifa*, which sought to provide the basis for positive law in the community thus created – an *Ummah*. The *Sahifa* was signed, as we learned earlier, by the new converts to Islam and by the Jews.

This *Ummah*, as envisioned by Muhammad and formalized in the *Sahifa*, could work only with the willing cooperation of all its constituents: the *Muhajirun* (Emigrants), the *Ansar* (the Medinan supporters of Muhammad) and the Jews. The first five years of Muhammad's work in Medina were spent in trying to gain such cooperation. Ahmad suggests that some within the *Ansar* and some among the Jews tended to withhold their cooperation, which led to the deteriorating relationship between Muhammad and the Jews, and to the military encounters between them.

Ahmad surmises that the Jews could not forget that they were the original settlers of Yathrib and that they represented a superior culture which,

Ahmad believes, accounts for their reluctance to accept a contract implying that it was made among equals. Muhammad's extreme disappointment with the Jewish refusal to recognize him as a prophet, led to his hostility towards them and to the wars against them. Ahmad now gives us some fresh insights into the strengths and weaknesses of siege warfare.

A key factor in the defeat of the Jews, Ahmad avers, was their reliance on their *atam*, fort-like castles built on heights. Within the strongholds, as observed earlier, were stores of food, silos, halls for conferences, schools, synagogues, a treasury and armory, and springs of fresh water. These strongholds were assumed to provide protection against the raiding Bedouin, a relatively sound assumption in *pre*-Islamic Arabia, where the Arab raiders had neither the equipment nor the patience for a prolonged siege. Arab warfare started with the hurling of insults against the adversary and extravagant praise for one's own clan or tribe. Ahmad now makes the perspicacious observation, that the most important and indeed decisive factor in a siege is the endurance and determination of both sides. Siege warfare is fundamentally different from ordinary warfare where the combatants on both sides are soldiers. But in the siege of a fort, which is not of an exclusively garrison nature, the majority of the besieged are non-combatant men, women and children. The children and the elderly unavoidably suffer the same privations, wounds and threat of death as the soldiers. Hunger and disease can easily undermine even the best-fortified strongholds. So for a realistic explanation of the extraordinary success of the Prophet's followers in war, we need to take seriously not only their considerable martial prowess resulting from their new religious zeal, but also the fact that in all four major encounters with Muhammad, the Jews of the Hijaz chose the shelter and protection of their *atam*, and were defeated in all four encounters.

It is in these terms that Muhammad and his followers learned something new about the power equation between the desert and the sown. The "something new" was the recognition of the vulnerability of even the best-fortified settlements and towns, a recognition that became an all-important element of Muslim military strategy in their spectacular conquests after the death of the Prophet. In those terms, Muhammad's war against the Jews of the Hijaz was a "dress rehearsal" for the wars of Islam against the empires.

Ahmad refers to four encounters, the fourth being Khaybar, which may require some qualification of the proposition stated in the previous paragraph. For Ahmad observes that Muhammad, as a gifted and experienced commander, could foresee the risks of imposing a siege on Khaybar – located on a heavily fortified, high mountainous plateau, surrounded by cultivated valleys and malarial swamps. Muhammad took the field nevertheless, but the battle was inconclusive and a peace was negotiated, but only after a great loss of life. The Jews agreed, as we saw earlier, to pay a tribute of 50 percent of their yield, and Muhammad recognized the advantage he gained by leaving the Jewish communities intact. The Jews, though they had not in this case decisively lost, were compelled to negotiate because they had underestimated their new kind of adversary. Their impressive fortification that had served them so well in pre-Islamic times, now turned out to be not quite adequate.

Ahmad, turning his attention to the advance of Islam after the death of the Prophet, proposes that the advance benefited the Jews and, indeed, was concomitant with the Jewish renaissance. It is the great, Jewish–Muslim symbiosis that accounts for the golden age of their fruitful encounter. In the light of that history, Ahmad regards it as misleading to speak of a "break with the Jews." The Jews faded out of the limelight, but did not disappear from Medina. When the Apostle died, his coat of mail was mortgaged to a Jew who had supplied him with food grains. The Jews, says Ahmad, were obviously conducting business as usual. For the Muslim chroniclers of wars, however, and for the biographer of the Prophet, the Jews of the Hijaz ceased to be of interest after the peace of Khaybar. The Jews of the Hijaz were neither expelled nor did they leave the region during Muhammad's lifetime.

Ahmad continues with these reflections:

> In less than twenty years after the death of the Apostle they [the Jews] demolished the walls of their mental and spiritual *utum* [fortress] and walked out to accept the challenge of a Muslim society which opened for them the doors of its mosques, schools, bazaars, markets and civil service, for education, social assimilation and their participation in the civic and political life. They took the full advantage of . . . all the intellectual and spiritual resources offered by the dominant elite without disappearing as a marginal minority. They joined [in effect] the Muslim *Ummah* as sustaining members. For 700 years their destiny was bound up with that of the Muslims. (125)

Ahmad cites Ellis Rivkin's *The Shaping of Jewish History*: "Every phase of Islamic growth was accompanied by a positive and creative reaction among Jews. Every phase of Muslim breakdown was accompanied by a [Jewish] disintegration: a golden age when [Muslim] Spain's wealth grew; humiliation and exile when it dwindled" (138). And in the same vein, Ahmad cites the perceptive comment by Joel Carmichael in his *The Shaping of the Arabs*, who considers it "very strange that while Christianity was gradually to disappear in most parts of the Muslim empire, Jewish communities survived and flourished – in Bukhara, formerly a great Christian center; in Yemen, once a Christian bishopric; and in North Africa, the home of St. Augustine" (p. 54). Ahmad remarks: "It would not look strange if the restricted nature and the limits of the Muslim-Jewish conflict were seen in their proper perspective" (125).

When Ahmad thus makes the case that after Muhammad's death Jews fared comparatively well under Muslim hegemony, he stands on rather firm ground where the historical evidence is concerned. But some of his other assertions about the Prophet, in particular, appear to fly in the face of historical facts. For example, Ahmad writes that all of the Prophet's

> marriages aimed to promote friendly relations in the political sphere. The union with Rayhana [the wife of one of the Jewish men of the Qurayza who were beheaded at Muhammad's command] was in fact a political announcement that Muhammad had closed the chapter of bitterness and was making another attempt to win the friendship of the B. Qurayza through marriage with a lady of their clan. *The gesture would have been meaningless and empty if all the male adults had been slain and their women and children sold as slaves.* (123, italics added)

If we read the italicized passage literally, Ahmad appears to deny that the massacre of the men of Qurayza and the sale of the women and children into slavery, is a historical fact. If that is what Ahmad meant to say in this passage, one wonders on what ground he chose to make such a claim when Ibn Hisham states the fact without hesitation or qualification:

> Saad gives the judgment as the so-called umpire, [Ibn Hisham writes], that the men should be killed, their property confiscated, and the women and children taken and sold as slaves. Then Muhammad went out to the market of Medina and dug ditches in it. Then he sent for the men of this Jewish tribe and struck off their heads in those ditches as they were brought out to him in batches . . . There were 600 or 700 in all, though some put the figure as high as 800 or 900. (461)

Ahmad makes another claim about the Prophet's marriages with Jewish women: "Muhammad tried to strengthen his negotiated peace with the state of Khaybar by the same sign of goodwill. He took Safiah in marriage and thus sealed his alliance with the most important Jewish power in the Hijaz" (124). In the first place, one wonders why Ahmad calls it an "alliance" rather than an acceptance by the vanquished of the terms imposed by the victor – 50 percent of the agricultural yield of the vanquished. And how can this relationship be called an "alliance," when a key provision of the imposed terms stipulated that Muhammad was entitled to expel the Jews from Khaybar any time he wished? (Ibn Hisham, p. 516). Secondly, how can Muhammad's taking of Safiah as his wife be a sign of goodwill, when he had just tortured and murdered her husband Kinana and her brother-in-law? Furthermore, as we saw earlier in William Muir's analysis of the event, Safiah's reputation as a great beauty, and the fact that the Prophet sent for her immediately following Kinana's execution, suggests that Muhammad's motive in destroying Kinana was the desire to obtain his wife (Muir, IV, 68). But Ahmad concludes his study without providing any evidence for his notion that no massacre of the Qurayza had occurred, and that Muhammad's taking of Rayhana and Safiah were diplomatic marriages and signs of goodwill.

## Muhammad and the Jews: G. D. Newby's Re-Examination of the Evidence

Newby implicitly agrees with our sociological argument that Muhammad's move from Mecca to Medina, the Hijrah of 622 CE, was a watershed event in the life and career of the Prophet. It was a turning point, as we have argued, because, if he had remained in the city of his birth and had failed to receive the opportunity for the Hijrah, it is a near certainty that a world-historical religion would never have resulted from his efforts. The Hijrah, far from being a voluntary act on Muhammad's part, was a necessary move owing to the growing hostility toward him by his fellow Meccans, some of whom went so far as to attempt to kill him. His early converts were few in number and persecuted to the extent that they had to seek refuge in Abyssinia. Moreover, Muhammad's last-resort attempt to find favor in Taif, Mecca's sister-city, was a total failure. Newby reminds us that while there is some debate among scholars concerning the reasons for Muhammad's sending his followers to Abyssinia, it seems clear that he wished to place emerging Islam in the Byzantine–Abyssinian camp. This was made possible, as noted earlier, by the considerable resemblance between Muhammad's teachings and elements of Byzantine–Abyssinian Christianity – so strong a resemblance, indeed, that Muhammad's followers who fled to Abyssinia may have been perceived as a Christian sect.

Muhammad's opportunity to migrate to Medina emerged when a few members of a polytheistic Arab tribe, the Banu Qaylah, better known by the two branch names, the Banu Aus and the Banu Khazraj, came to Mecca for the annual fair. Traditions relate that the Banu Qaylah had come to Medina from Yemen sometime in the middle of the sixth century CE and settled among the inhabitants, most of whom were Jewish. Originally sub-ordinate to the Jewish tribes, the B. Qaylah had to settle on agricultural land of lesser quality. In time, competition over scarce natural resources put them at odds with the Jewish inhabitants, and in the resulting conflicts the Arab tribe gained a measure of independence from the Jews, and perhaps even dominance.

Newby proposes that, "For the Aus and the Khazraj, linking their fate with Muhammad's rising fortunes would have been seen as a means toward further independence from the Jewish control of the city of Medina."[4] This proposition of Newby's might require a corrective, in that Muhammad was experiencing no rising fortunes at that moment. On the contrary, he was experiencing serious setbacks and discouragement. What Muhammad pos-sessed, however, despite the setbacks, was a reputation that had gone before him as a prophet and perhaps even as a messianic figure. A more likely expla-nation, then, of the Arab individuals' motives and aims in inviting Muhammad to Medina, is their having learned of his reputation. In their interactions and conversations with the Jews, members of the Arab tribes would have learned about Jewish eschatological beliefs, and their hopes and expectations for the coming of a Messiah. Given the apparent fact that Muhammad's reputation as a prophet had spread beyond Mecca during the years of his proselytizing, it is highly probable that the Arab members who met him at the fair, and invited him to Medina, wished to win him over to their cause before the Jews got to him first. In their conveyance of Jewish eschatological beliefs, the Jews might have asserted that the coming Messiah will first liberate them; but they might also have told their Arab interlocutors, that a universal deliverance would follow, as envisioned, perhaps, by Isaiah. Hence, the Arabs who negotiated with Muhammad may have reasoned that if they got to him in time, it is the Arabs who will first prosper and gain power.

Newby reviews the complexity of the Medinan social structure, the numerous clans, their mutual hostility, and the long war ending with the Battle of Buath shortly before the Hijra. The war had left everyone exhausted but not at peace. Earlier scholars had treated the Aus and the Khazraj as if each had been a distinct and unified tribe. But Newby, basing himself on more recent research, speaks of *clans* as armed camps, and agri-cultural land jealously guarded against raids by hostile neighbors. Tribal affiliations were weak, if not totally fictitious, and the cramped space of the oasis exacerbated the mutual hatreds. Jews and non-Jews formed alliances that were abandoned when one or another found an agreement to be no longer in its interest. Factors of location and occupation, Newby notes, were apparently as important as religion and tribal heritage in some of the alliances.

Newby now makes an observation that implicitly tends to support the cogency of our sociological argument concerning the significance of the Hijra. He points out that the agreement the Aus and the Khazraj had made with Muhammad allowed some seventy of his followers to precede him to Medina. These became guests in the homes of the Medinans who had, evidently, "accepted Muhammad on both religious and political grounds, although it is not clear to what extent religion played a part in the acceptance of Muhammad by the majority of the Aus and Khazraj. It appears most likely that Muhammad's appeal was as an arbiter among the warring factions in the town, which would fit perceptions that some had of him in Mecca" (80). In an endnote Newby explains why there were such perceptions: "Muhammad was called a *kahin* in Mecca by some of his detractors. Not only did this imply that he was a mantic seer, capable of giving minor prophecies in *saj*, 'rhymed prose'; it also meant that he could act as an intermediary in disputes as he had done when he cleverly solved the problem of replacing the cornerstone in the Kaaba by having a representative of each tribe lift the stone in place while holding onto a blanket in which it was wrapped, thus preventing any one of them from claiming priority over another" (146–7, n. 7).

Newby reminds us that after Muhammad's arrival in Medina, sources tell us of a treaty, or several treaties, called by Western scholars, the "Constitution of Medina," that established Muhammad in a central, leadership role in Medinan society. From Ibn Ishaq we learn that the Prophet made an agreement with the *Muhajirun*, those who had come from Mecca with Muhammad on the Hijra, and the *Ansar*, the "Helpers" of Medina who supported them. Included in this agreement in the form conveyed by Ibn Ishaq, were the Jews of the city, although a serious question remains about which Jews, and when the agreement was made. Ibn Ishaq dated the agreement at the beginning of Muhammad's stay in Medina, and later Muslim historians agreed. But Newby alerts us, to the fact, that by dating what was purportedly a general agreement with all of the Jews of Medina early, Muhammad was credited with an honor and power he acquired only later; the importance of the early dating being that subsequent Jewish opposition to Muhammad could thereby be characterized as a violation of the agreement, thus justifying his retaliations against them.

Newby draws our attention to two questions about the agreement, its authenticity and its dating. He cites Moshe Gil's well-known article, "The Constitution of Medina: A Reconsideration," where Gil convincingly argues for the unity and authenticity of the document, supporting observations made by some earlier scholars, that non-Muslims are included in the *ummah*, that Ibn Ishaq appears to make no corrections or interpolations, and that Muhammad is presented as occupying a relatively minor position. In response to Gil's view, however, some scholars have asked, if the document is authentic, why then are not all the Jews and Arabs mentioned in the document? And what is the relationship between this document and the tradition cited by al-Waqidi, that Muhammad had made a pact with *all* the Jews, which they are alleged to have subsequently broken? Newby now proceeds to offer an adequate response to these questions.

While still in Mecca, Muhammad may very well have believed that Jews and Christians would recognize him as a prophet and embrace his message, given his apparent self-understanding as a prophet in the line of Jewish prophets. And in Medina, as he was invited to serve as judge and mediator, he felt he had the authority to legislate both for his group of Muslims and for the Jews. Newby cites Quranic passages to make his case. In the fifth chapter of the Quran, for example, we find outlines of dietary laws, laws of inter-confessional marriage, and ritual hygiene. In verse 5 we read: "Today the good things are made lawful for you. The food of those who have been given the Scripture is lawful for you, and your food is lawful for them." That this is stated with the Jews in mind is confirmed by verse 7, where the audience is told, "Remember the kindness of God to you and His covenant by which He bound you, and you said, 'We hear and we obey.'" Newby remarks how dietary laws, historically, tended to bind Jews together while separating them from non-Jews. It therefore seems reasonable to suppose that Muhammad intended to use the same method to unify his new community. From the standpoint of Muhammad's legislation Jews could be included in the *ummah* if they accepted his definition of *kashrut*.

That Muhammad might have discerned a fundamental harmony between Islam and Judaism is further attested by the common observance of the fast on the tenth of the month of Tishri, the Yom Kippur fast, which was eventually replaced by the month-long fast of Ramadan, but not abrogated. Early Muslims, as we have seen, prayed facing Jerusalem along with the Jews, and some Muslims continued to read the Torah along with the Quran in their devotionals. Moreover, Muslim ideas about the sanctuary at Mecca, seem to have emerged in a Jewish environment. To support this proposition, Newby cites the relevant scholarly debate. In an 1982 article, Gerald Hawting addressed the old issue of the origins of the Muslim sanctuary at Mecca and challenged the notions of the similarities between Muslim sanctuary ideas and those of Judaism. Hawting rejected as unconvincing the explanations put forth by both Dozy and Snouck Hurgronje. Dozy's argument for successive migrations of Jews into Arabia from a time even before the establishment of Jerusalem as a Jewish sanctuary was successfully replaced by Snouck Hurgronje's arguments, that the acceptance of the Meccan sanctuary was a result of Muhammad's rejection by the Jews. Hawting argues, instead:

> It seems that the Muslim sanctuary at Mecca is the result of a sort of com-
> promise between a pre-existing pagan sanctuary and sanctuary ideas which
> had developed first in a Jewish milieu. I envisage that Muslim sanctuary ideas
> originated first in a Jewish matrix, as did Islam itself . . . It seems likely that
> the Meccan sanctuary was chosen only after the elimination of other possi-
> bilities – that in the early Islamic period a number of possible sanctuary sites
> gained adherents until finally Mecca became established as the Muslim sanc-
> tuary. And it also seems likely that one reason for the adoption of the Meccan
> sanctuary was that it did approximate to the sanctuary ideas which had
> already been formed – although they had to be reformulated, the physical
> facts of the Meccan sanctuary did not mean that already existing notions and
> terminology had to be abandoned . . . The Muslim sanctuary at Mecca
> should no longer be regarded as simply a remnant of Arab paganism. (cited
> by Newby, p. 84)

Newby proceeds to explore the significance of Hawting's proposition. First, the Jewish rejection of Muhammad's message in Medina prompted him neither toward an accommodation of pre-Islamic paganism, nor to a general condemnation of Jews and Judaism. Second, Muhammad appears to have continued to act within categories shared with the Jews of the Hijaz, even after he and his message were attacked by them. For Newby, what is fundamental in Muhammad's message is that

> Muhammad appeared to himself and to some others as a genuine continu-
> ation of the process of divine revelation; he was not crassly "accommodat-
> ing" to the Jews to try to win them over, only to abandon them in the face
> of opposition. Such cynicism falls short when it comes to explaining
> Muhammad's appeal and successes. Islam and Judaism in Arabia during
> Muhammad's lifetime were operating in the same sphere of religious dis-
> course: the same fundamental questions were discussed from similar per-
> spectives; moral and ethical values were similar; and both religions shared the
> same religious characters, stories and anecdotes. We can see this when we
> look at the implied context of the Quranic message. There is no expectation
> that the stories we call biblical are anything but familiar to the Arabian lis-
> teners, whether they are pagan, Jewish, or Christian. And to this argument
> we must also add the element of paganism. Not only is there the implication
> from the Quran that pagans knew the Jewish, Christian, and Muslim stories,
> but it is also implied that Jews, Christians, and Muslims knew the pagan

stories. When there was disagreement, as between Muhammad and the Jews, the disagreement was over interpretation of shared topics, not over two mutually exclusive views of the world. (84–5)

Newby argues that Muhammad had earlier expected to convert the Jews and that this expectation was not unreasonable in the light of his aim of reforming the Abrahamic heritage among the Jews and Christians of Arabia. There were in fact very few Jews who accepted Muhammad's message, and Newby is probably right to assume that even the very few such converts served to raise the level of anxiety in the Jewish communities. Newby convincingly proposes that Jewish opposition to Muhammad appears to be a combination of religious and political motives which were not separated in the minds of either the Jews or the Arabs. Indeed, it was the fusion of Muhammad's political–military and prophetic roles in Medina that eventually accounted for his success. For it was after the "miraculous" victory of the Muslims over the Quraysh at Badr that Muhammad gained considerable prestige in Medina and among the surrounding Bedouin tribes, a prestige he soon transformed into political power. The victory at Badr, however, was followed by a raid on the Muslims by Abu Sufyan, the Meccan commander. According to Muslim traditions, it was the leaders of the Banu Nadir who hosted Abu Sufyan and his raiders, supplying him with up-to-date intelligence about the Muslim forces. Although the raid itself was militarily insignificant, it revealed the relationship between the Jewish tribe, B. Nadir, and Muhammad's Meccan enemy. The Jewish public rhetoric against Muhammad together with the B. Nadir's secret dealings with his enemies, compelled him to act decisively, and to show that he was not weakened by the Meccan attacks. Ibn Ishaq reports that the Jewish tribe, the B. Qaynuqa, were the first to abrogate what was between them and the messenger of God. Ibn Ishaq fails to explain the cause of the breach, but Ibn Hisham tells the story with which we are now familiar, that some Jewish men of the B. Qaynuqa pinned the skirt of an Arab woman while she was seated in their market, so that when she stood up her nudity was exposed. A Muslim who was present took revenge on the Jew responsible for the prank, by killing him; and the Jews retaliated afterward, killing the Muslim.

Although W. Montgomery Watt asserts that the B. Qaynuqa were besieged in their strongholds and then expelled, Barakat Ahmad contends that the expulsion of the B. Qaynuqa never took place during Muhammad's lifetime. Following Ibn Ishaq and Ibn Hisham, he observes that only al-Waqidi introduced the expulsion feature of the story, and that two famous Hadiths date the expulsion after Muhammad's death. For

Muhammad, Ahmad argues, the defeat of the Qaynuqa and the confiscation of their arms sufficed, because he succeeded in separating them from their allies, while none of the other Jewish groups came to their defense. Newby believes that Ahmad's argument is further strengthened by the traditions reporting that the needy *Muhajirun* were not given confiscated land until after the expulsion of the B. Nadir.

As the Jewish resistance to Muhammad continued, it took the form of a propaganda campaign. As we learned earlier, poetry fulfilled the function of journalism in Arabia, informing, but also inciting, and serving as the opening salvo in battle. One of the Jewish leaders, Kaab al-Ashraf, whose mother was from the B. Nadir, wrote a poem that was intended to be vulgar and insulting, the offensive nature of which ensured that it would be broadcast. Muhammad's reaction was predictable anger, and he asked, "Who will rid me of Ibn al-Ashraf?" The volunteer was Muhammad b. Maslama, who became one of the first secret assassins in the Muslim force. Evidently, he was urged to fill that role by Saad b. Muadh, the leader of the B. Abd al-Ashal, the man who effectively brought about their conversion to Islam. He served as Muhammad's personal bodyguard at Badr, and urged the slaying of all the Quraysh. Described as a man of bad temper, he is the individual who played a key role in the massacre of the men of the B. Qurayza. So this Maslama devised a plot, gained permission from Muhammad to tell lies in order to gain entry to Kaab, and murdered him. This act cast terror among the Jews, and according to Ibn Ishaq, Muhammad followed this with a blanket order to "kill any Jew who falls into your power."

The battle of Badr was a delightful surprise for the Muslims who had never expected victory over a military force twice the size of their own. Their victory, Muhammad assured them, was due to God having been on their side. But in Muhammad's next major military encounter, the famous battle outside Medina around the hill of Uhud, the Muslims were routed when they thought Muhammad had been killed; they regrouped, however, and managed to hold off the Meccan army that somehow had failed to pursue its early advantage when it had it. Although the result of the battle was certainly no victory, neither was it interpreted as a defeat by Muhammad, since the Muslims had demonstrated that they could not be eliminated by the largest army the Meccans could mobilize.

We now come to the chain of events that led to the expulsion of the B. Nadir and the even more tragic end of the B. Qurayza. According to Barakat Ahmad, whose work we discussed earlier, when Muhammad approached the B. Qurayza and the B. Nadir for a renewal of the mutual non-aggression pact, the B. Nadir refused. Ibn Ishaq reports that Muhammad had asked the B. Nadir to pay the blood-money due under the existing agreement, which they refused. According to custom, blood–money or a blood–fine was paid when one was responsible for the killing of an individual. Muhammad had assumed responsibility for two murders committed by one of his followers, and set about collecting funds. Among those in Medina whom he approached for contributions were the B. Nadir, but as they had had nothing at all to do with the murders, they saw no good reason for making a contribution. Ibn Ishaq also relates that the B. Nadir had plotted to drop a rock on Muhammad's head, but he was divinely forewarned and saved from assassination. Newby agrees that the conjectures found in the sources leads one to the conclusion that the explanations for Muhammad's assault upon the B. Nadir are after-the-fact justifications for his move against them. As we have already learned, the B. Nadir were forced into their strongholds where they were besieged by Muhammad's troops. They had been promised support by the B. Awf, a group within the B. Khazraj, but the support never materialized and the Nadir were forced to surrender. In the terms of their capitulation, they were to be expelled from Medina, and allowed to take with them only such goods as they could carry on camelback, except, of course, weapons of war. Reports concerning this event relate that they dismantled their houses and carried away the doors and the lintels, departing with great pomp. The tribe's land was then distributed to the *Muhajirun*, thus eliminating their dependency on the *Ansar*. As Newby remarks, "by the fourth year after the Hijrah, Muhammad had neutralized the B. Qaynuqa and deported the B. Nadir. That left only the B. Qurayza as a major block of Jewish opposition" (90).

In the fifth year of the Hijra, the Meccans mobilized a huge military force with the aim of crushing Muhammad and his followers once and for all. Muhammad's forces may have been outnumbered by as much as three to one. In this so-called Battle of the Trench, as we have seen, the Muslims, on the advice of a Persian, adopted the stratagem of digging a ditch around the unprotected areas of the city thus succeeding in the repulsion of the Meccan invaders. As word spread of Muhammad's success, the Meccan alliance of neighboring allies and large Bedouin tribes proceeded to crumble. Now was the time, Muhammad decided, to remove the last obstacle to his total control of Medina, the B. Qurayza. According to Ibn Ishaq, Gabriel appeared to the apostle, with the message that Allah commands him to go to the B. Qurayza, for He is about to shake their stronghold. With this divine sanction, according to Ibn Ishaq, Muhammad deployed the recently victorious Muslim army around the strongholds of the B. Qurayza, forcing them to surrender unconditionally. They had requested the same terms as those granted to the B. Nadir, but were denied them; and because they were outnumbered, without allies and besieged in a stronghold in which, as we have seen, there were women, children, elderly and sick individuals, in addition to the male warriors, they had to submit to whatever Muhammad decided.

The B. Aws entreated with Muhammad that he deal with the B. Qurayza as he had with the B. Qaynuqa, who had been allies of the B. Khazraj. Tribal pride and rivalry demanded that each component of the *Ansar* be treated equally, and the Aws did not want it said that they were less able to protect their allies than their rivals. In response to the Aws' request, Muhammad persuaded them to agree to his appointing a *hakam*, a judge, from among them. When they agreed, he appointed Saad b. Muadh – whom we heard about earlier, as a man of bad temper who had urged the slaying of all the Quraysh. Newby recognizes, therefore, that Muhammad ". . . must have been certain that Saad's judgment would be harsh, and in line with the Prophet's wishes. And, since Saad was not only one of the Aws but had been wounded at Uhud, there was little that anyone could do to speak against the choice. They could only urge him to treat their allies with kindness. Saad replied, 'the time has come for Saad, in the cause of God, not to care for any man's censure.' After obtaining the explicit permission that they would abide by his decision, Saad ordered that the men should be killed, the property divided, and the women and children taken as captives. Muhammad supported the judgment by saying that it had come from God 'above the seven heavens.' It is reported that anywhere from 400 to over 900 adult males were killed and buried in trenches in the market of Medina" (92).

Newby's review of the evidence tends to support Ibn Hisham's account, which we cited earlier. The women and children of the B. Qurayza were sold into slavery to purchase horses and weapons for the Muslims, and Muhammad chose one woman, Rayhana, who is said to have remained with him until she died. Some of the women and children were ransomed by Jews in Medina, Khaybar, Tayma, and Wadi al-Qura. The tribe of the B. Qurayza was destroyed, thus eliminating all organized Jewish opposition to Muhammad in Medina. A small number of Jews seem, nevertheless, to have remained in the city. Muhammad, having secured the city for Islam, could now turn his attention to other Jewish enclaves in the Hijaz.

Previously we noted that from the time of William Muir's study, if not earlier, Western scholars have viewed the mass execution of the men of the B. Qurayza as a barbarous act unworthy of one with claims to religious leadership. This has prompted what Newby describes as "some recent revisionist examinations of the topic by two Muslims, W. N. Arafat and Barakat Ahmad" (92). Ahmad, as we have seen, maintained that the massacre had never occurred, arguing that Muhammad's taking of Rayhana was a *diplomatic* marriage and gesture. Ahmad then asks the rhetorical question, what good would such a gesture have been, if Muhammad had actually destroyed the B. Qurayza. Newby, describing a work by M. J. Kister as a "penetrating and thorough survey of the sources," avers that Kister provides a convincing argument that the main outline of events as presented in the *Sirah* (biography) is correct, "even if there has been some embellishment by later authors. It should not come as a surprise that the massacre of the B. Qurayza took place as it did. The escalating tension between Muhammad and the Jews was bound to force a military confrontation. It is clear, however, that the underlying policy was not totally anti-Jewish, because Jews remained in the city of Medina and in the territories under Muhammad's control until after his death" (93).

The massacre of the B. Qurayza did not, however, bring to an end Jewish resistance in the Hijaz; it continued from the strongly fortified Jewish city of Khaybar. In the sixth year after the *Hijra* Muhammad concluded the agreement of Hudaybiyya. This came about, we recall, as Muhammad marched to the outskirts of Mecca with the proclaimed intention of making an *umra*, a "lesser pilgrimage." Stopped at the borders of the sacred territory surrounding Mecca, he negotiated a withdrawal from Mecca for a year, thus providing the Meccans with a face-saving clause. But the agreement stipulated that in the following year, Muhammad and his followers would be allowed to enter the city, which the Quraysh would, accordingly, vacate for three nights. As Newby aptly remarks, "Despite the face-saving clause of immediate withdrawal, the treaty of al-Hudaybiyya showed that Muhammad had won and that there was no longer any serious Meccan opposition possible" (94).

Several months later, in the seventh year, Muhammad besieged Khaybar. He now had no fear that the Meccans would come to the aid of their erstwhile allies, and no need to worry about a force at his back from Medina. As we have already learned, the economic basis of Khaybar's wealth was agriculture, and date-palms in particular, as was true of the other oasis towns in the Hijaz. Considerable expertise was required for artificial irrigation, horticulture and all the other skills needed for successful farming in the desert climate. Possessing these skills, the Jews were able to negotiate terms that allowed them to remain on their land in return for the payment to Muhammad of half the annual harvest. The Jewish town of Fadak capitulated on similar terms; and since it was not besieged or taken in warfare, it was not subject to the Muslim division-of-booty rules. So Muhammad kept the proceeds for himself. Newby avers that capitulation became a regular feature of "submission" agreements mentioned in the *Sirah*. "In a large sense," writes Newby, "Muhammad's actions became the paradigm for the later Muslim community and, when Islamic society was established outside Arabia with hegemony over large numbers of Jews and Christians, the models of capitulation in Arabia were used to regulate non-Muslim communal life. There is the charge that many of the capitulation traditions have been tendentiously shaped by later transmitters to reflect their desires for how things ought to be, but in the main it seems that Muhammad was willing to tolerate a non-Muslim population in his *ummah* as long as it was willing to submit to the Muslim will" (95).

# 11

# Concluding Sociological Reflections

If we reflect on the Medinan phase of Muhammad's career – the last ten years of his life – it seems indisputable that it was in the Medinan context that he achieved astounding success in laying the foundation for a world-historical, political-religious movement. And if we again employ the counter-factual, thought-experiment introduced earlier, and ask whether the Prophet might have achieved similar success by remaining in Mecca, the answer appears to be beyond doubt: Muhammad's followers would either have remained a minuscule sect, or have been absorbed by Judaism or Christianity, or have vanished altogether.

Earlier we introduced a sociological framework consisting of four factors or necessary pre-conditions for the successful transformation of a demo-graphically small sect, of a few hundred followers, into a mass movement. The four factors were: (1) widespread discontent; (2) ideology; (3) charis-matic leadership; and (4) organizational strategy and tactics. As applied to the Meccan phase of Muhammad's career, it appears to be a near certainty that *none* of the factors were operative so as to produce a mass movement. If discontent existed at all, it was restricted to a small minority of individuals drawn, for the most part, from the lowest strata of Meccan society. The religious ideology that Muhammad preached there appealed only to those "have-not" individuals. Indeed, this ideology, far from appealing to the majority, seemed, on the contrary, to threaten their religious sentiments and material interests. The majority of the Quraysh, or at least their leaders and spokesmen, feeling antagonized and provoked, proceeded to persecute the Muslims to the point of their seeking refuge in Abyssinia. As for the third factor, charismatic leadership, it follows from the fact that discontent was negligible and the ideology correspondingly ineffectual, that there were objective constraints on the power of the Prophet's personality. Finally, there is the factor of organization, including strategy and tactics. In Mecca, the Prophet preached and warned, but had no strategy beyond that.

If now we turn to the Prophet's Medinan phase, and assess the causal weight of the respective factors, we can see rather clearly that each factor actively contributed, so to speak, to the Prophet's success. *Discontent* at Medina was in fact widespread; it was discontent in the form of a prevalent sense of insecurity and unease, stemming from the bloody civil strife between the Aws and the Khazraj and their respective allies. The tribal conflicts at Medina and throughout the Hijaz were such, that the social life of the desert tribes was "solitary, poor, nasty, brutish and short," to use Hobbes' phrase to describe the condition that Ibn Khaldun had recognized long before him. There was no Hobbesian "common power" in the northern Peninsula that might have put an end to the tribal wars of each against all. When Hobbes says that in the absence of a common power war prevails, his meaning is not that fighting is literally incessant. He explains that the notion of time is as relevant to war as it is to weather: "For as the nature of Foule weather lyeth not in a showre or two of rain; but in an inclination thereto of many dayes together: So the nature of war, consisteth not in actual fighting; but in the known disposition thereto, during all the time there is no assurance to the contrary. All other times is peace" (ch. 13, 89).

When Muhammad arrived at Medina, it was in a Hobbesian state of war, a condition in which all vitally necessary and worthwhile human activities were uncertain. This was the indispensable *opportunity* for Muhammad's success. If the Aus and/or the Khazraj had not learned from the Jews about their eschatological hopes for the coming of the Messiah; and if those men of the Arab tribes had not entertained the notion that the Prophet of Mecca might be that Messiah; and if they had not hastened to meet Muhammad and to invite him to Medina as a mediator with magisterial powers, it is almost certain that he would have had no other opportunity to migrate with his followers and find a favorable position from which to rethink things, adopt a new strategy and revitalize his mission.

Medina presented Muhammad with a new opportunity, a new starting point and a new organizational strategy. For the Prophet was now compelled to reflect – more carefully than ever before – on the tribal quarrels that prevailed in the Arabian Peninsula. If, therefore, we state what Muhammad reflected upon in Ibn–Khaldunian–Hobbesian terms, it must have been the fundamental disunity of the Arab–Bedouin tribes, each standing in the posture of an armed gladiator against every other; each with a strongly particularistic *asabiya* or "group feeling," but without any overarching, pan-Arabian *asabiya*. For Muhammad, then, the question, task and project was how to overcome the divisiveness and how to create a new, pan-Arabian "group feeling" or solidarity. What such solidarity presupposed, of course, was putting an end to the "war of each against all" of the tribes; and what was required for putting an end to that war, was the Hobbesian *conditio sine qua non*: a common power that would keep them all in awe.

It was now that Muhammad began gradually to create the "common power" by propagating his new religious ideology as an *armed* prophet, and by performing the functions of lawgiver, religious leader, chief magistrate, commander of the army, and civil head of an incipient state – all in one. And it was in this context that Muhammad, as the Prophet of Allah, acquired charisma – a gift of grace – and became a charismatic leader with the corresponding authority. The task of unifying required a new strategy and new tactics. The *Muhajirun* or Emigrants were poor, with no secure source of livelihood; and the *Ansar* Muhammad's Medinan supporters, even had they been willing, could not indefinitely have sustained the emigrants with the necessities of life. So Muhammad urged the Emigrants to adopt the sole remaining option, raiding merchant caravans. As we have learned from Ibn Khaldun and others, raiding, for the desert Arabs, was a "natural," morally acceptable occupation. These raids, under Muhammad's leadership, and especially the victory over the Meccans at Badr, enhanced the stature of the Prophet and increased the wealth, power and prestige of the *Ummah* in Medina. The Muslim warriors won much booty, and their success was interpreted by the Prophet as a manifestation of Allah's favor.

The battle of Badr was viewed as a turning point, as one senses from the Medinan revelations in the Quran as compared with those of Mecca, the Medinan dealing with practical, political questions, such as how to distribute the booty. The Muslim victory made possible an aggressive policy toward the Jews and, eventually, also toward the Christians whom Muhammad now charged with having falsified their own scriptures in order to conceal the prophecies foretelling his emergence. As compared with his career in Mecca, Muhammad was now clearly preaching a religious ideology deliberately designed to appeal first to the Arabs, and to serve, together with the material rewards gained from raiding, as the means of creating in the Peninsula a pan-Arabian "group feeling" or solidarity. The Arab-centered nature of the new religion that slowly took shape in Medina becomes all too evident in Muhammad's retention of virtually all of the pre-Islamic religious institutions – Allah, the Kaaba, pilgrimages, the Black Stone, Mecca, Ramadan – but imparting to them a new, monotheistic meaning. Therein lay the Prophet's originality.

There was one more salient ideological and practical–political development during the late Medinan phase of the Prophet's career. This is best brought out by reviewing briefly events we have already touched upon. In the spring of 628 Muhammad felt that his forces were strong enough for an assault on Mecca. On the way, however, he came to realize that the attempt might be premature, so he converted the expedition into a peaceful pilgrimage. He and other Muslim leaders met Meccan negotiators at a place called Hudaybiya, near the sacred area around Mecca, in which, according to strict pre-Islamic customs, no fighting was to take place in certain months of the year. There a pact was reached in which Meccans and Muslims were to be treated on equal terms. This treaty effectively ended the war with Muhammad's people, the Quraysh, and gave the Muslims the right to perform the pilgrimage to Mecca in the following year and to stay there for three days. Apparently, however, there was among the Prophet's more zealous warriors considerable dissatisfaction with this meager result.

How, then, did Muhammad deal with this dissatisfaction? In quite the same way that he had earlier dealt with the murmurs of restlessness among his chief warriors. As a rule, it was after a victory or a temporary setback or during a lull in fighting, that it became Muhammad's policy to attack the communities of the Jewish tribes – the Banu Qaynuqa, the Banu Nadir, and the Banu Qurayza. Now in the face of the murmuring after Hudaybiya he resolved to go after the Jewish oasis of Khaybar. Ibn Khaldun's theory is once again pertinent. For the Muslim victory at Khaybar, though incomplete, marked the first interaction between the Muslim State and a conquered, non-Muslim people; and the imposition upon the Jews of the tribute, formed a precedent for later conquests of settled peoples. It is in that sense that Muhammad's assaults upon the Jewish communities constituted a "dress rehearsal," for the Muslim conquests and dealings of the era following the death of the Prophet.

For Ibn Khaldun, we shall recall, "Both Bedouins and sedentary people are natural groups" (I, 249). In the context of the Prophet's Medina, the Arab–Bedouins were a natural group; and the Jews, as the only sedentary, agricultural people in the area, constituted the other natural group. What Ibn Khaldun means by "natural groups" is that owing to the distinctive social and economic conditions of sedentary peoples and Bedouins, it becomes second nature for the respective groups to lead the ways of life characteristic of them. The way of life of the Bedouin is to raid, and the way of life of the settled, agricultural people is to till the soil, to engage in arts and crafts, and to try to protect themselves by constructing fortified habitations.

In pre-Islamic Arabia, where there was no intertribal unity, and where tribal particularism and a Hobbesian "war of each against all" prevailed among the Bedouin tribes, the respective "natural groups" of the Hijaz found a *modus vivendi*: tribes raided and robbed, but the settled peoples could still survive and even prosper, often by coopting a tribe and making it worth its while materially to desist from attacking the community, or to serve as a client, protecting the settled people from other marauders. In such circumstances – that is, in pre-Islamic Arabia – the "natural groups" were "naturally" inclined to "live and let live"; the strongholds of the Jews tended to suffice for their protection and security; and the raiding way of life tended to suffice for the provision of a subsistence-level livelihood for the Bedouins. Indeed, there prevailed a symbiotic relationship between the desert and the sown.

But with the rise and development of Islam in Medina and its environs, the Khaldunian interplay between desert and sown underwent a fundamental change. As Ibn Khaldun reflected on the rise of Islam, he came to understand that a new religion can establish itself only by strife, and will succeed only if it enlists the support of a powerful, social solidarity; and once established, a new religion can greatly reinforce social solidarity, mend tribal divisions, at least temporarily, and create larger and larger solidarities by mobilizing and concentrating men's wills and emotions around a common purpose. The combination of religion and intertribal solidarity is formidable, and to it Ibn Khaldun attributed the sweeping conquests of the Muslim Arabs in the seventh century.

The difference, then, between the pre-Islamic and the Islamic interplay of desert and sown lay in the fact that the "live and let live" attitude was replaced first by the attitude of conquer and expel, and then of conquer and kill. That became Muhammad's policy first toward the Banu Qaynuqa and the Banu Nadir, and then toward the Banu Qurayza, whose men were massacred – an action apparently unheard of in pre-Islamic Arabia, and thus a Muhammaden novelty in the Peninsula. In these new circumstances, even the best fortified Jewish communities, such as those of Khaybar, acquired a vulnerability they had never had before. The confrontation between the desert and the sown under Muhammad was no longer an interplay in which the poorer Bedouins felt justified in making their living by raiding the prosperous settlements and robbing some of their goods. No, it now became, under Muhammad, a deadly quarrel in which conquest and tribute was the aim, and killing or the threat of it, the means. In these terms, Muhammad's deal with the Khaybar Jews was, in fact, a precedent and model for Islam's early conquests.

Moreover, as Ibn Khaldun observed, the Prophet's political practice gave rise to a religious corollary:

> In the Muslim community [he wrote] the holy war is a religious duty, because of the universalism of the Muslim mission and the obligation to convert everybody to Islam either by persuasion or by force. (I, 473)

In citing this passage, the point is not to propose that "holy war" is an "essential" or eternal trait of the Islamic faith. However, Ibn Khaldun's statement may, at the very least, be interpreted as a valid characterization of Islam's religio-political ideal in the era of her early conquests. This ideal followed logically, it seems, from the belief in only one God, a belief implying that there can be only one political sovereign and one law on earth. The Muslim State may tolerate unbelievers under its rule, as long as they are not polytheists, and follow one of the permitted religions such as Judaism or Christianity. But the Muslim State may not recognize the permanent existence of a non-Islamic polity. It seems, therefore, to be a valid historically specific characterization of the Islamic ideal in the period of the early conquests, that all humankind must accept Islam or submit to Muslim rule. It was the moral duty of Muslims to struggle until this was accomplished. This duty is called *jihad* in Arabic, meaning "effort" or "striving." For an adequate understanding of Islam's early conquests, it is, therefore, necessary to recognize that their animating spirit was inspired by the theory and practice of the Prophet.

It is Fred M. Donner who has made a highly significant contribution to our knowledge by documenting the extent to which Islam's early conquests were a continuation and application of Muhammad's theory and practice in Medina.[1] Donner fully recognizes the causal priority of Medina and Muhammad's role there, in explaining how Islam became a world movement and militant polity. For it was Muhammad's initiative in striving to create a unified Islamic community, or *umma*, in Medina and its environs, that eventually acquired a revolutionary significance in the Arabian Peninsula and beyond. Unique in the idea of the *umma* was the uncompromising monotheism of the Islamic community, which by its active rejection of polytheism, laid claim to the bodies *and* souls of the entire Arabian populace. The *umma* claimed to be the community of believers in the one and universal God. The one universal God implied that the *umma* must also become universal, which, in turn, implied that it must continue to expand until it has converted the entire pagan population, if not the whole of humankind. The growing acceptance of this idea was bound to prove quite effectual in developing a conquest movement of a political and religious character.

Membership in the *umma* as a monotheistic religious community, gradually implanted a new individual consciousness. For belonging to the *umma* meant loyalty to a community greater than one's tribe or kinship group. Because there was only one Islamic *umma*, breaking from it was not only a social or political act, but a moral act as well. Breaking ties with the *umma* was an offense against God and man, a sin and a crime. The teachings of Muhammad and the Quran posited a divine law and an absolute higher authority. The *umma* was to be the embodiment of that authority, regulating the lives of the members by a set of rules transcending the boundaries of tribal identity. Islam's strict monotheism made it easier, most likely, to accept the idea of one single locus of political authority in the realm of worldly affairs. Donner cites the fact that some of the separate documents forming the "Constitution of Medina" conclude with the phrase, "whenever you differ about a matter, it must be referred to God and Muhammad." "Implicitly," Donner observes, "Muhammad was in a position to claim absolute religious and political authority in the *umma*, and, indeed, over the whole world" (61). But however strong a Muslim's attachment to Muhammad might have been, one's primary allegiance was to Islam, to God and to the *umma* as the manifestation of God's will for man. So although Muhammad played a key role in the centralization of power in the *umma*, it did not prevent the transfer of authority after his death, because ultimate authority resided not in him, but in the community as a whole and the divine law that guided it. Hence, the creation of the *umma*, with the concept of absolute divine authority, provided the ideological foundation for the institutions of an incipient state hitherto unknown in the region. And it was in Medina and only in Medina where Muhammad found it possible to rise in power and to consolidate it.

Donner discerns several phases in the process of consolidation, the first being the struggle to establish himself firmly as the ruler of Medina, against the opposition of the groups resident in the oasis, notably, of course, the Jewish clans of the Qaynuqa, Nadir, and Qurayza. The second phase in Muhammad's political career was his struggle to humble the Quraysh of his native city, in the battles of Badr, Uhud, and the Trench, and his ultimate success in conquering Mecca. The third phase in Muhammad's struggle to consolidate his power becomes evident in his relations with nomadic groups, first in Medina's vicinity and increasingly farther afield. It seems clear that toward the end of his career, nomadic groups found that they had to come to terms with the new Islamic State because it now controlled the main agricultural and market centers in the Hijaz – Medina, Khaybar, and Taif – on which the nomads depended.

Donner reminds us that Muhammad was a skilled diplomat when it came to winning over certain important individuals and groups of a former enemy. He granted gifts and larger shares of booty, as after the victory at Hunayn, even shocking his old supporters by favoring the new converts. The Prophet knew, too, how to use promises of official posts in the new Islamic regime. Despite the long opposition and late conversion of the members of his own tribe, Muhammad nevertheless appointed several Qurayshis to key positions as military commanders, governors and close advisers. Some of these prominent members of the Quraysh may, in fact, have embraced Islam in return for a direct commitment from Muhammad to bring them into the upper circles of power in the new Islamic State.

Donner calls attention to a fundamental element of the emerging state, the introduction and implementation of a centralized system for the collection of taxes and the administration of justice. It was Muhammad himself who had set in motion the process of creating a centralized state authority in the Peninsula. And with centralization came a new, Muslim ruling elite. As the originally small Islamic community grew gradually into a State, conquering Jewish and Christian areas, the vanquished non-Muslims who were brought under the authority of the Islamic State, paid tribute in exchange for protection and decent treatment by their new overlords. Donner cites as the beginning of this tributary system the predominantly Jewish oasis of Khaybar in the northern Hijaz, and the large Christian community at Najran in the northern Yemen.

Quite striking about the new State and its political elite, is the new policy toward the nomadic groups. The rise of a Hijazi ruling elite meant a direct dominance over nomadic groups, and their subordination, within the State's sphere, to the sedentary groups that constituted the elite. It was, evidently, a deliberate policy of Muhammad's to bring nomadic groups under the firm control of the Islamic State. Muhammad appears to have required nomadic groups who embraced Islam, to abandon their nomadic way of life and to settle permanently in Medina – that is, to make a *hijra* of their own. Only those who agreed to settle were promised full rights with other Muslims. Although Donner provides no explanation for this new policy, it seems that one plausible reason for it was the Prophet's recognition that there was no other way to counteract the particularistic and centrifugal forces of the nomadic way of life. It is as if Muhammad had anticipated the Ibn–Khaldunian–Hobbesian insight, that it is only by means of instituting a "common power" that the centrifugal can be turned into centripetal forces. Muhammad accordingly barred powerful nomadic chieftains from the emerging political elite. This process of gaining control over the nomads was accentuated with the ascension of the Quraysh after the conquest of Mecca. If we follow Donner's lucid and, indeed, profound analysis, we can see the new Islamic State, with its ruling elite, producing three types of domination: (1) the hegemony of Muslims over non-Muslims; (2) the dominance of a preponderantly Hijazi ruling elite over other tribal groups; and (3) the hegemony of a sophisticated sedentary elite over nomadic groups (81).

## Abu Bakr and the *Ridda*

Muhammad's death in 632 plunged the new Islamic State into a crisis of succession, raising the question of who now will lead the *umma*. The *ridda*, meaning secession or apostasy, refers to the fact that several or perhaps even many tribes who earlier had sworn allegiance to Muhammad, took that to mean that their contract was with him *personally*. Even in his lifetime they resisted paying *zakah*, or tax, to the central government in Medina. Now that the Prophet was dead, it seemed logical to them that their obligations had come to an end and that they were no longer subject to taxation. It is likely that one of the underlying motives of the secessionists was their resentment of the rising hegemony of the Hijaz capital. The old and traditional centrifugal forces of Arabian nomadic life were once again expressing themselves. To allow those forces to gather momentum would mean, ultimately, the dissolution of the *umma* and the death of Muhammad's vision. Rising to the challenge, Muhammad's successor, Abu Bakr, mobilized a formidable force and demanded from the "seceders" unconditional surrender or war unto destruction. Khalid ibn-al-Walid, the hero of these wars, had within some six months of his generalship, reduced the tribes of central Arabia to submission. The *ridda* represented a massive challenge to Islamic domination of the Arabian Peninsula, and victory under Abu Bakr completed the process of political and military consolidation of the Islamic State. By the time of his death, the new Islamic regime had successfully conquered the entire Arabian Peninsula.

Donner argues that the *ridda* wars were therefore the culmination of the process of political consolidation that Muhammad had begun. It was the process in which an Islamic ruling elite gained full control over the tribal population of the entire Arabian Peninsula. Included in that process was the success of the sedentary sector of the new State in attaining virtually complete control over the nomadic elements, a remarkable achievement in the light of their long, historical success in avoiding such domination (89). Although Donner nowhere mentions Ibn Khaldun in his study, it is apparent that his theory of the interplay of the desert and the sown has a continuing relevance to what Donner calls the "foundations of conquest." Muhammad initiated a process culminating in the victory of the sown over the desert. And as that victory appears to have been a conscious and deliberate aim of Muhammad's, it would seem that an aspect of his genius was the recognition that without the consolidation of a "common power" or "leviathan," in the Hobbesian sense, consisting of a *sedentary* ruling elite, the *umma* was bound to disintegrate, with the unavoidable consequence that the nomadic elements would revert to their pre-Islamic condition.

In these terms, we must recognize the organic continuity between Muhammad's work and that of Abu Bakr. For if the *ridda* wars were the culmination of a process Muhammad had begun, the wars were also the beginning of something new –

> the Islamic conquest movement that so transformed the face of the ancient world. It was, first of all, the efforts of the Islamic State to extend its domination to all Arab tribal groups – including those in the steppes and towns of Iraq and Syria – that led to the first clashes between the new Islamic State and the Byzantine and Sasanian Empires. But the conquests also developed from the events of the *ridda* wars in a more integral way. For it was the firm subjugation of the nomadic warrior tribesmen of Arabia by the Islamic State that put into the hands of the new ruling elite the means to undertake an expansionist movement of unparalleled proportions . . . (89–90).

Donner thus rightly underscores the continuity between Muhammad's work and what followed. "The Islamic conquest of the Near East," Donner avers,

> cannot be viewed, then, as something separate from the career of Muhammad the Apostle or from the conquest of Arabia during the *ridda* wars. It must be seen as an organic outgrowth of Muhammad's teachings and their impact on Arabian society, of Muhammad's political consolidation, pursued by traditional and novel means, and especially of his efforts to bring nomadic groups firmly under State control, and the extension of that process of consolidation by the Islamic State and its emerging elite under the leadership of Abu Bakr. These elements, together, formed the foundations on which the Islamic conquest movement rested. (90)

Donner addresses the question of what led the ruling elite of the new Islamic State to embark on an expansionist policy. The most cogent reply to that question is that the religious–ideological message of Islam itself prompted the elite to believe, that they had an essentially religious duty to expand the domain of the Islamic State as far as practically possible. They saw it as their divinely ordained mission to do so. Even if mundane factors were at work, it was the religious ideology that gave sanction to the expansionist policy. The ideology was therefore a definite causal component of the warriors' motives and of the meaning they assigned to their actions. So although we cannot, of course, speak of one true cause of the conquests, we come close to such a cause by returning to the proposition stated earlier: one God implied one sovereign on earth, and the moral duty to strive for a universal Islamic republic.

Garth Fowden, a specialist in the history of antiquity, has also concerned himself with Islamic monotheism as a major factor in the aspiration to and realization of world empire.[2] Fowden reminds us that Muhammad and his successors had to conquer not just one but two empires, the Byzantine and the Persian. In just 73 years after the Prophet's death, the Islamic Empire reached its greatest extent, comprising all the lands from the Pyrenees through Spain and North Africa to the Indus Valley in the East. And, Fowden observes, "Not since the emergence of the Seleucid and Ptolemaic States in the aftermath of Alexander had there existed in this region an empire that had no serious competitor to fear" (141–2).

Fowden, like Donner, therefore addresses this question: Given the spectacular military and political success of early Islam, the durability of its Empire for a considerable stretch of time, its enormous size and its internal cohesion, what was the secret of its dominance and stability? "What made the Islamic Empire, however briefly, into a successful world empire," Fowden writes, "was the combination of imperial impetus with a universalist monotheism that was inflexible with regard to doctrinal essentials and full of missionary zeal toward polytheists, but flexible . . . in its dealings with other monotheisms" (160). Fowden, then, is inclined to agree that it was Muhammad's proclamation of a fresh revelation from the one God, together with his political theory and practice, that created such a powerful expansionist impulse.

However, the Islamic Empire, like all empires, was only a temporarily successful phenomenon, while the Islamic faith, in contrast, has endured. That is the living, lasting legacy of the historical Muhammad.

# Notes

## Introduction and Overview of the Life of Muhammad

1  F. E. Peters, *Muhammad and the Origin of Islam*, New York: State University of New York Press, 1994, p. 259. Hereafter, all page references to this work will be cited in parentheses immediately following the quoted passage.
2  Fred M. Donner, *Narratives of Islamic Origins: The Beginings of Islamic Historical Writing*, Princeton, NJ: The Darwin Press, Inc., 1998. In the present discussion I rely heavily on Donner's work. Hereafter, all page references to this work will be cited in parentheses immediately following the quoted passage.
3  Ibn Hisham, *The Life of Muhammad*, a translation of Ishaq's *Sirat Rasul Allah*, with Introduction and notes by A. Guillaume, Pakistan Branch: Oxford University Press, 1955, pp. 118–22. Hereafter, all page references to this work will be cited in parentheses immediately following the quoted passage.
4  Philip K. Hitti, *History of the Arabs*, revised 10th edn, New York: Palgrave Macmillan, 2002. Hereafter, all page references to this work will be cited in parentheses immediately following the quoted passage.

## 1  Ibn Khaldun's Social and Economic Theory

1  Ibn Khaldun, *The Muqaddimah: An Introduction to History*, translated from the Arabic by Franz Rosenthal, in 3 volumes, London: Routledge and Kegan Paul, 1958. All page references to this work will be cited in parentheses immediately following the quoted passage.
2  For Ibn Khaldun, the term "Arab," as a sociological term, is synonymous with "Bedouin" or "nomad" regardless of the ethnicity of the group in

question. But he also uses "Arab" for its ethnic meaning, as we shall see, in his discussion of pre-Islamic Arabia.

3  I remind the reader that Ibn Khaldun's term "Arab" refers not only to the ethnically Arab tribes of the Arabian Peninsula, but to all types of desert-dwelling Bedouin.

4  Charles Issawi, *An Arab Philosophy of History: Selections from the Prolegomena of Ibn Khaldun of Tunis* (1332–1406), translated and arranged by Issawi, London: John Murray, 1950.

## 2  Pre-Islamic Arabia

1  Philip Hitti, *History of the Arabs*, revised 10th edn, London: Palgrave Macmillan, 2002, p. 21. Hereafter, all page references to this work will be cited in parentheses immediately following the quoted passage.

2  Vol. I, edition, translation, and commentary by Alan Jones, published by Ithaca Press Reading for the Board of the Faculty of Oriental Studies, Oxford University, 1992. The quotations are from his Introduction.

3  *The Koran*, translated from the Arabic by J. M. Rodwell. Foreword and Introduction by Alan Jones, *Everyman*, London: J. M. Dent; Vermont: Charles E. Tuttle, 1994. Hereafter, all page references to this work will be cited in parentheses immediately following the quoted passage.

4  Henri Hubert and Marcel Mauss, *Sacrifice: Its Nature and Function*, translated by W. D. Halls, foreword by E. E. Evans-Pritchard, Chicago: University of Chicago Press, 1964.

5  Marshall G. S. Hodgson, *The Venture of Islam*, vol. I, *The Classical Age of Islam*, Chicago and London: University of Chicago Press, 1958–9, p. 159.

## 3  The Role of Abraham, Hagar, and Ishmael

1  In the Quran and in other Muslim texts Abraham is rendered as Ibrahim and Ishmael as Ismail.

2  See Muhammad Husayn Haykal, *The Life of Muhammad*, translated from the 8th edn by Ismail Ragi A. al-Faruqi, USA: North American Trust Publications, 1976. Hereafter all page references to this work are cited in parentheses immediately following the quoted passage.

3  William Muir, *The Life of Mahomet and History of Islam* in four volumes, London: Smith, Elder and Co., 1858, vol. I. Hereafter, all page references to this work will be cited in parentheses immediately following the quoted passage.

## 4 Recent and Current Scholarship

1  F. E. Peters, *A Reader on Classical Islam*, Princeton: Princeton University Press, 1994. Hereafter, all page references to this work will be cited in parentheses immediately following the quoted passage.

2  F. E. Peters, *The Arabs and Arabia on the Eve of Islam*, Ashgate-Variorum, 1999; vol. III of *The Formation of the Classical Islamic World*, Lawrence I. Conrad, General Editor. Hereafter, all references to this volume will be cited with the author's name and the page number of his article, immediately following the quoted or paraphrased passage. The chapters in this volume are taken from the sources listed below.

3  *Mawali*, sing. *Mawla*, a non-Arab embracing Islam and affiliating himself with an Arabian tribe. Gil evidently uses the term analogously to refer to an Arab who embraces Judaism.

4  This figure has been duplicated from U. Rubin, *Arabs and Arabia*, p. 314.

## 5 Possible Influences on Muhammad's Inspiration

1  New York: Ktav Publishing House, Inc., 1967, p. 1. Hereafter, all page references to this work will be cited in parentheses immediately following the quoted passage.

2  See Heinrich Graetz, *History of the Jews*, vol. III, Philadelphia: The Jewish Publication Society of America, 1939, ch. 3, pp. 53–85.

3  See his *History of the Jews*, tr. from the Russian by Moshe Spiegel, New York: Thomas Yoseloff, 1968.

4  Salo Wittmayer Baron, *A Social and Religious History of the Jews*, vol. III, New York: Columbia University Press, 1957. Hereafter, all page references to this work will be cited in parentheses immediately following the quoted passage.

5  D. S. Margoliouth, *The Relations Between Arabs and Israelites Prior to the Rise of Islam*, Oxford: Oxford University Press, 1924. Hereafter, all page references to this work will be cited in parentheses immediately following the quoted passage.

## 6 The Jews of Arabia: A Recent Re-Examination

1  See Gordon Darnell Newby, *A History of the Jews of Arabia From Ancient Times to Their Eclipse Under Islam*, University of South Carolina

Press, 1988. Hereafter, all page references to this work will be cited in parentheses immediately following the quoted passage.

2 Gershom G. Scholem, *Major Trends in Jewish Mysticism*, New York: Schoken Books, 1941, p. 42.

## 7 Richard Bell's Origin of Islam in its Christian Environment

1 Richard Bell, *The Origin of Islam in its Christian Environment*, London: Macmillan, 1926. Hereafter, all page references to this work will be cited in parentheses immediately following the quoted passage.

## 8 W. Montgomery Watt's Muhammad

1 W. Montgomery Watt, *Muhammad at Mecca*, Oxford: Clarendon Press, 1953. All references to this work will be cited as Watt and the page number, in parentheses, immediately following the quoted passage.

2 Patricia Crone, *Meccan Trade and the Rise of Islam*, Princeton University Press, 1987. Hereafter, all references to this work will be cited in parentheses immediately following the quoted passage.

3 Bibliotheca Persica, ed. by Ehsan Yar-Shater, "The History of Al-Tabari," vol. VI, *Muhammad at Mecca*, translated and annotated by W. Montgomery Watt and M.V. McDonald, SUNY Press, 1988. Hereafter, all references to this work will be cited in parentheses immediately following the quoted passage.

4 Muhammad Husayn Haykal, *The Life of Muhammad*, translated from the 8th edn by Ismail Ragi A. al-Faruqi, USA: North American Trust Publications, 1976, p. 107. Hereafter, all references to this work will be cited in parentheses immediately following the quoted passage.

5 Max Weber, *The Methodology of the Social Sciences*, tr. and ed. Edward A. Shils and Henry A. Finch, Glencoe, Illinois: The Free Press, 1949, pp. 164 and 166.

6 W. Montgomery Watt, *Muhammad at Medina*, Oxford at the Clarendon Press, 1956. Hereafter, all page references to this work will be cited in parentheses immediately following the quoted passage.

## 9 Muhammad at Medina: William Muir's Analysis

1 William Muir, *The Life of Mahomet and History of Islam*, in four volumes, London: Smith, Elder and Co., 1858, vol. II, p. 207. Hereafter,

all references to this monumental achievement will be cited in parentheses immediately following the quoted passage.

2  Sir William Muir, *Mahomet and Islam*, London: Darf Publishers Ltd, 1986, pp. 151–2.

3  Michael Lecker, *Jews and Arabs in Pre-Islamic and Early Arabia*, Ashgate-Variorum, 1998, article number 10, p. 71.

## 10  Muhammad and the Jews

1  Barakat Ahmad, *Muhammad and the Jews: A Re-Examination*, New Delhi: Vikas Publishing House, Ltd, 1979. Hereafter, all page references to this work will be cited in parentheses immediately following the quoted passage.

2  H. G. Reissner, "The Ummi Prophet and the Banu Israel," *The Muslim World*, vol. 39, 1949, p. 278, cited in Ahmad.

3  Israel Friedlaender, "The Jews of Arabia and the Gaonate," *The Jewish Quarterly Review*, 1910–11, vol. I, p. 252, cited in Ahmad.

4  Gordon Darnell Newby, *A History of the Jews of Arabia from Ancient Times to Their Eclipse Under Islam*, 1988. Hereafter, all page references to this work will be cited in parentheses immediately following the quoted passage.

## 11  Concluding Sociological Reflections

1  See Fred McGraw Donner, *The Early Islamic Conquests*, Princeton, NJ: Princeton University Press, 1981. All page references to this work will be cited in parentheses immediately following the quoted passage.

2  See his *Empire to Commonwealth*, Princeton, NJ: Princeton University Press, 1993. All page references to this work will be cited in parentheses immediately following the quoted passage.

# Bibliography

Abduraheem, M. R. M., *Muhammad, the Prophet*, Madras: Garnet Books, 1971.

Ahmad, Barakat, *Muhammad and the Jews: A Re-Examination*, New Delhi: Vikas, 1979.

Ali, Maulana Muhammad, *The Religion of Islam*, Cairo: Arab Writers, Publishers, and Printers, 1950.

Ali, Syed Ameer, *The Spirit of Islam*, London: Methuen, 1965.

Ali, A. Yusuf, tr. *The Holy Quran*, Washington, DC: American International Printing Company, 1946.

Altheim, F. and R. Stiehl, *Die Araber in der alten Welt*, 5 vols, Berlin: W de Gryter, 1964–9.

Andrae, Tor, *Muhammad: The Man and His Faith*, tr. Theophil Mengel, New York: Harper, 1960.

Arberry, A. J., tr. *The Koran: Interpreted*, London: Oxford University Press, 1964.

Armstrong, Karen, *Muhammad: A Western Attempt to Understand Islam*, London: Victor Gollancz Ltd, 1991.

Asani, Ali S., Kamal Abdel-Malek, and A. Schimmel, *Celebrating Muhammad: Images of the Prophet in Popular Muslim Poetry*, Columbia: University of South Carolina Press, 1995.

Atiyah, Edward, *The Arabs*, Penguin, 1955.

Ayoub, Mahmoud, *The Quran and its Interpretors*, vol. I, Albany: SUNY, 1984.

Balyuzi, H. M., *Muhammad and the Course of Islam*, Oxford: G. Ronald, 1976.

Baron, Salo Wittmayer, *A Social and Religious History of the Jews*, vol. III, New York: Columbia University Press, 1957.

Beeston, A. F. L., "Pre-Islamic Languages of Arabia," *Arabica*, 28 (1981), pp. 178–86.

Bell, Richard, *The Origin of Islam in its Christian Environment*, London: Macmillan, 1926.

Burton, John, *The Collection of the Quran*, Cambridge: Cambridge University Press, 1977.

Choudhury, G. W., *The Prophet Muhammad: His Life and Eternal Message*, London: Scorpion, 1993.

Cook, Michael, *Muhammad*, Oxford: Oxford University Press, 1983.

Cragg, Kenneth, *The Event of the Quran: Islam in its Scripture*, London: Allen and Unwin, 1971.

Crone, Patricia, *Meccan Trade and the Rise of Islam*, Princeton: Princeton University Press, 1987.

Crone, Patricia, *Slaves on Horses*, Cambridge: Cambridge University Press, 1980.

Crone, Patricia, and Michal Cook, *Hagarism: The Making of the Islamic World*, Cambridge: Cambridge University Press, 1977.

Dashti, Ali, *Twenty-Three Years: A Study of the Prophetic Career of Muhammad*, tr. F. R. C. Bagley, London: Allen and Unwin, 1985.

Dermenghem, E., *Muhammad and the Islamic Tradition*, tr. J. M. Watt, New York: Harper, 1958.

Donner, Fred McGraw, *The Early Islamic Conquests*, Princeton, NJ: Princeton University Press, 1981.

Donner, Fred McGraw, *Narratives of Islamic Origins*, Princeton, NJ: The Darwin Press, Inc., 1998.

Dubnov, Simon, *History of the Jews*, tr. Moshe Spiegel, New York: Thomas Yoseloff, 1968.

*Encyclopedia of Islam*, Leiden: E. J. Brill, 1954.

Fowden, Garth, *Empire to Commonwealth*, Princeton, NJ: Princeton University Press, 1993.

Friedlaender, Israel, "The Jews of Arabia and the Gaonate," *The Jewish Quarterly Review*, vol. I, (1910–11).

Fueck, J., The Originality of the Arabian Prophet," *Studies on Islam*, tr. M. L. Swarts, New York: Oxford University Press (1981), pp. 86–98.

Gabrieli, F., *Muhammad and the Conquests of Islam*, tr. Virginia Luling and Rosamund Linell, London: Weidenfeld & Nicholson, 1968.

Geiger, Abraham, *Judaism and Islam*, New York: KTAV Publishing House, 1970.

Gerth, H. H. and C. Wright Mills, eds., *From Max Weber: Essays in Sociology*, London: Routledge & Kegan Paul, 1948.

Gibb, H. A. R., *Islam: A Historical Survey*, Oxford: Oxford University Press, 1989.

Gibb, Hamilton A. R., "Pre-Islamic Monotheism in Arabia," *Harvard Theological Review* 55 (Cambridge, MA, 1962), pp. 269–80.

Gil, Moshe, "The Origin of the Jews of Yathrib," *Jerusalem Studies in Arabic and Islam* 4 (Jerusalem, 1984), pp. 203–24.

Graetz, Heinrich, *History of the Jews*, vol. III, Philadelphia: The Jewish Publication Society of America, 1939.

Graham, W., *Divine Word and Prophetic Word in Early Islam*, The Hague: Mouton, 1977.

Grunebaum, G. E. von, "The Nature of Arab Unity before Islam," *Arabica* 10 (Leiden, 1963), pp. 4–23.

Haykal, Muhammad Husayn, *The Life of Muhammad*, tr. Ismail R. al-Faruqi, Indianapolis: American Trust Publications, 1976.

Henninger, Joseph, "Pre-Islamic Bedouin Religion," in Merlin Schwarz, ed. and trans., *Studies on Islam* (New York, 1981), pp. 3–22.

Hinds, Martin, *Studies in Early Islamic History*, ed. by Jere Bacharach, Lawrence I. Conrad, and Patricia Crone with an Introduction by G. R. Hawting, Princeton, NJ: The Darwin Press, Inc., 1996.

Hitti, Philip K., *History of the Arabs*, London: Macmillan, rev. 10th edn, 2002.

Hodgson, Marshall G. S., *The Venture of Islam*, Chicago and London: University of Chicago Press, vol. I, 1961.

Holt, P. M., Ann K. S. Lambton, and Bernard Lewis, eds., *Cambridge History of Islam*, Cambridge: Cambridge University Press, 1970.

Ibn Hisham, *The Life of Muhammad*, a translation of Ishaq's *Sirat Rasul Allah*, with intro. and notes by A. Guillaume, Pakistan Branch: Oxford University Press, 1955.

Ibn Ishaq, Muhammad, *The Making of the Last Prophet: A Reconstruction of the Earliest Biography of Muhammad*, Columbia: University of South Carolina Press, 1989.

Ibn Khaldun, *The Muqaddimah: An Introduction to History*, tr. Franz Rosenthal, 3 vols., London: Routledge and Kegan Paul, 1958. New material copyright 1967 by Bollingen Foundation, Princeton: Princeton University Press.

Issawi, Charles, *An Arab Philosophy of History: Selections from the Prolegomena of Ibn Khaldun of Tunis*, London: John Murray, 1950.

Jones, Alan, *Early Arabic Poetry*, vol. I, Oxford: Oxford University Press, 1992.

Jurji, E. J., "Pre-Islamic Use of the Name Muhammad," *The Muslim World*, 26, (1936), pp. 389–91.

Kister, M. J., "Al-Hira: Some Notes on its Relations with Arabia," *Arabica* 15 (Leiden, 1968), pp. 143–69.

Kister, M. J., "The Campaign of Hulaban: A New Light on the Expedition of Abraha," *Le Muséon* 78 (Paris, 1965), pp. 425–36, and *Studies in Jahiliyya and Early Islam* (London, 1980), no. 18.

Kister, M. J., *Studies in Jahaliyya and Early Islām*, Variorum Reprints, 1980.

Lecker, Michael, *Jews and Arabs in Pre-Islamic and Early Arabia*, Ashgate-Variorum, article 10, 1998.

Lecker, Michael, "Muhammad at Medina: A Geographical Approach," *Jerusalem Studies in Arabic and Islam*, 6, (1985), pp. 29–62.

Lecker, Michael, *Muslims, Jews and Pagans: Studies on Early Islamic Medina*, Leiden: E. J. Brill, 1995.

Lecker, Michael, "On Arabs of the Banu Kilab Executed Together with the Jewish Banu Qurayza," *Jerusalem Studies in Arabic and Islam*, 19, (1995), pp. 66–72.

Levy, Reuben, *The Social Structure of Islam*, being the second edition of the Sociology of Islam, Cambridge: Cambridge University Press, 1969.

Lewis, Bernard, *The Arabs in History*, New York: Harper & Row, 1966.

Margoliouth, D. S., *Relations Between Arabs and Israelites Prior to the Rise of Islam*, Oxford: Oxford University Press, 1924.

Margoliouth, D. S., *Lectures on Arabic Historians*, Calcutta: University of Calcutta, 1930.

Margoliouth, D. S., *The Early Development of Muhammadanism*, New York: C.Scribner's Sons, 1914.

Montgomery Watt, W., "Belief in a 'High God' in Pre-Islamic Mecca," *Journal of Semitic Studies* 16 (Oxford, 1971), pp. 35–40.

Muir, William, *The Life of Mahomet and History of Islam* , 4 vols, London: Smith, Elder and Co., 1858.

Muir, William, *Mahomet and Islam* , an abridgement of his monumental 4-vol. study, London: Darf Publishers Ltd, 1986.

Newby, Gordon Darnell, *A History of the Jews of Arabia* , Columbia, SC: University of South Carolina Press, 1988.

Peters, F. E., *The Arabs and Arabia on the Eve of Islam* , Ashgate-Variorum, 1999, vol. III of the Formation of the Classical Islamic World, Lawrence I. Conrad, gen. ed. Introduction by Peters and articles by G. E. Grunebaum; M. J. Kister; Joseph Henninger; Moshe Gil; Fazlur Rahman; Uri Rubin; H. A. R. Gibb; Montgomery Watt.

Peters, F. E., *Muhammad and the Origins of Islam*, Albany: SUNY, 1994.

Peters, F. E., *A Reader on Classical Islam*, Princeton: Princeton University Press, 1994.

Peters, F. E., *Allah's Commonwealth*, New York: Simon and Schuster, 1973.

Rahman, Fazlur, *Islam*, Chicago: University of Chicago Press, 1979.

Rahman, Fazlur, "Pre-Foundations of the Muslim Community in Mecca," *Studia Islamica* 43 (Paris, 1976), pp. 5–24.

Reissner, H. G., "The Ummi Prophet and the Banu Israel," *The Muslim World*, vol. 39, (1949).

Rodinson, M., "The Life of Muhammad and the Sociological Problem of the Beginnings of Islam," *Diogenes*, 20, (1957), 28: 51.

Rodinson, M., *Muhammad*, tr. Anne Carter, New York: The New Press, 1971. Introduction and foreword 1980 by Maxime Rodinson.

Rodwell, J. M., tr., *The Koran*, Foreword and Introduction by Alan Jones, Everyman, London: J. M. Dent, 1994.

Rubin, Uri, "The Ka'ba: Aspects of its Ritual Functions and Position in Pre-Islamic and Early Islamic Times," *Jerusalem Studies in Arabic and Islam* 13 (Jerusalem, 1986), pp. 97–131.

Rubin, Uri, *The Eye of the Beholder: The Life of Muhammad as Viewed by the Early Muslims*, Princeton: Darwin, 1995.

Rubin, Uri, *Between Bible and Quran: The Children of Israel and the Islamic Self Image*, Princeton, NJ: The Darwin Press, Inc., 1999

Scholem, Gershom G., *Major Trends in Jewish Mysticism*, New York: Schoken Books, 1941.

Smith, Wilfred Cantwell, *The Meaning and End of Religion*, New York: Macmillan Company, 1962.

Tabari al-, *The Last Years of the Prophet*, Albany: SUNY Press, 1990.

Torrey, Charles Cutler, *The Jewish Foundation of Islam*, New York: KTAV Publishing House, Inc., 1967.

Trimmingham, J. Spencer, *Christianity Among the Arabs in Pre-Islamic Times*, London: Longman, 1979.

Wasserstrom, Steven M., *Between Muslim and Jew: The Problem of Symbiosis Under Early Islam*, Princeton: Princeton University Press, 1995.

Watt, W. Montgomery, *Muhammad at Medina*, Oxford: Clarendon Press, 1956.

Watt, W. Montgomery, *Muhammad at Mecca*, Oxford: Clarendon Press, 1953.

Weber, Max, *The Sociology of Religion*, tr. Ephraim Fischoff, Boston: Beacon Press, 1963.

Weber, Max, *The Methodology of the Social Sciences*, tr. and ed. Edward A. Shils and Henry A. Finch, Glencoe, Illinois: The Free Press, 1949.

Zakaria, Rafiq, *Muhammad and the Quran*, London: Penguin, 1991.

# Index